The Information Retrieval Series

Volume 30

Information Retrieval (IR) deals with access to and search in mostly unstructured information, in text, audio, and/or video, either from one large file or spread over separate and diverse sources, in static storage devices as well as on streaming data. It is part of both computer and information science, and uses techniques from e.g. mathematics, statistics, machine learning, database management, or computational linguistics. Information Retrieval is often at the core of networked applications, web-based data management, or large-scale data analysis.

The Information Retrieval Series presents monographs, edited collections, and advanced text books on topics of interest for researchers in academia and industry alike. Its focus is on the timely publication of state-of-the-art results at the forefront of research and on theoretical foundations necessary to develop a deeper understanding of methods and approaches.

This series is abstracted/indexed in EI Compendex and Scopus.

Asif Ekbal • Rina Kumari

Dive into Misinformation Detection

From Unimodal to Multimodal and
Multilingual Misinformation Detection

 Springer

Asif Ekbal
Computer Science and Engineering
Indian Institute of Technology Patna
Patna, India

Rina Kumari
KIIT University
Bhubaneswar, India

ISSN 1871-7500   ISSN 2730-6836   (electronic)
The Information Retrieval Series
ISBN 978-3-031-54833-8   ISBN 978-3-031-54834-5   (eBook)
https://doi.org/10.1007/978-3-031-54834-5

This Springer imprint is published by the registered company Springer Nature Switzerland AG
The registered company address is: Gewerbestrasse 11, 6330 Cham, Switzerland

If disposing of this product, please recycle the paper.

This book is dedicated to our parents who enlightened us with the value of strong work ethic and our families who always motivated for taking new challenges.

Preface

This book provides a brief introduction to misinformation and various novel approaches for solving misinformation detection problems. In recent times, most people get information through social media platforms. Social media news and information contain several attributes like text, image, audio, and video. False news creators manipulate any or all of these attributes to create false information. Misinformation has undoubtedly become a significant issue affecting businesses, economies, election outcomes, and societies. The dissemination and effects of inaccurate, distorted, or false information spread rapidly and reached millions of people within minutes through various communication channels. False information may be of various forms, such as fake news, disinformation, misinformation, rumors, satire, etc. This book considers all kinds of false information as fake news or misinformation and uses the terms *fake news* and *misinformation* interchangeably. The primary purpose of this book is to provide a foundation for the problems of misinformation or false content detection including various challenges and approaches to solve them. This book is helpful for academicians, researchers, postgraduate as well as undergraduate students, and industry people who wish to explore various dimensions of misinformation detection regardless of their past knowledge and experience.

The book starts with an overall description of misinformation. It briefly introduces the history, various issues or challenges, several reasons for creating and spreading misinformation, several forms, and its impact on individuals and society. The second chapter discusses the prior works on misinformation detection that helped structure the book to solve the various problems. This chapter explores various datasets, recent advancements, and state-of-the-art mechanisms for misinformation detection. The third chapter demonstrates that the presence of surprising content in the story draws instant attention and appeals to strong emotional stimuli in the story reader, which is one of the significant characteristics of the virality of misinformation. It first introduces *novelty, novelty detection, emotion, and emotion recognition*, briefly. After that, it discusses various terminologies that are used throughout the chapter. Subsequent sections explore the application of novelty and emotion in the misinformation detection domain. It also explores a case study demonstrating a methodology for misinformation detection using emotion recognition and novelty detection. The primary goal of this chapter is to use this concept and implement emotion recognition novelty detection as supporting tasks for automatic misinformation detection. This chapter repurposes textual entailment for novelty detection and classifies disinformation using models trained on extensive entailment and emotion datasets. The fourth chapter explores the importance of the joint learning of interrelated tasks to improve the performance of the primary task. This chapter first introduces multitasking and then discusses its advantages. It focuses on developing a framework for joint learning of interrelated tasks such as emotion recognition, novelty detection, and misinformation detection. More specifically, this chapter justifies that affective information and textual novelty are the main ingredients to consider while designing an automatic misinformation detection framework.

After Chap. 4, this book majorly focuses on the role and importance of multimodality in misinformation detection. The fifth chapter explores various datasets and mechanisms leveraging multimodal information. It first introduces multimodality, its importance, and its applications in various domains for solving different tasks. In continuation, this chapter also talks about challenges in the multimodality. It further discusses a case study for developing a multimodal misinformation detection framework. It aims to leverage various information from different sources (e.g., text, image, video, etc.) to build an efficient system. It justifies that an effective combination of different input modalities may assist the system in proper learning. This chapter also demonstrates the fusion mechanisms of text and image modalities to obtain an efficient multimodal feature that ultimately helps to classify multimedia fake news. The sixth chapter discusses how novelty and emotion can be helpful in multimodal misinformation detection. It justifies that detecting misleading information is difficult without earlier knowledge about that particular news and explores the possible solutions to tackle this problem. Chapter 7 introduces the concept of multilingualism. It starts with discussing multilingual content, its importance, and applications in the NLP domain and continues with the challenges and benefits. It implements an effective neural model to detect fabricated multilingual information, which overcomes the research and development gap in misinformation detection for regional languages as a case study. Finally, the last chapter (Chap. 8) summarizes the contents of the book.

Each chapter starts with an introductory section to briefly introduce the topic. Wherever required, each chapter includes pictorial descriptions of methods and concepts to improve clarity and facilitate better understanding.

Bihar, India   Asif Ekbal
Bhubaneswar, India   Rina Kumari
December, 2023

Suggestions and opinions have always proved very helpful in enhancing any endeavor. We request all readers to write us their valuable feedback/comments/suggestions for the betterment of the book at *asif@iitp.ac.in* or *rina.kumarifcs@kiit.ac.in.*

Acknowledgments

This book is the outcome of a fruitful cooperation between researchers and academicians that has spanned many years. It would not have been possible without the many contributors whose names did not appear on the cover. We thank our institutions (The Indian Institute of Technology Patna (IITP), India, and The Kalinga Institute of Industrial Technology, Bhubaneswar Odisha, India) for giving us the time and opportunity to write the book. We would like to thank all the faculty and staff members of our institutions, who helped us by providing the necessary resources and in various other ways in completing this book. We would like to thank our family, friends, and colleagues for their continuous support and motivation. We also thank the Springer staff for their very professional support and discussions.

Many others not named above contributed to the outcome, and we wish to express our gratitude to all of them.

Contents

About the Authors

Asif Ekbal is currently an Associate Professor in the Department of Computer Science and Engineering, IIT Patna and an Associate Dean, Resources at IIT Patna. He has been pursuing research in the broad areas of artificial intelligence, natural language processing (NLP), and machine learning (ML) since the last 20 years.

He has authored around 300 papers in top-tier conferences and journals. Asif has been involved in several sponsored research projects, funded by industries, such as Elsevier, Accenture, EZDI, LG, Skymap, Samsung Research, Wipro, and Flipkart, and government agencies such as MeitY, MHRD, and SERB, . He has been serving as an area chair, PC member, and reviewer to several well-known conferences. He is currently the associate editor and/or in the editorial board of several reputed journals. He is an awardee of the "Best Innovative Project Award" from the Indian National Academy of Engineering, Govt. of India; "JSPS Invitation Fellowship" from Govt of Japan; and the "Young Faculty Research Fellowship Award" of the Govt. of India. He is among the top 2% of scientists, published by Stanford University findings in Elsevier (2021, 2022, 2023), and top computer scientists, published by Openrsearch.com

Rina Kumari is currently an assistant professor in the School of Computer Engineering, KIIT Deemed to be University, Bhubaneswar, Odisha, India. She holds a PhD from the Indian Institute of Technology Patna, India. Her main area of research is natural language processing, deep learning, and fake news detection. She has published papers in various peer-reviewed conferences like IJCNN and IJCNLP and journals of international repute like *Information Processing and Management* (IPM), *Expert Systems With Applications*, *Journal of Intelligent Information Systems* (JIIS), etc. She is a recipient of the IEEE CIS Participation Grant IJCNN 2021. She has also reviewed several manuscripts of conferences like ICONIP and ICON and journals like IEEE Transactions, Springer, Elsevier (IPM), etc. She has chaired a session in ASSIC 2022.

Acronyms

AMFB	Attention-based multimodal factorized bilinear pooling
ANN	Adversarial neural network
APR	Amazon product review
AUC	Area under the curve
BERT	Bidirectional encoder representations from the transformer
Bi-GRU	Bidirectional gated recurrent unit
Bi-LSTM	Bidirectional long short-term memory
CARN	Cross-modal attention residual network
CNN	Convolutional neural network
CSV	Comma-separated values
DCNN	Deep convolution neural network
DT	Decision tree
EANN	Event adversarial neural network
FNC	Fake news challenge
FND	Fake news detection
FNID	Fake news inference dataset
GCAN	Graph-aware co-attention network
HFFN	Hierarchical feature fusion network
ICMR	Indian Council of Medical Research
IIM	Inter-modal interaction module
KNN	K-nearest neighbor
LARS	Layer-wise adaptive rate scaling
LR	Logistic regression
LSTM	Long short-term memory
MBFC	Media bias/fact check
MCB	Multimodal compact bilinear pooling
MFB	Multimodal factorized bilinear pooling
MKD	Multilingual knowledge distillation
MLB	Multimodal low-rank bilinear pooling
MLP	Multilayer perceptron
MMFND	Multisource multiclass fake news detection

MMM	Multilingual multimodal misinformation
MVAE	Multimodal variational autoencoder
NB	Naive Bayes
NER	Named entity recognition
NLG	Natural language generation
NLI	Natural language inference
NLP	Natural language processing
NPS	Net promoter score
PCA	Principle component analysis
PMTM	Proposed multitask model
QQP	Quora question pair
RBF	Radial basis function
RFC	Random forest classifier
RL	Reinforcement learning
RNN	Recurrent neural network
ROC	Receiver operating characteristics
RTE	Recognizing textual entailment
SCL	Supervised contrastive learning
SGD	Stochastic gradient descent
SOTA	State-of-the-arts
SPO	Subject predicate object
SVM	Support vector machine
TAG	Topic-Agnostic
TER	Textual entailment recognition
TI-CNN	Text and image information-based convolutional neural network
t-SNE	T-distributed stochastic neighbor embedding
USA	United States
VAE	Variational autoencoder
WBG	Without background
WHO	World Health Organization

Chapter 1
Introduction

News and reports contain numerous details, such as author, source, prominent headlines, attractive writing styles, photos, videos, etc. Any variations created to these details result in fake or misleading news. Misinformation or false information is created by manipulating any one or all of these attributes. Misinformation has undoubtedly become a significant issue affecting businesses, economies, election outcomes, and societies. The dissemination and effects of inaccurate, distorted, or false information spread rapidly and reach millions of people within minutes through various communication channels. Fake news aims to emulate the presentation of news and information to obtain legitimacy and credibility. However, fake news is not only limited to gaining the emergence of the news. It seeks to follow journalistic writing, how an authentic news article includes an image, and how a reliable news site presents itself. The quick spread of information has been facilitated by the development of the Internet and the quick uptake of social media sites like Facebook and Twitter. With the help of these platforms, users generate and disseminate more information than ever before, some of it false or misleading and has no bearing on reality. The resemblances of fake news with journalistic news reports amplify the seriousness of this threat regarding the other elements of disinformation. Subsequent sections in this chapter briefly discuss the history of fake news, different definitions, various forms, modalities, clues in fake news, the purpose and reason for creating and spreading misinformation, and the impact of misinformation on society and individuals. It also explores the objective and challenges of misinformation detection.

A. Ekbal, R. Kumari, *Dive into Misinformation Detection*, The Information Retrieval Series 30, https://doi.org/10.1007/978-3-031-54834-5_1

1.1   History

Information or stories designed to mislead or confuse readers are called fake news. Misinformation or false content is not a recent development. During the 1890s, when dramatic news stories were frequently published in newspapers, the term "fake news" was initially coined. In 2017, fake news gained legitimacy as the Collins English Dictionary's word of the year and has remained in the headlines ever since. Although the phrase might emerge as the latest innovation, it has been a part of media history long before social media, since the invention of the printing press. There are lots of examples of false news throughout history.

The invention of the printing press in the fifteenth century has promoted the spread of both real and fake news faster than ever before. In the mid-seventeenth century, this technology helped in spreading false information about George II, the king of Britain and Ireland at that time. The king struggled to stop a rebellion against him and had to prove himself as a strong leader to make this rebellion unsuccessful. During that period, various sources on the side of the rebels published false information about the king. This ruined the King's reputation, showing how misinformation can change people's opinions. By the nineteenth century, newspapers were a popular, cheap, and easy way of transmitting news to the public. Printing became so cheap in America that some papers could be bought for just a penny. By taking this advantage, some newspapers in the United States (USA) published various false stories about African Americans during racist sentiment in the 1800s, leading to deficiencies and crimes. Nazi propaganda machines further used this to build anti-Semitic fervor. **Yellow Journalism** is the crucial term for the publication of biased or sensationalistic stories in the newspapers. The term yellow journalism evolved during the 1890s, and at that time, it competed with the audience by reporting rumors and shocking stories. In 1898, the incredulous news of yellow journalism also led to the Spanish-American War. During the First World War in 1917, British officials spread various false information against Germans, which convinced the people to support British personnel. During the twentieth century, people started demanding more reliable news sources, which resulted in the establishment of the New York Times and other reliable news sources. It fed the light of yellow journalism, and false content dissemination almost stopped until the acceleration of Web-based news drove it back into full swing.

Nowadays, people like to read the news online, which has given massive popularity to social media platforms. Recently, social networking has become a necessary component of life for every person. It has led to an explosion of misinformation, false stories, and fake news, widely spread on various social media platforms without being fact-checked. Cheap and easy Internet access has also accelerated the dissemination of fake news within seconds rather than days or weeks. As visual content attracts readers more, fake news creators have started to create and spread the news with false visual content. Over the years, the development of technology has supported the dissemination of fake news through innovations like the printing press, photography, and social media. Video tampering is not easy, so videos were initially considered a reliable news source. However, the development of deepfakes has also threatened video news sources. Deepfakes normally superimpose the face of a person in a news video into the face of another person, which makes the news statement fake.

As per the above discussion of fake news history, it is clear that it has a long journey. However, along with the popularity of social media, fake news has changed its representation, form, and propagation speed, which makes modern fake news different from traditional journalistic misinformation and false content.

1.2 Definition of Misinformation

The news refers to a report of a specific recent and actual event of common interest, which somehow affects the community and disseminates something new to its audience. News is the outcome of journalism, which follows the principles of verification and independence to report the truth. Therefore, the notion of fake news and misinformation is contradictory in the real sense of the word. According to researchers, journalists, psychologists, and scientists, fake news has different definitions. Most of them agree that fake news contains articles that mimic the exact format of a report or news with false information created with malicious intent to deceive the reader and manipulate their opinion. The enlisted definitions are popular for fake news from several different vital perspectives.

Definition 1 Fake news is fabricated news articles deliberately intended to deceive or mislead the readers. It usually appears on sites that masquerade as authentic news Web sites.

Definition 2 Fake news is intentionally and verifiably false news articles that could mislead readers.

Definition 3 Fake news is pertinent to the look and feel of real news, but this news is low in facticity and high in the immediate intention to deceive the reader.

Definition 4 Fake news is best defined as the intended presentation of misleading or false claims as news, where the claims are misleading by design.

Definition 5 A fake news story claims to describe events in the real world, usually by mimicking the protocols of traditional media news, yet is known by its creators to be remarkably false and is spread with the two goals of being widely disseminated and of deceiving at least some of its audience.

Definition 6 The news that exhibits a lack of truth or the news that is either false or misleading and propagated with an intention to deceive or mischief or in the manner of bullshit.

Definition 7 Fake news is counterfeit news or a story if and only if it is not credible news but is presented as credible news, with the intention and propensity to deceive the reader.

Definition 8 The fabricated or false information mimics news media content in form but not in intent or organizational process.

Definition 9 Partly or entirely false information, appearing as news and typically expressed as visual, textual, or graphical content with an intention to confuse or mislead the population

Definition 10 The content that seems like a news piece that makes objectively false claims in a materially false manner that the given events have occurred. By design, this definition avoids any intent requirement because improper intent is not essential for a piece to be fake news.

Definition 11 Fake news is defined as deliberately false information. It is written with the intent to deceive the reader to gain political or financial benefits. It is factually incorrect and usually has sensational headlines that grab immediate attention.

1.3   Types of Misinformation

To get a deeper understanding of misinformation in social media, this section enlists various types of misinformation below, though the classification is not exclusive. All the types have different specific definitions and semantics. However, all are correlated and broadly have similar semantics. Different kinds of misinformation vary remarkably in their intent, tactics, and impact. Therefore, a new misinformation dictionary is essential for better clarification about it, which can help the reader think about these differences. Figure 1.1 depicts the different types of misinformation, and subsequent paragraphs discuss these types in detail.

Misinformation It is inaccurate, false, or out-of-context information created or disseminated without deliberate intent to cause harm. For example, when friends or family members share false health claims, political plans, or theories on social media platforms, they do not try to deceive. They have the impression that they are passing along credible information. But, in reality, they spread misinformation.

Disinformation Disinformation is inaccurate, distorted, or misleading content knowingly created with the intention to deceive and cause harm. It is influenced by three factors: political power, profit, or the aim to sow chaos and confusion. So, intentionally spreading misinformation is disinformation. It may be the false information about the military strength or plans of any country, proliferated by a government or intelligence agency in a militant act of tactical political subversion.

Fig. 1.1 Different types of misinformation

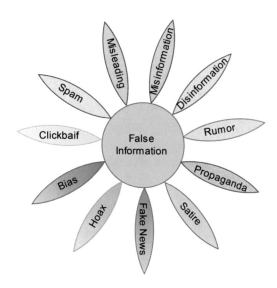

Misleading News It is false information in which the semantic meaning of the headline and body is different. It usually includes out-of-context information. Misinformation is also unintentionally shared, misleading information, whereas disinformation is false information that is intentionally shared and intended to deceive the reader. It can also consist of false or outdated information. In the natural language processing (NLP) community, misleading information detection has attracted many researchers nowadays.

Rumor A rumor can be defined as an unverified claim about some statement or story. People usually share on social media or pass it around without confirmation that the information is valid.

Propaganda The information, opinions, ideas, or images spread by a community, an organized group, or a government to influence people's opinions are known as propaganda. It is disseminated without offering all the information or covertly highlighting a single perspective on the concepts, details, information, or rumors. People spread it widely to help or harm an individual, group, institution, nation, etc. The word "propaganda" is generally used negatively, especially for political persons who falsely claim to get elected. Thus, propaganda is spreading information in support of a cause where the credibility of information is not so important.

Satire It is the technique of making someone or something look ridiculous, raising laughter to embarrass or discredit its targets. Satire is a way of making fun of people using exaggerated or silly language. Politicians are easy targets for satire, especially when acting hypocritical or self-righteous.

Fake News The fabricated news or stories without verifiable facts or sources are known as fake news. It is any article containing false information, tampered image or video, etc.

Hoax A practical joke, a comment to cause embarrassment or to induce political or social change by increasing people's awareness about something, is called a hoax. A hoax is a false story created purposefully and passed as truth by a person or group.

Bias It is the personal opinions influencing the judgment in favor of or against an idea or thing. Someone may develop biases for or against an individual, a group, or a belief. It is an act of unfairly supporting or opposing a particular person or thing based on hostile feelings or opinions. It may also include false claims and wrong facts and figures.

Clickbait (The now: What is clickbait 2023) It is an overemphasized or sensationalized headline that encourages one to click a link to an article, image, or video. We can define clickbait as ads that claim to disclose secrets or other sensationalist information. It includes wording like *You won't believe what happened next...*, *Click here to learn more...*, *etc.* Instead of presenting facts, clickbait headlines often appeal to curiosity and emotions. Once someone clicks the link, the hosting Web site of that link earns money from the advertisers. Clickbait can be harmful when it is used along with the creation of fake news. Clickbait headlines are generally found in social media posts and blogs. Researchers have proposed several methods for clickbait detection.

Spam Any undesirable, unprompted digital communication broadcasted in bulk is called spam. Generally, spam is transmitted via email but can also be disseminated via phone calls, text messages, or social media. Spam includes marketing messages selling unwanted goods. Spam can propagate malware, trick for disclosing personal information, or scare messages to think someone needs to pay to get out of trouble.

1.4 Modalities in Misinformation

False information can span a range of topics, platforms, and styles. It is distinguished by various entities such as news creators, content, surrounding social context, and news spreaders. Modalities are related to the news content, which includes various attributes, such as news titles and bodies containing textual and visual information. In ancient days, traditional news articles contained only textual information, so fake news creators created false information by manipulating text content only. But in recent years, news articles have been composed of several parts, including text, images, audio, and videos. As visual information attracts people's attention quickly, fake news creators are creating and spreading false information with visual content nowadays. Based on the news contents, the misinformation is divided into two types.

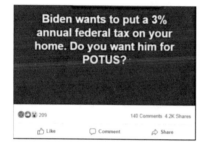

Fig. 1.2 Examples of unimodal misinformation

Unimodal Misinformation The misinformation created by manipulating only the text content of the news stories and spread only in the text form is usually called unimodal misinformation. Figure 1.2 shows a few examples of the unimodal misinformation collected from various social media platforms.

Multimodal Misinformation The misinformation created by manipulating images, audio, and video along with the text content of the news articles is called multimodal misinformation. Figure 1.3 shows examples of multimodal misinformation collected from various social media platforms.

1.5   Clues in Misinformation

Although the misinformation and fake news creators are intelligent enough to create the misinformation exactly like the real news, some clues are present in the tampered information. These clues can be identified by careful analysis of the news articles. The following paragraphs briefly discuss some general clues present in misinformation. Some images shown in different clues have been collected from various social media platforms.

Fig. 1.3 This news is misleading. The news contains some images with a textual description, so it is multimodal misinformation

Unknown or Unusual Web Addresses False information can mislead people by mirroring trusted Web sites or using similar names and Web addresses to trustworthy news organizations. Some misinformation contains a URL or a link supposedly to an official Web site, but the hyperlink accesses a fake domain that mimics the original one. Figure 1.4 depicts such an example of the misinformation that clearly shows the unusual Web addresses in the link. In the first view, the user will not notice that the Web address differs from the original website.

Inflammatory or Sensational Words One of the primary purposes of misinformation is to attract the news reader's attention, which can accelerate news dissemination.

Fig. 1.4 The URL of the Web page is similar except double zero (00) instead of double "o" in Facebook. The page is also almost similar to Facebook, but it is not an authentic Facebook page

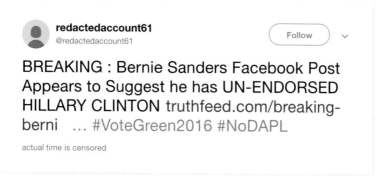

Fig. 1.5 The news starts with a word "breaking," which is an inflammatory word that accelerates sensation and compels the people to share the news

Therefore, the news creators add some inflammatory words, such as BREAKING NEWS, GOOD NEWS, HEARTBREAKING, AMAZING, UNBELIEVABLE, WOW, etc. in almost all the false information. These provocative words are generally found in the title of fake news and misinformation. Figure 1.5 depicts the example of the misinformation, which includes the sensational words.

Element of Surprise Sometimes, news articles describe some unusual and rare events and activities that surprise the news reader. These uncommon events may or may not be verified by the proper channel. The unverified rare events are also important clues to false information. Figure 1.6 shows examples of the misinformation that embeds the element of surprise. This is multimedia news in which a person is lying down over the aircraft. It is impossible to fly over the aircraft and surprises the reader. In this scenario, the reader can think the news may be fake.

An Afghan citizen trying to flee his country after Taliban occupation.

Fig. 1.6 The news shows that a person is lying down over aircraft, which embeds element of surprise

User Credibility Misinformation and fake news are generally created and spread by some antisocial people through unauthorized sources and social media accounts. If a piece of breaking news originates or becomes viral through an unofficial channel, it can be false information. Thus, user credibility is an essential clue to misinformation. Figure 1.7 explains an example of such clues in misinformation. The user account itself does not seem credible or official. So, the news posted by this account may or may not be credible news.

Title and Article Mismatch Sometimes, the news title does not exactly explain and support the news body. To spread the news faster, the news creators manipulate the heading of original news to make it more surprising and attractive, but they give less attention to manipulating the entire news body. It leads to the lack of correlation between news titles and news bodies in misinformation.

Emotional Appeal Emotion appeal in news articles is also an indication of the misinformation. The emotions and sentiments are embedded with the false information to compel and excite the readers to share it in their family and friends' network through various channels. Some sentences like "Please share it with your loved ones," "It is a matter of life and death of your family and friends," "It is a matter of our pride," etc. are generally added in the misinformation to activate

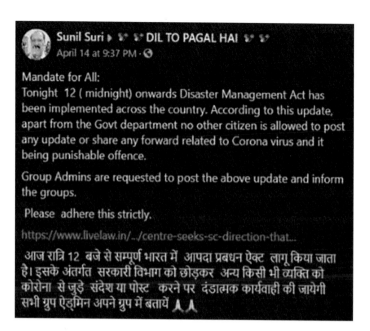

Fig. 1.7 It shows that the account of the user is not credible

the emotions of news readers. Figure 1.8 shows an example of misinformation that contains emotional appeals. This example has been published by Freedom Daily in which the textual information includes the words like "IMMEDIATELY REGRET IT." The word regret affects the public emotions and opinions, and people started to share the news without any investigation. Due to the emotion, this news has been frequently shared on social media even if the news does not have any relation with black lives.

Social Media Comments and Replies Social media is a great pool of credible and false information. In recent times, almost everyone uses some social media platforms to read the news. People also share their thoughts, knowledge, and opinions regarding any news in the form of comments and replies. Analysis of these comments also gives some indication of the credibility of the news article. Figure 1.9 sheds light on such clues in misinformation. The first part of the Fig. 1.9 shows the pilot taking a selfie in the air. The second part of the Fig. 1.9 shows some comments indicating that it is a tampered image. The third part of the image depicts some comments that describe the anger of people. Thus, comments themselves have some clues to analyze whether the news is fake or not. Also, the image caption itself suggests that it is a photoshopped image.

Fig. 1.8 The words "IMMEDIATELY REGRET IT" show the emotional appeal in the example

1.6   Purpose and Reason for the Creation and Spread of Misinformation

The Internet and advanced digital technology accelerate the dissemination of false information enormously. False information often has the goal of attracting a large audience, promoting self-reputation, and spoiling the reputation of an individual or community. Sometimes, it is created to be widely shared online for the purpose of making money through advertising revenue via Web traffic, disgracing a public figure, business competitor, political movement, organization, etc. Sometimes, false stories are created to influence people's thoughts, opinions, and views against a political agenda to manipulate the election outcomes. It is also used to create confusion about any public events, which can often be a money-making business for online publishers. For the fake news creators, the second goal after the false information creation is its fast dissemination. For this purpose, the false news

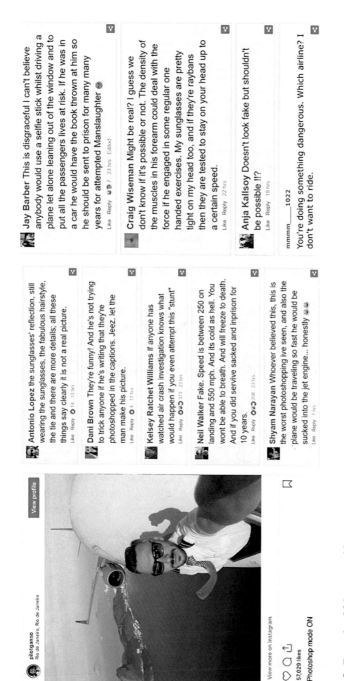

Fig. 1.9 Example of fake news with comments

creators manipulate the news with high expertise, which makes it difficult for the general people to identify. It is a huge reason for the spread of misinformation. The invention of social media platforms delivers the news to millions of people within a second, and false content creators are taking advantage of it. It is another big reason for the spread of misinformation. A few more reasons for the fast dissemination of misinformation are as follows:

Low Literacy Level In recent days, around 86% people in developed countries like the USA are using Android phones and the Internet. This percentage is around 50% in India. As the Internet is available at a very cheap rate, almost everyone is reading and sharing the news on social media, but they do not have proper knowledge about it. Cheaper Internet access and the habit of using social media without efficient knowledge lead to faster spread of misinformation.

Lower Attention Span Sometimes, if we receive news from family, friends, or some known person, we forward it directly without investigating the credibility of the news. Most of the time, everyone generally reads the title only and forwards it without paying much attention to the news body, which may have some tampered information. In this way, the lower attention span is a big reason for misinformation spread.

Emotional Appeals Fake news creators use emotion and sentiment as weapons for the spread of misinformation. They incorporate emotional content in the fabricated news and appeal to the readers to share it in their network. The false content creators invoke emotions in the articles in such a way that it compels the news readers to believe and share. So, the emotional appeal in the news articles is also a considerable reason for the rapid spread of false information.

Less Knowledge of Fact-Checking Methods The day-to-day advancements in technology introduce several state-of-the-art algorithms for fact-checking. But these technologies do not reach each and every individual within a short span of time. Due to less knowledge of fact-checking methods, everyone shares the news without checking the credibility. Sometimes, even the readers think that news may be false, but due to a lack of credibility checking knowledge, they do not justify and share it without verification. So it also leads to the faster spread of misinformation on social media.

1.7 Impact of Misinformation

False news has acquired social media and is becoming a part of life for many people. Misinformation is an emerging issue and can be challenging to detect. It is also highly transmissible, which not only frightens the well-being of individuals but also poses significant threats to the integrity of democracies and elections worldwide. It can change the views, opinions, thoughts, and decisions of people. Misinformation shows the negative impact on individuals and society. False information results in health hazards and distrust in media, undermining the democratic process and serving as platforms for hate speech and harmful conspiracy theories. People feel social, economic, political, and mental distress due to false and misleading content on social media during health emergencies, riots, wars, pandemics, and humanitarian crises. Misinformation also results in a rise in erroneous analysis of scientific knowledge, escalating fear, opinion polarization, panic situations, and decreased access to relevant information. Unreliable evidence on events amplifies and accelerates the spread of misinformation.

Many examples are available that show the negative impact of misinformation. The US presidential election 2016 is a suitable example. Fake news was produced during this election to support one of the multiple candidates. Many people have believed and forwarded approximately 37 million times on Facebook. As the new coronavirus disease spreads around the world, the fast dissemination of news causes anxiety among the population. In 2020, the World Health Organization (WHO) announced the COVID-19 disease as a pandemic. After that, many false information and rumors started floating on social media platforms. Later, WHO described the dangers caused by the spread of misinformation about COVID-19 as an infodemic. The adverse impact of misinformation has been shown during this life-threatening disease when many workers left the workplace to their native place during the lockdown despite the advice to stay wherever they were. Much misinformation regarding the cure of coronavirus was also rapidly disseminated over social media platforms, resulting in thousands of people's deaths. A popular misconception that drinking pure alcohol could kill the virus in the contaminated body killed approximately 800 people in Iran, while about 5,876 people were hospitalized for methanol poisoning. Due to another myth that chloroquine and hydroxychloroquine can cure the coronavirus disease, many people have lost their lives, and many others have lost their vision. Thus, false information broadly affects the individual and society.

1.8   Objective and Challenges of Misinformation Detection

With the advancement of news reading methods from standard newspapers to social media Web sites, false content creators have started spreading misinformation on social media. As social media produces a large quantity of digital information, it becomes impossible to detect fake news by manual fact-checking. Due to this, it becomes essential to develop some automatic algorithms to reduce the impact of misinformation and stop the harm or loss of lives because of its negative impact. The previous section briefly discusses the impact of misinformation on individuals and society. In light of the discussed harmful effects, the first objective of misinformation detection is to identify the false content in the initial phase (i.e., before spreading), and the second objective is to stop its dissemination as soon as possible (i.e., before reaching the people). If the misinformation is already spread, the third objective is to spread awareness about the credibility of the news among people. These three are the broad objectives of misinformation detection, which demands various strategies and algorithms. The second chapter in this book briefly demonstrates the existing algorithms for misinformation detection, and the third chapter onward introduces various state-of-the-art methods to detect false news on social media.

Researchers and scientists have faced numerous challenges in designing various algorithms to solve the above objective of misinformation detection. Some of the common challenges are as follows:

Lack of Good Resources A good work or research and development (R&D) depends on the sufficient amount of available resources. These resources may be some datasets, practical examples, existing fact-checking algorithms, source credibility-checking methods, etc. In the beginning, fake news creators manipulated text content only to form false information. They also published information from a fake account, and it was challenging to check the credibility of the source. With the advancements in multimedia news, false content creators started tampering with images and videos. The unavailability of image/video fact-checking methods became a challenge for multimedia misinformation detection. Inventions of deep learning methods for fake news detection demand enormous amount of data. But the available datasets are not efficient enough to deal with all types of misinformation. Due to the large multimedia datasets, links for images and videos are provided. But after some time, these images and videos are deleted for security purposes. The missing photos and videos on the given link reduce the quality and efficiency of the dataset. Thus, missing data is a massive challenge in designing robust multimedia mechanisms for misinformation detection.

High-Quality Tampering in Textual and Visual Information The aim of fake news creators is to create false content that exactly looks like the real news. So they developed misinformation with high expertise in such a way that the people could believe and share the information with others. Therefore, apart from resources, this high-quality tampering becomes challenging to detect.

1.9 Summary

This chapter briefly introduces fake news and misinformation, historical background, various definitions, and different types and modalities of misinformation. It also briefly discusses various clues present in misinformation, the purpose and reason for creating misinformation, and the broad impact of misinformation on individuals and society. The latter part of this chapter broadly talks about the objective of misinformation detection and various challenges that may be encountered during misinformation detection. The next chapter briefly talks about the recent advancements in the misinformation detection domain. More specifically, it demonstrates various existing algorithms and how these algorithms detect false or misleading information in the early stages.

Chapter 2
Recent Advancements in Misinformation Detection

Chapter 1 briefly introduces the misinformation and the need for its detection. After having sufficient knowledge about misinformation, it is essential to know the recent trends and advancements in misinformation detection. As journalists, scientists, and researchers have realized the negative impact of misinformation, they have conducted various investigations to identify fake news and misinformation before they become viral. Initially, journalists have started manual verification of the news, but in the era of social media, credibility checking of a large volume of news articles is difficult and time-consuming. To avoid this limitation, researchers have developed various automatic methods using machine learning, which detects misinformation quickly. Researchers have also introduced different deep learning methods to strengthen these automatic methods. As deep learning methods demand large datasets to train, people have developed several datasets that help train fake news detection models. Initially, these datasets and techniques were developed only for textual news articles, but with the developments in visual modalities in news articles, multimodal datasets and methods have come into existence. This chapter discusses the recent trends and developments that represent the recent advancements of the datasets and methods for misinformation detection. The following sections briefly describe these two aspects of advancement.

2.1 Datasets

Most researchers, industrialists, and academicians nowadays are focused on building machine learning and deep learning frameworks to solve emerging problems using existing datasets. Data is the backbone of any deep learning and machine learning models. Therefore, it is essential to understand what a dataset is, its significance, and its role in designing robust deep learning and machine learning solutions.

A. Ekbal, R. Kumari, *Dive into Misinformation Detection*, The Information
Retrieval Series 30, https://doi.org/10.1007/978-3-031-54834-5_2

A dataset is a group of different types of information stored in a digital format. It comprises texts, images, audio, videos, numerical data points, etc. Deep learning and machine learning models require large datasets to design the best model with high fidelity. Recently, numerous datasets have been introduced to solve real-life problems in many fields, and misinformation detection is one of them. Despite the availability of various datasets, the lack of quantitative and qualitative datasets is still a cause of concern. With time, misinformation detection datasets have grown tremendously and will continue to grow with high momentum in the future. So, after explaining the importance of datasets, the following subsections discuss various existing datasets developed to solve the misinformation detection problems.

2.1.1 Unimodal Misinformation Detection Dataset

The unimodal dataset is a collection of data instances only containing textual information. Section 1.4 briefly discusses the concept of unimodal. The first fact-checking dataset has been constructed by Vlachos and Riedel (2014). This dataset includes 221 statements collected from CHANNEL4[1] and POLITIFACT.COM.[2] Each statement is labeled with detailed judgment and fine-grained labels, such as *true, mostly true, half true, mostly false*, and *false*. After introducing this dataset, various other datasets have been developed to solve misinformation detection problems. This section provides a detailed description of various unimodal misinformation detection datasets.

LIAR (Wang 2017) It is a publicly available dataset for misinformation detection that consists of 12,836 human-labeled short statements. Each dataset instance includes a short statement, speaker, context, label, and justification as attributes. Statements have been collected from POLITIFACT.COM, and the average length of these statements is 17.9. The data instances belong to six different classes, *viz.*, true, mostly-true, half-true, barely-true, false, and pants-fire. In the LIAR dataset, 1050 instances belong to the pants-fire class, and other labels include the range from 2,063 to 2,068. Table 2.1 depicts one sample from the LIAR dataset.

FEVER (Thorne et al. 2018) FEVER stands for Fact Extraction and VERification. It includes 185,445 claims classified into three classes, such as *supported, refuted, and notenoughinfo*. The data instances of the first two classes also include necessary evidence for their judgment. Table 2.2 depicts some examples of the FEVER dataset, and Table 2.3 shows the dataset distribution across various classes for training, test, and development sets. Here, the training set is used to train the model, the development set is used to fine-tune the parameter of the training algorithm, and the test set is used to predict the class of the unseen data or new data instances.

---

[1] https://www.channel4.com/.

[2] https://www.politifact.com/.

Table 2.1 Sample of LIAR dataset

Attribute	Value
Statement	The last quarter, it was just announced our gross domestic product was below zero. Who ever heard of this? It's never below zero.
Speaker	Donald Trump
Context	presidential announcement speech
Label	Pants on Fire
Justification	According to the Bureau of Economic Analysis and National Bureau of Economic Research, the growth in the gross domestic product has been below zero 42 times over 68 years. That's a lot more than "never." We rate his claim Pants on Fire!

Table 2.2 Sample of FEVER dataset

Attribute	Value
Claim	The Rodney King riots took place in the most populous county in the USA.
Sentence	Los Angeles County, officially the County of Los Angeles, is the most populous county in the USA
Label	Supported

Table 2.3 FEVER dataset distribution across different classes for training, development, and test set. Here, NEI represents the Not Enough Information class

Class	Training	Development	Test
Supported	80,035	3,333	3,333
Reffuted	29,775	3,333	3,333
NEI	35,639	3,333	3,333

BuzzFeedNews (Potthast et al. 2018)   The BuzzFeedNews dataset is the collection of news published on Facebook by 9 news agencies. It comprises the news published from September 19 to 23 and September 26 and 27, which is close to the 2016 US election. To prepare this dataset, five BuzzFeed journalists fact-checked every post and the linked article. This dataset contains two sets of data, *viz.*, fake news and real news in CSV file format. Each file has 91 samples and 12 features. Each data sample contains an ID, title, source, image, and visual information links. The dataset includes a total of 1627 news articles. Along with binary annotation (fake/real), these articles are classified into four categories: mostly true, mostly false, a mixture of true and false, and no factual content. Table 2.4 shows the detailed data distributions of the BuzzFeedNews.

BuzzFace (Santia and Williams 2018)   BuzzFace is the extension of BuzzFeedNews dataset. It integrates data on Facebook comments and reactions along with news articles. In this dataset, each article includes news body text, images, links, Disqus plugin comments, Facebook plugin comments, and embedded tweets. This dataset contains over 1.6 million text items, approximately 400 times larger than the BuzzFeednews dataset. The class labels of the BuzzFace data instance are the same as the BuzzfeedNews data instance, i.e., *mostly true, mostly false, mixture of true and false, and no factual content.*

Table 2.4 BuzzFeedNews
data distributions across
various classes and publishers

Publisher	True	Mix	False	n/a	Total
Mainstream	806	8	0	12	826
ABC News	90	2	0	3	95
CNN	295	4	0	8	307
Politico	421	2	0	1	424
Left-wing	182	51	15	8	256
Addicting Info	95	25	8	7	135
Occupy Democrats	55	23	6	0	91
The Other 98%	32	3	1	1	30
Right-wing	276	153	72	44	545
Eagle Rising	107	47	25	36	214
Freedom Daily	48	24	22	4	99
Right Wing News	121	82	25	4	232
Total	1264	212	87	64	1627

Some-like-it-hoax (Tacchini et al. 2017)   As the name suggests, this dataset has been prepared to classify the hoax and non-hoax news. It is also a collection of news articles published on Facebook. To prepare this dataset, the author first listed two types of Facebook pages: scientific news sources and conspiracy news sources. The news articles collected from scientific news sources are considered credible and annotated as non-hoax. In contrast, the news articles collected from conspiracy news sources are considered non-credible and annotated as hoaxes. The resulting dataset includes 15,500 posts from 32 Facebook pages (14 conspiracy and 18 scientific). Among total posts, 8,923 (57.6%) belong to the hoax category, and 6,577 (42.4%) belong to the non-hoax category.

PHEME (Zubiaga et al. 2016)   PHEME dataset has been prepared for the rumor detection. This dataset contains rumors and non-rumors posted on Twitter during breaking news. It includes rumors related to nine breaking events. Most of the events were related to deliberately killing some people. In this dataset, each rumor is annotated with one of the three veracity labels: either True, False, or Unverified. It contains 330 rumor threads and 4,832 tweets.

CREDBANK (Mitra and Gilbert 2015)   CREDBANK is a corpus that consists of tweets, events, topics, and associated human reliability judgments. This dataset has been prepared by performing the real-time tracking of approximately 1 billion streaming tweets for more than 3 months. It is also based on proper routings of the tweet streams to human annotators within a short period after those events unfold on Twitter. It also considers the computational summarization of those tweets. This dataset contains more than 60 million tweets from 1,049 real-world events. Thirty human annotators annotated each event into different categories: credible and non-credible. The tweets related to credible events are considered credible, and those related to non-credible events are considered non-credible.

NELA-GT-2018 (Nørregaard et al. 2019)   It is the collection of 713k articles collected from 194 media and news outlets. These news articles were collected between February 2018 and November 2018. The sources of these articles also include hyperpartisan, mainstream, and conspiracy Web sites. The data instances (articles) have been annotated as per the credibility of the sources. In this dataset, the ground-truth ratings of the sources have been provided from eight different assessment sites, which cover multiple dimensions of veracity, including bias, adherence to journalistic standards, reliability, transparency, and consumer trust. These eight assessment sites are NewsGuard, Pew Research Center, Wikipedia, Opensource, Media Bias/Fact Check (MBFC), AllSides, BuzzFeed News, and PolitiFact.

FA-KES (Salem et al. 2019) Most of the above-discussed dataset spin around US political, entertainment, and satire news. These datasets have been prepared by scrapping news Web sites and annotated according to the credibility of the Web sites. Despite the earlier datasets, FA-KES is the collection of fake news revolving around the Syrian war. Apart from news Web sites, this dataset contains news articles from various media outlets representing loyalist press, mobilization press, and diverse print media. The resultant dataset consists of 804 news articles annotated as true or fake. Table 2.5 shows some samples from the dataset.

COVID-19 Fake News Dataset (Patwa et al. 2021) In the year 2020, the COVID-19 was on its peak. During that period, the entire world was facing an infodemic of fake and misleading news along with life-threatening diseases. Misinformation about the cure, vaccine, and disease prevention were circulating on different social media outlets. To tackle this problem, researchers have developed various datasets and methodologies, and the COVID-19 Fake News Dataset is one of them. It consists of 10,700 COVID-19-related social media posts. Each post has been manually annotated as fake or real. Table 2.6 shows some samples from the dataset. Out of the total, 5600 instances belong to the fake class, and 5100 instances belong to the real class, which reflects that this dataset is approximately balanced.

Table 2.5 Samples of FA-KES dataset

Article Title	Event	Label
At least 40 killed in Syrian weapons depot blast	Ghouta Chemical Attack	fake
80 Civilians Killed by Russian Airstrikes on Aleppo despite 48-Hour Truce	Multiple Offensives All Over Syria	fake
Syrian Army Kills 11 ISIL Terrorists Destroy Their Posits in Deir Ezzor	Khan Sheikhoun Chemical Attack	true

Table 2.6 Samples of COVID-19 fake news dataset

Text	Source	Label
All hotels, restaurants, pubs etc will be closed till 15th Oct 2020 as per tourism minister of India.	Facebook	Fake
Scene from TV series viral as dead doctors in Italy due to COVID-19	Fact checking	Fake
Indian Council of Medical Research (ICMR) has approved 1000 #COVID19 testing labs all across India. There was only one government lab at the beginning of the year. #IndiaFightsCorona. #ICMRFightsCovid19	Twitter (ICMR)	Real

Table 2.7 Fine-grained labels of the tweets for different tasks

Tasks	Values
Contains hate	Yes, No, Can't decide
Talk about a cure	Yes, No, Can't decide
Give advice	Yes, No, Can't decide
Rise moral	Yes, No, Can't decide
News or opinion	News, Opinion, Can't decide
Dialect	Modern Standard Arabic, North Africa, Middle East, Can't decide
Blame and negative speech	Yes, No, Can't decide
Factual	Yes, No, Can't decide
Worth fact-checking	Yes, Maybe, No, Can't decide
Contains fake information	Yes, Maybe, No, Can't decide

AraCOVID19-MFH (Ameur and Aliane 2021) It is a COVID-19-related fake news and hate speech dataset. It is a multi-labeled dataset in Arabic language that consists of manually annotated tweets. This dataset includes 10,828 Arabic tweets associated with various labels to perform ten tasks. These tasks are *Contains hate, Talk about a cure, Give advice, Rise moral, News or opinion, Dialect, Blame and negative speech, Factual, Worth fact-checking,* and *Contains fake information.* Further, the tweets are associated with fine-grained labels for each task, as shown in Table 2.7. Therefore, it can solve numerous other tasks (9 tasks) along with fake news detection tasks.

BanFakeNews (Hossain et al. 2020) In recent years, fake news has also circulated on social media in regional languages, which is an emerging and challenging problem. To tackle this problem, researchers are developing various datasets and methodologies in regional languages. The BanFakeNews dataset is also an outcome of this investigation. This dataset was created for the Bengali language for fake news detection. It includes 50k news articles associated with two classes: *authentic* and *fake*. Out of the total news, 48,678 news articles belong to the authentic class, and 1,299 are associated with the fake class. Authentic news articles were collected from different mainstream trusted news portals in Bangladesh, and fake news articles were collected from some Web sites publishing misleading, clickbait, and satire.

Fake News Filipino Dataset (Cruz et al. 2020) It is also a fake news dataset developed in low-resource language, i.e., Filipino. This dataset contains 3,206 news articles associated with fake or real class. Among the total instances, 1,603 instances belong to the fake class, and 1,603 instances belong to the real class, which implies the perfect balance of the dataset across the two classes. Fake news articles have been collected from fake news Web sites active in the Philippines, and real news articles have been collected from mainstream news Web sites active in the Philippines.

Fake News Challenge (FNC) (Slovikovskaya and Attardi 2020) It has been introduced during Fake News Challenge Stage-1. This dataset has been obtained from Emergent, a digital journalism project for rumor detection. The dataset includes 49,972 instances in total. Each instance is the headline-body pair. Each pair is associated with a stance labeled by expert journalists. This dataset specifically has been designed for stance detection, determining whether the viral news agrees, disagrees, discusses, or is unrelated to the verified claims. It is true if the viral news agrees with the real, verified claims. If the viral news disagrees, it is false. The same concept is applied to verified false claims. Discusses and unrelated labels do not help that much in fake news detection. Thus, even if the dataset instances (headline body pairs) do not have direct fake and real labels, with the help of stance labels, it becomes relevant for fake news detection. FNC dataset contains a title and a body text pair, either from two different news articles or from the same news article associated with one of the stance labels among *agrees, disagrees, discusses, and unrelated.*

Bytedance (Xiaoye 2019) Similar to the FNC, ByteDance has also been developed for solving the stance detection task. Global Internet technology business ByteDance, with its headquarters in China, is the creator of this dataset. It is now available as the Fake News Classification competition dataset. The training and test sets compose this dataset. There are 320,767 news pairs in the training set. Each pair of news is linked to one of the three class labels: unconnected, disagreed, or agreed. There are 80,126 unlabeled news pairs in the test set. The dataset includes an English translation of each news article, whereas the originals are in Chinese.

Covid-Stance (Mutlu et al. 2020) It is also an stance detection dataset. It is the collection of user-generated COVID-19-related content on Twitter. It consists of approximately 14,000 tweets in the form of manually annotated opinions of the tweet initiators concerning the use of "chloroquine" and "hydroxychloroquine" to treat or prevent COVID-19 disease. Each instance of this dataset associated with one of the three classes, such as *against, favor,* and *neutral.*

Fake News Inference Dataset (FNID) (Sadeghi et al. 2022) This dataset has been developed for misinformation detection using natural language inference. The entire dataset is composed of two parts. Each part is further split into training, test, and validation sets. In the first part, the training set includes 15,212 instances, the validation set contains 1,058 instances, and the test set is a collection of 1,054 test instances. In the second part, the training set contains 15,052 training samples, 1,265 validation samples, and 1,266 test samples.

2.1.2   Multimodal Misinformation Detection Dataset

In prior studies, authors have detected fake news utilizing textual or linguistic features extracted from the text content of the news. Still, the news comes with different modalities like image, audio, video, etc. Any or all of them may provide helpful evidence for detecting misinformation. This motivation has inspired the researchers to develop numerous multimodal datasets that help solve the problems across various dimensions of misinformation detection. The subsequent paragraphs explain some popular datasets used to perform this task.

Image Verification Corpus (Maigrot et al. 2016) This dataset is a part of Verifying Multimedia Use at MediaEval challenge. It is the collection of multimedia tweets that include tweet text, contextual information, and associated images. The tweets are associated with a label fake, real, or humor. The dataset comprises two parts: a training set and a test set containing tweets from different disaster-related events. The training set contains a total of 14,483 tweets, in which 6848 tweets belong to the fake class, 5001 tweets are of the real class, and humor class contains 2634 tweets. The test set includes 3781 tweets. In this dataset, the humor class instances are not present in the test set. As this dataset is a multimodal dataset, it includes images and text. The dataset contains 360 images in the training set and 50 in the test set.

Weibo (Jin et al. 2017) This multimodal Chinese dataset was gathered from a Chinese microblogging platform. These Web sites usually urge users to report questionable tweets on Weibo, which are confirmed as real or fake by a group of well-known users. This dataset includes these verified tweets and the labels collected from May 2012 to June 2016. It consists of 9527 news posts, which are further divided into train and test sets. The train set includes 7531 data instances, and the test set contains 1996 data instances. It is a multimodal dataset comprising 5320 real and 7954 fake images.

FakeNewsNet (Shu et al. 2020) It is a data repository that contains two datasets (PolitiFact and GossipCop) with a variety of features. It is the first fake news dataset that includes spatiotemporal information, news content, and social context. PolitiFact includes political news associated with fake or real classes, whereas GossipCop includes the entertainment-related news again associated with fake or real class. The news content in the dataset includes news text and images. The social context includes tweet posts, retweets, replies, likes, the number of users involved in these activities, and followers. The spatiotemporal information in these two datasets includes geographical location, such as user profiles and tweets with location, timestamp for the news, and timestamp for the responses. FakeNewsNet is a large-scale dataset with 432 fake and 632 real news in the PolitiFact dataset and 5,323 fake and 16,817 real news from the GossipCop dataset. It also consists of 164,892 fake and 399,237 real tweets in PolitiFact and 519,581 fake and 876,967 real tweets in the GossipCop dataset.

Fauxtography (Zlatkova et al. 2019) Fauxtography dataset is the composition of two different datasets collected from two different fact-checking Web sites, such as Snopes[3] and Reuters.[4] It is the collection of viral, interesting, and even contradictory images with some piece of text (claim) that describes the image. Snopes dataset includes image-claim pairs labeled as either true or false. The collected data consists of 838 instances, 197 true and 641 false. Reuters dataset includes 395 true image

---

[3] https://www.snopes.com/.

[4] https://www.reuters.com/.

claim pairs. After summing up both the datasets, it reaches 592 true and 641 false image claim pairs.

Fakeddit (Nakamura et al. 2020) The multimodal fake news datasets discussed above consist of the link of the images or videos. As time passed, those images and videos were deleted from that link. Therefore, in recent times, these datasets have a tiny number of images or videos. To overcome this limitation, researchers have introduced a dataset named Fakeddit. It comprises text and image data, comment data, metadata, and fine-grained fake news labels. It is a large-scale dataset containing over 1 million multimodal samples from various categories of fake news. These samples are labeled according to 2-way, 3-way, and 6-way classification categories. The 2-way label includes *fake* and *real* categories, and the 3-way label includes *completely true, fake* and *sample with false content*. The 6-way label includes *true, satire, misleading content, imposter content, false connection* and *manipulated content*. This dataset contains 1,063,106 samples, which is the summation of 628,501 fake and 527,049 real samples.

Factify (Suryavardan et al. 2022) Factify is a multimodal fact verification dataset. It comprises textual claims, images, and reference textual documents. Factify is the collection of 50,000 claims accompanied by 100,000 images. The main purpose of designing this dataset is to solve the task of classifying the claims into support, refute, and not-enough-evidence classes with the help of the supporting data.

TI-CNN (Yang et al. 2018c) Text and Image information-based Convolutional Neural Network (TI-CNN) is a multimodal fake news dataset containing news article associated with an image. According to the article that publishes this dataset, it includes 20,015 news articles, out of which 11,941 are fake, and 8,074 are real news articles. Authors have scrapped text and metadata from more than 240 Web sites for fake news. Megan Risdal has given the list of these Web sites on Kaggle.[5] The real news has been crawled from well-known authentic news Web sites such as the Washington Post, the New York Times, etc. This dataset contains attributes like title, text, image URLs, author, and Web site. Since the image URLs are given instead of the actual images, and many images are not now available on those URLs, we avoid the dataset instances for which the images cannot be downloaded. Finally, we make this dataset with a size of 5221 instances. This modified dataset includes 2,612 real news and 2,609 fake news articles. Further, we divide this dataset into 60:20:20 as training, testing, and validation sets. Researchers use the title, text, and image information to discover the intrinsic differences between fake and real news to train the different misinformation detection models.

CHECKED CHECKED is the first multimedia Chinese dataset related to COVID-19, developed for misinformation detection in the Chinese language. It includes 2,104 verified COVID-19-related microblogs spread on Weibo and collected from December 2019 to August 2020. Along with microblogs, CHECKED includes

---

[5] https://www.kaggle.com/mrisdal/fake-news.

1,185,702 comments, 1,868,175 reposts, and 56,852,736 likes. The dataset also includes an efficient set of multimedia information for each microblog, including textual, visual, temporal, network information, and ground-truth labels. This dataset has two ground-truth labels, i.e. *fake* and *real*.

2.1.3 Multilingual Misinformation Detection Dataset

Multilingual means the composition of multiple languages. The advancements and ease of use of social media platforms have accelerated the spread of news and information in various languages instead of only English. This has motivated the creation and spread of misinformation in various languages, which demands multilingual misinformation detection for which multilingual datasets are required. Although many datasets for misinformation detection exist, these are mostly monolingual in nature. To fulfill the scarcity of annotated multilingual misinformation datasets, researchers have developed a few datasets that can make progress in the field of multilingual and domain-independent fake news detection. The below section discusses some of the popular datasets among them.

MM-COVID (Li et al. 2020b) During 2020, the COVID-19 pandemic had been declared as the global health crisis of the entire world. During that period, the misinformation about COVID-19 was spreading at a high speed. To prevent fake news, people have introduced various multilingual algorithms and datasets, and MM-COVID is one of them. This dataset contains multilingual misinformation and the related social context. It is a collection of 3,981 fake news and 7,192 credible information from six different languages: *English, Portuguese, Spanish, French, Hindi*, and *Italian*.

MuMiN (Nielsen and McConville 2022) MuMin is basically misinformation graph dataset. It comprises social media data like tweets, images, articles, user information, replies, and hashtags. It contains approximately 21 million tweets collected from 26,000 Twitter threads. Each thread is semantically linked to over 13,000 fact-checked claims across various events, topics, and domains in 41 different languages.

FakeCovid (Shahi and Nandini 2020) FakeCovid is the first multilingual cross-domain dataset, which includes 5,182 fact-checked COVID-19 news articles. It is a collection of news articles from 92 different fact-checking Web sites. The data instances have been manually annotated into 11 different classes according to the labels provided by the fact-checking Web sites. The dataset has been collected in 40 languages from 105 different countries.

Mul-FaD (Ahuja and Kumar 2023) The Mul-FaD introduces a multilingual dataset that includes approximately 43,488 articles in German, English, and French. To develop this dataset, the authors have collected various misinformation datasets from the Kaggle Web site. They have just adopted the text and labels from those datasets. Initially, this dataset contained a total of 43,488 articles in the English

Table 2.8 Dataset statistics of Mul-FaD dataset

	English	German	French
Fake	9475	7000	5996
Real	8018	6000	6999

language. The authors have randomly selected 26,000 instances and divided them into two equal parts. Further, they translated each part into French and German, respectively. Thus, the resultant dataset becomes multilingual. Table 2.8 depicts the data distribution and statistics of the Mul-FaD dataset across various languages.

2.2 Methods

In this chapter, Sect. 2.1 discusses the numerous datasets of various categories in details. After having proper and sufficient knowledge of the datasets, it becomes important to understand the role and the process of utilization of those datasets in implementing various misinformation detection methodologies. Along with the dataset development, researchers have also made efficient progress in designing the misinformation detection frameworks. This section discusses these frameworks from four different perspectives: *knowledge, writing style, propagation pattern*, and the *social context*.

2.2.1 Knowledge-Based Misinformation Detection

The knowledge-based method detects misinformation by checking whether the knowledge contained in news content is consistent with the known facts. More specifically, it is the comparison between the textual knowledge extracted from the news articles that have to be verified and the knowledge graphs that represent ground truth or facts. Therefore, before going deeper into this perspective to make the decision, it is necessary to have some understanding of knowledge and facts. In this domain, knowledge represents a set of *Subject, Predicate*, and *Object* (SPO) triples extracted from the given news article that effectively represents the given information. For example, the knowledge extracted from the sentence *Garlic water is a cure of COVID-19* can be represented as (Garlic water, cure, COVID-19) in SOP form. The knowledge verified as truth is termed as *fact*, and the set of facts is termed as *knowledge base*. *Knowledge Graph* provides a graph structure that represents the SPO triples in the form of a knowledge base, where the nodes are formed using either subject or object and edges are formed using predicates.

The fake news detection from the perspective of knowledge is done by fact-checking. Initially, fact-checking was developed in journalism to assess news credibility. For this purpose, journalists identify the differences between the extracted knowledge from the verifiable news content (statements or claims) and the known facts. Although this perspective of news credibility detection can be utilized for news containing both text and image, it has been majorly implemented for textual news articles. Initially, the authors have developed manual fact-checking methods, which have further been advanced to automatic fact-checking methods. The knowledge-based fact-checking includes *expert-based, crowdsourcing-based*, and *computation-based* methods. Some of them are manual, and some are automatic methods.

This section briefly presents some prior misinformation detection works designed using the expert-based perspective. The study presented in Zhang et al. (2018) solves the problem of misinformation detection by analyzing the news article in detail. It tries to identify the diverse connections among news articles, news topics, subjects, and their creators. By analyzing these features, the authors also designed a framework named "FakeDetector." In expert-based systems, some famous fact-checking Web sites are Snopes and PolitiFact. Expert-based credibility verification depends on domain experts as fact-checkers to investigate the credibility of the given news content. This fact-checking is basically performed by a small group of highly credible fact-checkers. It is easy to manage and results in the most accurate results, but it poorly scales with the increase in the volume of verifiable news content, and it is also very costly. As soon as the new claim comes, the investigator consults domain experts in that domain. It takes some time for a final judgment about credibility. To avoid this limitation, (Guha 2017) has given a strategy in which the credibility verification techniques provide the facility to the users, which allows reading all the related information along with the news article. After reading the complete information, the users provide a rating according to the predefined policy. This rating is further mapped to a threshold value, and if the rating is greater than the threshold, the news is classified as credible; otherwise, it is classified as fake. This analysis is generally done on three attributes of the news: text, source, and user response. By using these attributes, the authors in Ruchansky et al. (2017) designed a model that combines the text, source, and responses to capture the implicit characteristics of the news, which determine the news credibility.

In the crowdsourcing method, users are given the option to discuss and provide the credibility label of specific news. Therefore, this approach fully relies on the wisdom or opinion of the crowd to fact-check the news on the basis of their knowledge. Fiskkit[6] is a Web site that follows the crowdsourced mechanism for fact-checking. Another application provides a framework that allows users to report any malicious or false content. Then the reported contents are further verified by the expert scientists or journalists to determine the credibility of the news. If the news contains some false information, the application immediately removes it from the platform or stops its propagation. Facebook flag method is one of the popular methods of misinformation detection methods. On Facebook, the detective algorithm runs in the background, which selects some news every day and sends it

---

[6] https://fiskkit.com/.

to the expert. According to the response of the experts, it propagates or stops the news.

The main purpose of the computational fact-checking methods is to provide a fact-checking system to the users that can categorize the news content as false true. The computational fact-checking methods first identify the true claims and then try to discriminate other related claims from the verified claims. It works on the basis of users' point of view on the specific content. Structured knowledge graphs and the open Web are suitable examples of computational fact-checking methods. The work presented in Etzioni et al. (2008) and Magdy and Wanas (2010) differentiate true news and false news based on the news content and annotates fake news into three different classes: serious fabrication, humorous, and large-scale hoaxes. Further, the study presented in Rubin et al. (2015) discusses the pros and cons of computational-based misinformation detection. This work introduced data-centered applications that utilize the available datasets and apply machine learning and deep learning methods to design text classifiers for misinformation detection. The upcoming sections discuss such types of models in detail.

2.2.2   Style-Based Misinformation Detection

The style-based misinformation detection is similar to knowledge-based misinformation detection, which focuses on analyzing news content. However, the style-based methods identify the news intention (i.e., if there is any intention to mislead the people) in addition to evaluating the news authenticity by analyzing the news content. In contrast, knowledge-based methods can't identify the intention. Real news can be distinguished from fake news using a set of non-latent machine learning features called style. The main purpose of style-based misinformation detection is to identify the differences in writing styles between true and fake news. It often relies on NLP mechanisms and is implemented using a machine learning framework. The motivation behind style-based methods is that false stories prefer to write the information in a specific style, which encourages readers to trust. This style might include strong emotional appeal, some uncommon events or phenomena, use of special characters or punctuation marks, misspelled words, etc. Instead, real news mostly includes neutral words and also describes the events with facts. Such special content styles can be automatically identified by using some machine learning algorithms.

News style or linguistic features can be extracted from the text, images, and videos within to-be-verified content. The linguistic patterns are still poorly understood, and the linguistic aspects heavily rely on domain expertise and particular event characteristics. Thus, by enhancing the extracted linguistic features, the models can be improved even more. The linguistic characteristics and patterns of the textual content are examined in style-based literature. A technique that assesses the style of hyperpartisan (very biased) and bogus news has been reported by a study in Potthast et al. (2018). It demonstrates how the style analysis aids in differentiating between news that is hyperpartisan and mainstream. In Castelo et al. (2019), a Topic-AGgnostic (TAG) classification technique for identifying false news sites was presented. It makes use of linguistic traits and Web markup. Additionally, by detecting linguistic features, the authors in Pérez-Rosas et al. (2018) have developed a linear support vector machine (SVM) classifier based on linguistic features. Style-based methods also include the investigation of extreme affective information, such as emotion and sentiment. It also explores the role of novelty (non-common events) in misinformation spread. The following section provides some prior works in this domain.

2.2.2.1 Affect-Aware Misinformation Detection

Affect analysis (e.g., emotion and sentiment analysis) is an interdisciplinary study and has been one of the exciting areas in natural language processing (NLP) and computer vision (CV). This has been used in several NLP tasks, such as machine translation (Kajava et al. 2020), dialogue generation (Firdaus et al. 2020), sarcasm detection (Chauhan et al. 2020), etc. The study in Mai et al. (2019) proposed a Hierarchical Feature Fusion Network (HFFN) for multimodal affective computing. It introduces a new two-level strategy (Divide, Conquer, and Combine) for efficient multimodal feature fusion. A new work, presented in Chauhan et al. (2019b), explored the interaction between different modalities using the Inter-modal Interaction Module (IIM) for multimodal emotion and sentiment analysis. The study in Ghosal et al. (2018a) has proposed an inter-modal attention-based framework for multimodal sentiment classification. Another study (Akhtar et al. 2019) has developed an attention-based multitask learning framework for emotion and sentiment recognition.

Although affective information has been broadly investigated, it is a new dimension in the detection of misinformation. Affective information mining has recently drawn attention from scholars because false news context and content likely contain obvious emotional and sentiment biases. Below, we discuss the prior studies of affective information in the context of misinformation detection.

Emotions are essential to our existence since they represent sentiments like joy, fear, grief, and happiness that impact our day-to-day actions. Social media sites like Facebook, Instagram, and Twitter are the most widely used venues for people to express and share their thoughts and feelings. Data from social media posts, news headlines, song lyrics, and blog entries have been effectively used for the comprehensive investigation and development of emotion recognition models such as Liew and Turtle (2016); Abdul-Mageed and Ungar (2017). Researchers investigate fine-grained emotions and how they appear in the news and stories published through various social communication mediums. A system for predicting many emotions with diverse strengths in a single sentence was presented in Zhou et al. (2016). A mechanism using a dimensionality reduction method employing non-negative matrix factorization is proposed in Wang and Pal (2015). It provides the emotion distribution as an output. By fusing several constraints, including topic correlations, emotional bindings, and emotion lexicons, it has created a framework for constraint optimization. The system presented in Becker et al. (2017) used naive Bayes (NB), support vector machine (SVM), and radial basis function (RBF) to examine textual emotion categorization in a multilingual environment. Additionally, it used the outputs of these classifiers to create meta-classifiers for emotion prediction, specifically boosting and bagging (Maclin and Opitz 1997). The work published in Ren and Hong (2019) presented an emotion recognition method to obtain distinct emotions from internet reviews. It explored the divergent consequences of three distinct emotions (anger, fear, and sadness) on perceived review.

The emotional reactions to news posts, such as liking, commenting, and sharing, also inevitably contribute to the spread of false information. According to research in Zarrabian and Hassani-Abharian (2020) and Ghanem et al. (2020), there is a significant likelihood and severity of various emotional effective information, including disgust, fear, and surprise, in the response caused by fake news. Instead, real news shows a high probability and severity of sadness, joy, and trust. Another study presented in Giachanou et al. (2019) has investigated the importance of emotional signals in misinformation detection. To ascertain the veracity of claims, this work has illustrated an LSTM model that integrates emotional clues taken from the textual part of the claim. The research conducted by Giachanou et al. (2021) has also looked at extracting emotional clues from statements to examine how this affects the evaluation of credibility. An architecture based on deep learning presented in FakeFlow (Ghanem et al. 2021) analyzes the involvement of affective information that influences the opinions and emotions of the readers. This model considers the combined form of topics and the obtained affective information to study the movement of affective information content. Emotion and fake news are closely related, according to research by Guo et al. (2019); Zhang et al. (2021b) and Preston et al. (2021). Prior studies only used the emotional features of claims or real news content to identify false news. The study published in Zhang et al. (2021b) looked into the connection between social and publisher emotions. It also looks into the appearance of dual emotions in actual and false news. While social emotion is gleaned from the comments, publisher emotion is taken from the news content. According to a different study (Guo et al. 2019), fake news is inherently sensational and provocative, which may cause users to feel suspicious, anxious, or shocked. A bidirectional gated recurrent unit (Bi-GRU) is designed in this study to learn the emotional behavior of news and comments. Additional research (Preston et al. 2021) has been published on identifying fake news, particularly on Facebook. This study aims to determine whether people with high *emotional intelligence* are less prone to believe false information. Sentiment, in addition to emotion, is inevitably involved in identifying fake news.

Emotion is the presentation of a particular feeling or sentiment, and sentiment helps individuals convey their emotion through expression; hence, the two are co-related. Researchers have proved in their prior works that sentiment could provide an important signal for false news. The work investigated in Sivasangari et al. (2018) isolates the rumor based on the sentiment polarity of the tweets. The study in Ajao et al. (2019) has proved that there exists a relation between sentiments and fake news that improves the performance of the misinformation detection model. The work reported in Shrestha (2018) designs a machine learning model, i.e., Random Forest Classifier (RFC), that performs sentiment analysis in user comments. Many other studies, such as Kula et al. (2020); Bhutani et al. (2019) and Ajao et al. (2019), have analyzed the sentiment for effective fake news detection. These studies include a deep learning-based model implementation to prove that learning affective information with fake news detection improves fake news performance.

2.2.2.2   Novelty-Aware Misinformation Detection

The novelty, also known as an anomaly, exception, or outlier, is a pattern in the information that causes an unforeseen behavior in any system's performance. These days, novelty detection is becoming more and more popular in various fields, including image processing (Kerner et al. 2019), text mining (Kumar and Bhatia 2020), industrial monitoring (Jose et al. 2020), and healthcare informatics (An et al. 2020). This task is highly related to the *textual entailment recognition* (TER) (Xiong et al. 2020) work. A novelty detection method is commonly applied to check whether a document is non-novel or novel according to its content. Prior research attempted to identify novelty at the lexical or sentence level (Lee 2015) but could not address repetition at the semantic level. Researchers have developed these strategies using a traditional feature-based machine learning architecture or a rule-based one that depends on handcrafted characteristics obtained from the documents.

Recent research focuses on automatic feature extraction with neural networks and deep learning. A study (Ghosal et al. 2020) explored document-level novelty detection tasks to find the novelty of a document with reference to the source document. This work implements a neural attention method to identify document-level novelty without feature manipulation. It illustrates how the degree of originality in a target document could be established by simply comparing the texts in the source and target documents. The textual entailment task is closely related to novelty detection, which finds the relation between the text fragments. Several machine learning techniques, including SVM, RF, and multilayer perceptron (MLP), were proposed in the study published in Saikh et al. (2017). These algorithms use textual entailment to discover document-level novelty.

Novelty detection is also helpful for non-redundant document retrieval tasks. The mechanism developed in Breja (2015) presents a novel method for novelty identification in Web documents to collect pertinent and non-redundant information to investigate the unique document retrieval job. In addition, it has also provided a technique that can be added to a Web crawler to reduce redundancy and retrieve the most pertinent content. Semantic similarity and text summarizing are used in the development of this novelty detection method. The text is first summarized using the ontology, and from the summary, semantic similarity is computed. It determines whether a document is novel or non-novel using semantic similarity. The authors have presented a network-based method for the novelty identification of academic literature in a different study (Amplayo et al. 2018). This approach presents an autoencoder network by leveraging graph characteristics to train the novelty detection model.

Researchers have proposed novelty detection work in a few specific domains in addition to these broad ones. Novelty detection is very much related to the TER task, and people have started the TER task to perform stance detection tasks. The misinformation detection task is similar to the stance identification task (Hanselowski et al. 2018). Therefore, novelty detection and TER are frequently applied in misinformation detection. The work proposed in Rohit et al. (2018) explores novelty detection tasks in the news stream due to the high proliferation of redundant and misleading. Inspired by the assumption that *high novelty accelerates the possibility of the news post being fake*, the authors in Qin et al. (2016) have developed a method for rumor detection with the help of novelty detection tasks. The authors of this article employed similarity analysis to determine how closely a fresh news item matched the rumors that had already circulated and then used that knowledge as a novel feature for rumor identification.

The studies presented in Chaudhry et al. (2017) and Slovikovskaya and Attardi (2020) have solved the misinformation detection using stance detection task. The investigations introduced different variations of the bidirectional encoder representations from the transformer (BERT) model for the misinformation classification task. Literature Liu et al. (2019a); Pham (2019) and Yang et al. (2019a) have explored natural language inference (NLI) task (MacCartney 2009) using different variations of deep learning models to detect fake news. These mechanisms find the relation between existing news and newly viral news using natural language inference, which ultimately replicates whether the new news is novel concerning old verified news. The model determines whether the news is fake or real based on the NLI outcomes.

2.2.3 News Content-Based Misinformation Detection

A news article includes various information, including the author, source, attention-grabbing headlines, writing styles, photos, and videos. Any modifications to these elements result in false or misleading information. Social context, network information, and news substance are the main factors in identifying fake news on social media. This section covers a few well-known and current studies examining the context, news content, and social media diffusion process to identify fake news. Under this group, the literature is categorized into two classes, *viz.*, (i) unimodal misinformation detection and (ii) multimodal misinformation detection. The literature examining knowledge, style, and propagation patterns of false news is included in unimodal fake news detection. Multimodal talks about the image and video-embedded misinformation detection frameworks.

2.2.3.1   Unimodal Misinformation Detection

Research on unimodal (textual or visual) fake news detection methods typically makes use of social context-based (Shu et al. 2019a; Ma et al. 2018) and content-based (Ma et al. 2016; Yu et al. 2017a) features. A well-known work called FakeDetector (Zhang et al. 2020) introduced an automatic model for determining the trustworthiness of fake news by extracting a collection of latent features from the textual data. A deep diffusive network model that simultaneously learns the representations of news articles, subjects, and creators has been designed to identify fake news based on these aspects. The work explored in Liu et al. (2019b) attempted to record dynamic shifts in news spreaders, diffusion structures, and news contents. This study used an early rumor identification model based on long short-term memory (LSTM) to find rumors in their early stages. Capturing the dynamic variations between rumors and non-rumors' spreaders and diffusion structures is a novel idea. A different study (Zubiaga et al. 2018) has demonstrated that using discourse features taken from social media conversations to improve a sequential classifier's performance is beneficial. Additionally, LSTM has been investigated, which uses a smaller feature set to perform better than a sequential classifier. The techniques described in Rashkin et al. (2017) involved examining the linguistic characteristics of misleading texts by contrasting the linguistic patterns of propaganda, satire, and hoaxes with those of true news. It determines if the news article is true or false based on these language characteristics. The study proposed in Faustini and Covoes (2020) introduces a framework to identify fake news using only textual features. To classify fake news, it creates source textual features that are platform and language-independent and uses random forest (RF) (Gilda 2017), naive Bayes (NB) (Rish et al. 2001), support vector machine (SVM) (Huang et al. 2018), and K-nearest neighbor (KNN) (Zhang 2016). This system performs feature engineering that precludes a quicker or more automated method for identifying false news. The work reported in Castillo et al. (2011) has proposed automatic credibility assessment using classification techniques like SVM and decision tree (DT) (Song and Ying 2015) to determine the credibility of the tweets based on user and tweet features, which are primarily statistical and semantic types.

While handcrafted, general, and style-based features are crucial for identifying false news, selecting or extracting them requires human knowledge, which is impractical and takes time. On the other hand, models based on deep learning and machine learning (Ma et al. 2016; Huang and Chen 2020) automatically extract the characteristics from the data. A machine learning-based ensemble model for detecting fake news has been presented in research (Gravanis et al. 2019). It makes use of both content-based features and machine-learning techniques. Machine learning methods are effective, but because of a lack of domain knowledge and experience, collecting handcrafted textual features for the typical machine learning-based false news detection models is difficult. The authors recognized the rumors in Kwon et al. (2013) using the structural, temporal, and linguistic elements of propagation. This study has demonstrated the key structural and linguistic differences during the propagation of rumor and non-rumor posts. It extracts the features by examining the linguistic patterns distinguishing genuine news from propaganda, satire, and hoaxes. Using these linguistic characteristics, the model determines if the news article is true or false.

According to a study in Wu et al. (2020), the performance of the model is degraded by a large number of noisy and irrelevant characteristics that are extracted using deep learning. In order to eliminate redundant and unnecessary features from the extracted information for news credibility measures, a novel model built on an adversarial neural network (ANN) has been constructed. Even though the model's adversarial training produces better features, training it is challenging. In addition to being extremely resource-intensive, the model takes a long time to create the pertinent and noise-free features. A method that integrated data from several sources was presented in the study published in Karimi et al. (2018), along with a method called multisource multiclass fake news detection (MMFND). Additionally, it distinguishes between various levels of fakeness. In the end, this method combines automated feature extraction, multisource fusion, and degrees of fakeness to produce an interpretive and persuasive model for fake news detection. This effort ignores the comments and answers in favor of merely considering the news content from various sources and viewpoints. It can be further enhanced if it incorporates the comments on that news post since the dissemination of fake news also relies on the evidence offered in the comments. A different study (Saikh et al. 2020) created an attention-based system for categorizing false news. The Bi-GRU network encrypts the text, and word-level attention is applied to extract significant and pertinent textual elements. Later on, it used an MLP network to identify false news. A tri-relationship embedding method called *TriFN* has been introduced in a recent study (Shu et al. 2019b). It models user-news interactions and publisher-news relations simultaneously for the purpose of classifying false news. A related study (Ruchansky et al. 2017) presented a model based on a recurrent neural network (RNN) that determines if a post is legitimate or false by looking for trends in user activity.

Despite having exponential development, deep learning techniques don't explain internal behavior. The researchers are now considering explainable false news detection because of this constraint. The work described in Chi and Liao (2022) has created an explainable decision system for detecting fake news that interacts with people through dialog trees and automatically learns at the human level. It aids individuals in comprehending the system's internal thought process. The methods mentioned above for identifying bogus news articles from several domains have concentrated on a particular inefficient domain. The research presented in Mosallanezhad et al. (2022) has created a deep learning mechanism based on reinforcement learning (RL) (Kaelbling et al. 1996) to capture the interdomain feature.

Visual indicators are becoming increasingly popular for detecting fake news, but most research still relies on textual context and content. According to the research published in Jin et al. (2016b), there are differences in the distribution patterns of photos in false and true news. On the basis of this presumption, the visual characteristics of photos and statistics are extracted to categorize the news as authentic or fake. A multi-domain visual neural network has been shown in a paper published in Qi et al. (2019) to extract both physical and semantic aspects of a picture, which aids in the task of detecting fake news. Neural network-based methods for image forgery detection in fake news have been developed by the studies presented in Bappy et al. (2017); Kim and Lee (2017) and Qi et al. (2019).

During the COVID-19 infodemic, misinformation detection has gained much attention and popularity. The research discussed in Pennycook et al. (2020) has looked into the factors that contribute to the dissemination of false information regarding COVID-19. A different study (Kouzy et al. 2020) investigated the significance of early interventions and offered a preliminary estimate of the amount of false information. The study discussed in Cuan-Baltazar et al. (2020) assessed the readability and quality of COVID-19 disease-related Internet resources. The approaches discussed below don't offer a strong enough answer for multimedia news posts since deceptive news posts can contain more than just text and images. To get around this restriction, practitioners and researchers concentrate on multimodal false news identification.

2.2.3.2   Multimodal Misinformation Detection

Compared to unimodal false news detection, a literature survey indicates that multi-modal fake news detection is a relatively recent field. Researchers and practitioners have recently become interested in multimodal information analysis as a means of addressing several real-world issues, including emotion analysis (Chauhan et al. 2019a), sentiment analysis (Ghosal et al. 2018b), visual question answering (Antol et al. 2015), image captioning (Karpathy and Fei-Fei 2015), and misinformation detection (Jin et al. 2017). Recent advancements in fake multimedia news have drawn interest worldwide, making multimodal misinformation identification a burgeoning field of study. The study presented in Jin et al. (2017) has reported the very first work of multimodality. It is a deep learning-based method that integrates an attention mechanism with information extracted from the social environment and multimodal interactions. Because of this, the algorithm can only extract information relevant to an event and cannot be used to detect false information about recently announced events. By integrating the suggested model with an event and domain-independent feature extraction method, the performance of this study can be enhanced. Event adversarial neural network (EANN), a deep learning-based model, was proposed by the study reported in Wang et al. (2018) to address the shortcomings identified in Jin et al. (2017). Using an adversarial network, the model creates event invariant feature representations (Goodfellow et al. 2014). The shared representation of multimodal posts is beyond the capacity of this model to learn. To get around this representation learning problem, the study in Khattar et al. (2019) introduced a multimodal variational autoencoder (MVAE) for false news identification. To get the outputs, an additional sub-task (the decoder part of the VAE in MVAE and the event discriminator in EANN) has been implemented. The performance of these models is heavily reliant on the sub-task. If the sub-task is absent, the model performs worse. The inability to find shared multimodal representations is another drawback of the above-discussed research (EANN and VAE). These frameworks combine text and image feature representations to provide multimodal characteristics that might not properly align and interact with textual and visual elements. The study has introduced a multimodal technique called Spotfake reported in Singhal et al. (2019). It is capable of detecting fake news without the need for any sub-tasks. The first limitations in EANN and VAE were addressed by the investigation presented in Singhal et al. (2019), but it proceeds with another limitation of extracting better-shared representations.

As explained in the above literature, examining suitable fusion approaches to integrate data from various sources efficiently is one of the most important aspects of any multimodal learning framework. Multimodal compact bilinear pooling (MCB), which creates a very-high-dimensional joint feature representation based on the outer product of two feature vectors, was first introduced in Fukui et al. (2016). In order to deal with the problem of high dimensionality, the work in Kim et al. (2016) presented a multimodal low-rank bilinear pooling (MLB). This method performs the element-wise multiplication (Hadamard product operation) (Kim et al. 2016) of two feature vectors to generate the joint feature representation in the common space. The multimodal factorized bilinear pooling (MFB) module was recently employed in the works in Chauhan et al. (2019c) and Yu et al. (2017b). This module helps extract the combined representation of text and image features for the natural language generation (NLG) (Reiter and Dale 1997) task in the fashion domain. The current multimodal fusion methods are not reliable for detecting fake news. Consequently, there is a great demand in this field due to the successful fusion of text and visual modalities. An attention residual network (CARN) that is cross-modal and capable of extracting and fusing pertinent information from both textual and picture modality in relation to one another has been built via the misinformation detection mechanism described in Song et al. (2021b). A method for encoding text and picture data using cross-modal attention was introduced in the paper published in Sachan et al. (2021). It makes use of transformer-based techniques as well as deep convolution neural networks. A capsule network was used for visual feature extraction in the multimodal work examined in Palani et al. (2021), and BERT was used for textual feature extraction. It subsequently produced an attentive feature fusion technique. An attention-based fusion strategy to obtain highly meaningful interaction across multiple modalities has also been introduced by the work reported in Wang et al. (2022).

False multimedia news now includes audio and video content as well. Therefore, audio- and video-embedded misinformation detection has also become an exciting dimension of multimodal fake news detection. This direction is greatly advanced by the work shown in Choi and Ko (2021), which presents an artificial neural network for fake video identification in news articles after introducing topic modeling. Subsequently, the work in Choi and Ko (2022) has created multimodal video-embedded misinformation identification techniques. These mechanisms generate multimodal features by combining text features from the title, description, and comments with visual features from the video. To combine these features, it also makes use of attention mechanisms and subject knowledge. It determines whether the news is authentic or fake based on the multimodal features.

2.2.4 Propagation-Based Misinformation Detection

Propagation-based misinformation detection exploits information provided in news propagation on social media, which relies on self-defined graphs. Propagation-based methods detect misinformation based on how it spreads online. This approach generally discovers the interrelation of relevant events on social media posts to see the credibility of that news. The studies presented in Jin et al. (2014, 2016a) better exploit the propagation methods for news credibility verification implemented using graphs.

Despite its popularity in NLP, deep learning is limited to capturing semantic textual properties based on word sequences. Nevertheless, it cannot identify non-sequential semantic traits or information about news transmission. The research in Ghadiri et al. (2022) and Chiang and Zhang (2021) have presented graph-based approaches for fake news detection because the graph captures the non-sequential features and long-distance semantic dependencies. These approaches mine non-sequential long-distance semantics by converting the text sequences into a graph and applying deep learning over the produced graph. In addition to linguistic and textual characteristics, social context offers useful information for identifying false news. A noteworthy addition to the explainability field is the study by Lu and Li (2020), which creates a Graph-aware Co-Attention Network (GCAN) to determine if a source tweet is authentic or not by extrapolating an explanation from the news content (tweets and retweets). A study in Wu et al. (2021) has presented a knowledge graph enhanced framework, and another work (Sharma and Sharma 2021) has introduced comment filtering mechanisms for the explainability in fake news detection. A study in Song et al. (2021a) used a textual graph to augment knowledge, which was then merged with visual features to create a multimodal feature fusion. The application of the multimodal fusion method employing a graph for false news detection was spurred by the growing popularity of graph-based mechanisms to extract non-sequential characteristics. An attention network for graphs has been proven for multimodal fusion in Dhawan et al. (2022). It extracts the high-level semantic multimodal features for fake news detection.

2.3 Summary

This chapter describes a brief literature survey, and the recent advancements in the topics related to misinformation detection focused on in this book. The literature survey briefly explains prior misinformation detection works exploring news content, news context, linguistic style, and propagation. The chapter starts with the gradual advancements of the datasets, and later, it concentrates on the algorithms and frameworks developed for misinformation detection in recent years from various perspectives. After having sufficient knowledge about misinformation and the contributions to its detection, the significance of novelty and emotion in the detection of false information is covered in the following chapter. The next chapter briefly explores misinformation detection from the linguistic style perspective.

Chapter 3
Novelty and Emotion in Misinformation Detection

After having a general understanding of misinformation in Chap. 1 and awareness about the recent advancements in this domain (discussed in Chap. 2), this chapter puts the light on some specific features, such as *novelty* and *emotion*, which play an effective role in the spread of misinformation. According to the research reviewed in Chap. 2, the inclusion of *surprising content* in the story, which grabs the reader's attention immediately and causes a strong emotional response, is a key factor in the virality of false news. Starting from the basic introduction about novelty and emotion, this chapter discusses a machine learning- and deep learning-based method that incorporates implicit information like *textual novelty* and *emotion* in a pipeline process for addressing the misinformation detection problem instead of detecting the news credibility only by using content information. This chapter focuses on capturing the combined role and behavior of these implicit characteristics in credible and non-credible news. Before going deeper into this concept, the sections below briefly introduce the novelty and emotion.

3.1 Novelty and Novelty Detection

In the literature, novelty has different definitions. Novelty means something different from the existing one. It also refers to some uncommon phenomenon that incorporates an element of surprise. For example, a novelty in the data means an unusual instance or data instances with different characteristics or simply different from the existing data. For instance, considering the following news pair, the novelty information can be deduced that new news is non-novel with respect to verified news.

Verified news: 5G generates coronavirus in human skin cells—false.

New news: The 5G technology breaks up the cells in the human body to make the new coronavirus—having a similar semantic meaning as the verified news. Therefore, it will also be false.

It concludes that the new news is non-novel concerning the verified news. Nowadays, researchers are performing *novelty detection* tasks for solving variations of other related tasks that require anomaly detection, such as network intrusions, jet engine failure, machine learning, hacking, entailment recognition, fraud detection, and many more. For example, in fraud detection, credit card companies usually monitor the purchasing habits of a user. When they find any type of deviation from those regular habits, they immediately call the user to confirm whether the transaction was authorized or if the card was stolen or lost. Novelty detection recognizes whether the current input differs from the previous input, which is a fundamental ability for classification or any other learning systems in machine learning or deep learning.

Its challenging nature and practical importance have led to many approaches. Because of the novelty detection techniques, various applications can decide whether a new observation follows the same distribution as the existing observations or differs from the existing one. If the observation belongs to the same distribution, it is called an inlier, which is considered non-novel. It is called an outlier and considered in the novel category if it differs. Thus, the novelty detection task is a classification task that classifies the new observation into two different categories: *novel* and *non-novel*.

3.2 Emotion and Emotion Recognition

Emotion shows a vigorous impact on the daily lives of every individual. People decide whether they are sad, angry, bored, frustrated, or happy. The choice of hobbies and activities also depends on the emotions they incite. Understanding emotions can help people navigate their lives with greater stability and ease. Awareness of emotional state also helps in managing stress better. In actuality, emotion is the representation of a conscious mental reaction. Emotions have different representations based on the reactions of human beings in response to a situation or event. For instance, a person experiences happiness, surprise, and joy when they get some good news. Similarly, when threatened or receiving bad news, a person experiences fear, sadness, and disgust.

Emotion recognition identifies human reactions or experiences through text, images, or videos. Technological advancements in this domain play a major role in helping people recognize the emotions of others, which is a nascent research area nowadays. Generally, the technology works best if it uses multiple modalities in context. However, in this particular chapter, textual emotion recognition has been emphasized.

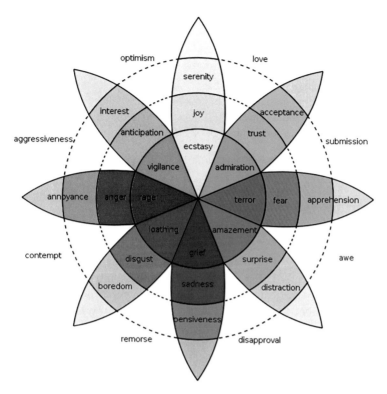

Fig. 3.1 It shows the wheel of emotion introduced by Robert Plutchik

Various researchers have explored emotions in different categories; accordingly, their definitions have changed over time. A psychologist, Paul Ekman, gave a theory in 1972 that suggests that emotions can be categorized into six classes: fear, anger, disgust, sadness, joy, and surprise. After that, Robert Plutchik introduced a wheel of emotion as an emotion classification system in the 1980s. Figure 3.1 (Angioni and Tuveri 2019) shows the graphical representation of the wheel of emotion.

This model explains that a combination of emotions can replicate different emotions. Plutchik has classified emotions into eight categories: sadness, joy, disgust, trust, fear, anger, anticipation, and surprise. Further, he has expanded the emotion categories by combining these basic emotions. For instance, the combination of happiness and anticipation corresponds to excitement. The following examples replicate different emotions, recognized from the text:

Text with emotion classes

Text-instance-1:"I was going to watch a movie yesterday, but I missed the bus."
Emotion:"Sad"

Text-instance-2:"Wow! I love this story"
Emotion:"Happy or joy"
Text-instance-3:"Please, don't put me in the lockup"
Emotion:"Fear"

In 1999, Ekman expanded his list to include several other basic emotions including excitement, embarrassment, contempt, pride, shame, amusement, and satisfaction (Dalgleish and Power 2000). In addition to the above-discussed emotion recognition works, various other works have been proposed to strengthen this domain.

3.3 Various Terminologies

3.3.1 Embedding

In natural language processing and machine learning, embedding is considered a technique that maps the textual contents (words, sentences, documents) to vectors of continuous number. It is frequently used for passing the text as input to the neural network. Embedding also measures the relationship between two text fragments. For example, it is difficult to map the relationship between two words, "Toyota" and "Honda." However, it becomes easy to find the relationship between their vector representations, which are set to very close according to some measure. Nowadays, various embedding techniques, such as One-hot encoding, Glove, Word2Vec, Elmo, BERT, etc., are available for solving various natural language processing tasks.

3.3.2 Natural Language Inference (NLI)

It is a task of determining the relationship between two text fragments called "premise" and hypothesis. This relationship is established based on the condition of whether the given "hypothesis" and "premise" logically follow (entailment), unfollow (contradiction), or are undetermined (neutral) to each other. NLI is also known as recognizing textual entailment (RTE). This can be viewed as a classification task that classifies the hypothesis into three classes based on the premise: entailment, contradiction, or neutral. The below example gives a clear understanding of the NLI.

Example 1

Premise: Two children are hugging each other.
Hypothesis: Two children are showing affection.
NLI Class: Entailment

Example 2

Premise: Ram is playing on the ground.
Hypothesis: Ram is sleeping.
NLI Class: Contradiction

Example 3

Premise: The magicians are performing for us.
Hypothesis: The magicians are famous.
NLI Class: Neutral

In the first example, "showing affection" is inferred from the "hugging each other." This means the hypothesis can be inferred from the premise. Therefore, the label is given as entailment. In the second example, Ram cannot sleep and play simultaneously. Therefore, both sentences contradict each other. In the third example, both premise and hypothesis have individual semantics. This means they do not depend on each other. Therefore, the label is neutral.

3.3.3 Evaluation Metrics

Evaluation metrics are used to measure the performance of the machine learning or deep learning models. To justify the model's performance, it is essential to compute the evaluation metrics. In machine learning and deep learning, various evaluation metrics are available to test a model. Some of them are used to evaluate the performance of the classification model, and some are used for the regression model evaluation. As this chapter discusses a classification model, we introduce some evaluation metrics relevant to this in this section. These include classification accuracy, confusion matrix, precision, and recall F1-Score.

Confusion Matrix It is a matrix that represents the performance of a classification model in terms of correctly classified and wrongly classified instances. Figure 3.2 shows the proper visualization of it.

Precision (P) It is defined as the ratio of correctly classified samples as positive and total actual positive samples. Equation 3.1 depicts it mathematically.

$$P = \frac{TP}{TP + FP} \tag{3.1}$$

Recall It is defined as the ratio of correctly classified samples as positive and total samples predicted as positive. Equation 3.2 depicts it mathematically.

$$R = \frac{TP}{TP + FN} \tag{3.2}$$

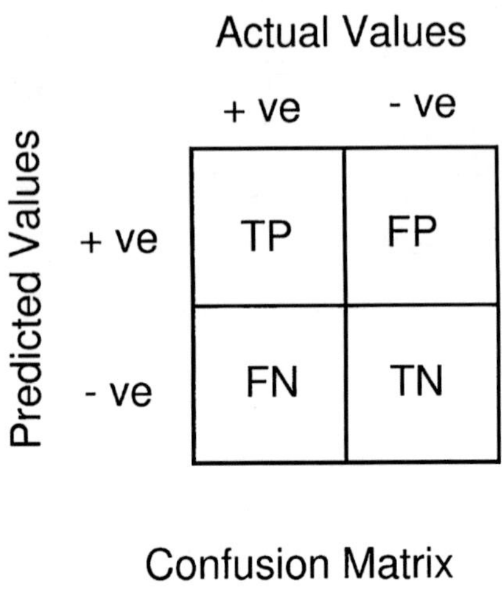

Fig. 3.2 COVID-Stance
ROC curve

Actual Values

	+ ve	- ve
+ ve	TP	FP
- ve	FN	TN

Predicted Values

Confusion Matrix

F-Score The F-Score is calculated as the harmonic mean of recall and precision. Equation 3.3 gives the mathematical representation of it.

$$F = \frac{2 * P * R}{P + R} \tag{3.3}$$

Accuracy It is the ratio of correctly classified samples and total samples. It is mathematically represented by Eq. 3.4.

$$F = \frac{TP + TN}{TP + FP + TN + FN} \tag{3.4}$$

3.4 Application of Novelty Detection in Misinformation Detection

Section 3.1 briefly discusses about novelty and novelty detection. This section presents the understanding of how misinformation replicates *element of surprise, i.e., Novelty* and how it acts as a key attribute for misinformation detection. This section also talks about how novelty makes a significant contribution to the spread of misinformation and social penetration. As the novelty implants surprising content in the news articles, it draws human attention and behaves as a catalyst for news sharing and decision-making. The main purpose of the misinformation is to grab our attention, and for this purpose, *novelty is the key*. Psychologists argue that the weird representation of the hyperpartisan claims is one of the reasons for its huge success (Pennycook and Rand 2019). According to different research on Twitter, false news is retweeted 70% more frequently than authentic news (Vosoughi et al. 2018). Users were considerably more likely to retweet a tweet that was *measurably more novel* than true news. This is because false news story was more novel than true news.

The implication of false news detection with novelty detection was first introduced by MIT scholars.[1] This article motivated to perform misinformation detection using novelty detection via entailment task with significance to textual similarity measures. In this process, the first novelty of the news is computed with respect to the verified prior (old) news with the aid of methods used in detecting textual entailment (TE) (Ghosal et al. 2022a). Section 3.3 describes the textual entailment in detail.

The relevance of novelty detection with TE is found in the sense that a certain hypothesis H entailed from premise P (a certain piece of source text) could be considered as non-novel with respect to P if a human reading the hypothesis H after reading T would find redundant information in H. In contrast, if H is not entailed from P, a human reading H after P would find a new piece of information in H. Hence, H could be considered novel information with respect to P. Textual entailment is a unidirectional relationship between the hypothesis and premise. In contrast, the textual similarity is a bidirectional relationship between two text fragments. Therefore, the basis of novelty detection in misinformation detection also carries on with this intuition and is grounded in the elementary relationships of textual entailment with textual similarity.

Further, the TE system is interpreted to detect the novelty of an incoming news article with respect to some old verified news articles that are already seen by the system. The verified news article acts as premise P. New incoming news acts as hypothesis H. Novelty detection from news implies figuring out new information from incoming news and subsequently arriving at the judgment of whether the news could be termed as a novel or not. The decision should always be with respect to some relevant verified information. If the verified news is true (real) and new incoming news is detected as non-novel with respect to the verified news, the incoming news is also real and vice versa. On the other hand, if the verified news is true (real) and new incoming news contradicts and is detected as a novel with respect to the verified news, the incoming news is fake and vice versa. In a misinformation detection system, verified news is considered as the premise, and the hypothesis is the new incoming news article. Table 3.1 shows some samples of the verified news and related new news.

After having the above discussion, in summary, it can be justified that novelty detection finds the similarities and differences between verified and new news articles. If the new news is similar to the verified news, it follows the same credibility label. If the new news is dissimilar, it follows the opposite credibility label.

---

[1] https://mitsloan.mit.edu/ideas-made-to-matter/study-false-news-spreads-faster-truth.

Table 3.1 Dataset characteristics visualize that the premise and hypothesis may be from the same or different news article in the form of news headline-headline pair, headline-body pair, body-body pair, or body-headline pair. It also gives the justification for novelty labels

Sl. No	Premise	Hypothesis	Remark
1.	"The plane is about to take off. A man knelt down at the hatch!" That was the tear-jerking scene.	The man on the front of the cockpit kneeling before takeoff? This story is made up!	The premise and hypothesis are from two different but related news. The premise is verified as false, and the hypothesis contradicts the premise. Therefore, the hypothesis is true.
2.	Chloroquine or hydroxy-chloroquine is a cure for the novel coronavirus	It is good that the UK is beginning patient trials of Remedies for treating the coronavirus. But there is no good reason not to begin similar trials of chloroquine and azithromycin which are much cheaper and now in use in both France and the USA.	Premise and hypothesis are from the same news article (Premise-News Headline, Hypothesis-News Body). The premise is verified as false, and the hypothesis supports the premise. Therefore, the hypothesis is also false.

3.5 Application of Emotion Recognition in Misinformation Detection

Literature in Chap. 2 reveals that the replies and comments against misinformation show different emotions, such as anger, disgust, surprise, and fear. Instead, the replies and comments in real news replicate sadness, anticipation, trust, and joy emotion. It suggests that viewers are more likely to instantly forward news items when they have a strong emotional appeal. As a result, it somewhat supports the necessity for regulatory control, especially during an incident when the spread of false information might make people fearful and panicked. This is a significant challenge, primarily because misleading information might pass for reliable news, leading readers to trust it and take appropriate action. Table 3.2 shows the analysis of an example that justifies how emotions have different characteristics in real and false information. The investigation of these characteristics supports misinformation detection.

Table 3.2 Table depicts an example of misinformation. It also explains that emotion is an implicit characteristic that can help in misinformation detection

Premise	Hypothesis	Remarks
Use of a surgical mask reduced the proportion of droplets and aerosols with detectable virus among children and adults with confirmed seasonal coronavirus and seasonal influenza infection.	Face masks are dirty, dehumanizing, and ineffective. Stanford University study: "The data suggests that medical and non-medical face-masks are ineffective in blocking human-to-human transmission of infectious COVID-19 disease".	The premise shows the "trust" emotion category. In contrast, the hypothesis shows the "disgust" and "sadness" emotion categories.

3.6 Misinformation Detection Using Novelty Detection and Emotion Recognition (A Case Study)

This section briefly discusses a framework for misinformation detection that leverages novelty and emotion as implicit features. According to the discussion presented in Sects. 3.4 and 3.5, it is clear that in every misinformation detection system, the critical task is to understand the novelty and emotional appeal of the news, which accelerates its dissemination. For the proper functioning of the misinformation detection system, it is necessary to perceive the implicit information from the news content, which can further be used as the implicit features in this work. This section devises a machine learning- and deep learning-based technique for misinformation detection. The primary goal of this approach is to implement a novel misinformation detection system that considers the novelty and emotional details of the source (verified news) and target news (new news) pairs and determines whether the target contains false or real content concerning the source. Figure 3.3 shows the overall framework of the proposed model. It consists of three modules, *viz.*, Novelty detection module, emotion recognition module, and misinformation detection module. The below sections describe each of these sub-models in detail.

3.6.1 Proposed Model

3.6.1.1 Novelty Detection Module

As per the above discussion, novelty is a crucial component of news articles, and identifying novelty in texts calls for a deep comprehension of their semantic relationships. This model displays intricate semantic relationships between the text pairs using natural language inference (NLI). This portion of the model takes the premise (source) and hypothesis (target) pairs and extracts the novelty-aware textual feature representations from them.

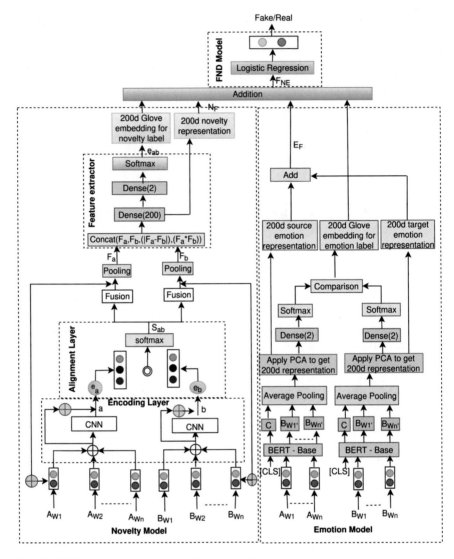

Fig. 3.3 Misinformation detection model using novelty and emotion information

Encoding Layers Given a text pair that contains source as $A_{W_1}, A_{W_2}, .., A_{W_n}$ and target as $B_{W_1}, B_{W_2}, .., B_{W_n}$, where n represents number of words in a sentence. As a neural network only takes numerical data as input, all the words in a sentence are first converted into vectors using a 300-dimensional pre-trained GloVe embedding. After that, sentence embedding is obtained using a simple Multichannel convolution neural network (CNN) (Sotthisopha and Vateekul 2018)-based sentence encoder. Further, each sentence S_i is encoded into the hidden representations $h_{A_{S_i}}$ and $h_{B_{S_i}}$, where S_i represents the concatenated word embedding. After finding embeddings,

Eqs. 3.5 and 3.6 are utilized to calculate the hidden representations for source text.

$$h_{A_{S_i}p} = Maxpool(Conv2d(S_A(p, p)))$$ (3.5)

$$h_{A_{S_i}} = concat(max(h_{A_{S_i}p})$$ (3.6)

Similarly, the hidden layer representation of the target sentence is also computed as shown in Eq. 3.7.

$$h_{B_{S_i}} = concat(max(h_{B_{S_i}p})$$ (3.7)

Here, $p \in [2, 3, 4]$. A residual link is created from the sentence representation (S_i) to the hidden vectors $(h_{A_{S_i}})$ and $(h_{B_{S_i}})$ to prevent information loss and improve the sentence's semantic representation. It produces a concatenated representation as shown in Eq. 3.8.

$$a = [S_i; h_{A_{S_i}}]$$
$$b = [S_i; h_{B_{S_i}}]$$ (3.8)

Alignment Layer The alignment layer encodes the feature representations for the source and target pairs that are obtained from the encoding layer. It determines how the source and target sentences interact semantically. Equation 3.9 is used to project the sentences into a latent space first, and Eq. 3.10 is used to calculate the dot product of the source-target pair. Further, a softmax classifier function is applied over the resultant vector using Eq. 3.11.

$$e_{a_i} = tanh((W_a a_i + bs_a)$$
$$e_{b_i} = tanh((W_b b_i + bs_b)$$ (3.9)

$$d_{ab} = e_{a_i}\dot{e}_{b_i}$$ (3.10)

$$S_{ab} = \frac{exp((d_{ab}^T d_w))}{\Sigma_t exp((d_{ab}^T d_w))}$$ (3.11)

The projected vectors of the source and target sentences are denoted by e_{a_i}, e_{b_i}, respectively. The dot product of both vectors is represented by d_{ab}. d_w, bs, and S_{ab} represent weight, bias, and the softmax output, respectively. The attended and semantic representation of the target sentence with respect to the source sentence is the output of the softmax function. Further, this output is passed as input to the fusion layer.

Fusion Layer Equation 3.12 illustrates how the fusion layer compares and fuses local representations with the aligned representations from three different perspectives. The output of the fusion layer is calculated independently for both the target and source sentences.

$$F_{a1} = G1([a; S_{ab}])$$

$$F_{a2} = G2([a, (a - S_{ab})]) \tag{3.12}$$

$$F_{a3} = G3(a; (a \circ S_{ab}))$$

$$F_a = maxpool(G([F_{a1}; F_{a2}; F_{a3}])) \tag{3.13}$$

Similarly,

$$F_b = maxpool(G([F_{b1}; F_{b2}; F_{b3}])) \tag{3.14}$$

Equations 3.13 and 3.14 define the representation generated from the fusion layer. This representation is then sent to a pooling layer, which encodes the pooled representations of the source and target phrase pairs into the feature extraction layer. G1, G2, G3, and G represent the single-layer feed-forward neural networks with independent parameters. F_a and F_b represent the pooled representations of source and target sentences, respectively. $\circ$ signifies the element-wise multiplication, which computes the similarity between two vectors, while subtraction emphasizes the difference.

Feature Extraction Layer It encodes the pooled representations and concatenates the many features of interactions between target and source sentences using Eq. 3.15. Equation 3.16 is then used to project this combined representation into 200-dimensional space, and Eq. 3.17 is used to transfer it to an output layer containing two neurons. Finally, this layer uses Eq. 3.18 to apply a softmax activation function on this output.

$$F' = [F_a, F_b, |F_a - F_b|, F_a * F_b] \tag{3.15}$$

$$N_F = tanh((W'_F * F' + bs'_F) \tag{3.16}$$

$$N'_F = tanh((W_{N_F} * N_F + bs_{N_F}) \tag{3.17}$$

$$e_{ab} = \frac{exp((N_F'^T e_w))}{\Sigma_t exp((e_{ab}^T e_w))} \tag{3.18}$$

Here, F' represents the vector obtained from the fusion layer. N_F depicts projected representation, N'_F represents the output layer. e_{ab} is the softmax output, which provides the final novelty labels (novel or non-novel). These novelty labels and the projected vectors are encoded into the *Addition* layer that instructs the model to perform a certain task.

3.6.1.2   Emotion Recognition Model

An original transformer model serves as the basis for the sequential composition of bidirectional transformer encoders, which make up the bidirectional encoder representation from transformer (BERT) model (Vaswani et al. 2017). As news headlines and/or article pairs compose the misinformation datasets, they lack in rich-emotive wording and explicit emotional content. While BERT provides contextual embedding and extracts implicit emotional cues from the text, GloVe embeddings are static and do not extract these types of data. This is why the emotion recognition model makes use of BERT. The concatenated representation of word embedding, positional embedding, and segment embedding of an input token sequence, w = $(w_1, .., w_n)$, is provided as the input to the BERT model. For every sentence, a special token ([CLS]) is added as the initial token, and a final special token ([SEP]) is added. The emotion prediction challenge is performed using the pre-trained $BERT_{Base}$ model (Layer = 12, Hidden size = 768, Attention heads = 12) (Devlin et al. 2019) context-dependent sentence representation. BERT produces $H = (h_1, .., h_n)$ as its output. Subsequently, average polling is used over the contextual sentence representation vector H. To obtain the 200-dimensional latent representation of the emotion-aware feature for both target and source sentences, Principle Component Analysis (PCA) (Bro and Smilde 2014) is then applied. Equation 3.19 accurately captures it.

$$E_{Fs} = PCA(Averagepooling(H_s))$$
$$E_{Ft} = PCA(Averagepooling(H_t)) \quad (3.19)$$

The emotion recognition component further adds 200-dimensional feature representations of both the target and source. Equation 3.20 is further used to generate the aggregated emotion-aware representation of the sentence pairs.

$$E_F = E_{Fs} + E_{Ft} \quad (3.20)$$

Here, E_{Fs} and E_{Ft} are the emotion feature representations for the source and target, respectively. E_F represents the combined emotion feature of the sentence. E_{Fs} and E_{Ft} are passed into a fully connected layer with a softmax function that computes the source emotion labels following Eqs. 3.21 and 3.22.

$$E'_{Fs} = tanh((W_{E_{Fs}} * E_{Fs} + bs_{E_{Fs}}) \quad (3.21)$$

$$e_{E'_{Fs}} = \frac{exp((E'^T_{Fs} e_w))}{\Sigma_t exp((E'^T_{Fs} e_w))} \quad (3.22)$$

The emotion labels for the target sentence are computed similarly to the source sentence and represented as $e_{E'_{Fs}}$. The Addition layer receives both the scaffold labels and the composite emotion-aware representation. The combined emotion-aware representation and the scaffold labels are added in the Addition layer.

3.6.1.3 Fake News Detection Model

The 200-dimensional novelty-aware and emotion-aware representations, novelty scaffold label, and emotion scaffold label representations are obtained. After that, these four representations are combined and fed into a logistic regression (LR) model to determine the authenticity of the news. In this work, the LR classifier is employed due to the extremely low model complexity. These operations are discussed mathematically in Eqs. 3.23 and 3.24. Here, F_{NE}, e_{ab}, F_{label}, and Prob(F_{NE}) represent the Addition layer output, novelty label, emotion label, and probability of a news post being fake or real, respectively.

$$F_{NE} = [N_F + e_{ab} + E_F + F_{label}] \qquad (3.23)$$

Now the logistic function is,

$$Prob(F_{NE}) = P(F_{NE}) = \frac{1}{1 + e^{-F_{NE}}} \qquad (3.24)$$

The model is first trained on some misinformation detection datasets to solve the misinformation detection tasks. Since the existing misinformation datasets lack novelty and emotion labels, they are not well suited for tasks involving the detection of novelty and emotion. Therefore, two tasks are essential to design a misinformation detection system. The first task is to prepare the dataset with novelty and emotion labels, and the second task is to predict whether the new news has some misinformation with respect to verified news. Therefore, in the first task, pre-trained models (similar architecture as (Yang et al. 2019b) for novelty and a BERT-based model for emotion) are used for the novelty and emotion label extraction.

The novelty model is first trained on (QQP) dataset[2] (Imtiaz et al. 2020), and after that, misinformation datasets such as ByteDance, Fake News Challenge-1, and Covid-Stance are used as test set for which the model returns the novelty label. The QQP dataset has been discussed in Sect. 3.6.2, and the misinformation datasets have been briefly mentioned in Sect. 2.1. A BERT-based emotion model is trained using Unified dataset[3] (Klinger et al. 2018). The unified dataset has been briefly discussed in Sect. 3.6.2. The premise and hypothesis of misinformation datasets are independently fed as test data to the model for emotion label prediction after the model has been trained. After having both the labels along with misinformation labels, the misinformation datasets are used for training the above-discussed model.

---

[2] http://qim.ec.quoracdn.net/$quora_duplicate_questions$.tsv.

[3] https://github.com/sarnthil/unify-emotion-datasets.

The ByteDance, Fake News Challenge-1, and Covid-Stance datasets have been used to train the developed misinformation detection model. Section 2.1 briefly describes all these datasets.

3.6.2 Datasets

This section explores the various datasets used for training the emotion and novelty models. NLI is approximated first for novelty detection, and this novelty is incorporated for misinformation detection. Since the QQP dataset is most suitable for extracting novelty information, it is employed for novelty detection. Since QQP is a well-known large-scale dataset for novelty detection via textual entailment (Li et al. 2018), this dataset is used to pre-train the novelty detection model. The Unified dataset (combined dataset of fourteen existing emotion datasets) is employed to pre-train the emotion model because eight emotion labels (fear, anger, surprise, happy, sad, joy, trust, and anticipation) have been considered for this work, and this dataset fully satisfies the requirements. Ultimately, ByteDance, FNC, and Covid-stance datasets are used to train the misinformation detection model. Only these datasets satisfy the requirements of the model, which needs a dataset containing pairs of premises and hypotheses. In two distinct subsections, an overview of these datasets is provided. The misinformation datasets have been briefly discussed in Sect. 2.1. The following paragraphs describe other datasets that were used to train the emotion and novelty models. All the datasets are publicly available, and they are of different sizes.

Quora Question Pair Dataset It is the first published Quora question pair dataset. Every sample of this dataset contains ID, Question1ID, Question2ID, Question1, Question2, and isduplicate attributes. *isduplicate* indicates whether two questions are identical or not, with a value of 0 or 1. There are 404,290 question pairs in this dataset.

Unified Dataset It is the combination of fourteen existing emotion classification datasets such as *Blogs (Aman and Szpakowicz 2007), Affective Text (Strapparava and Mihalcea 2007), CrowdFlower (Seyeditabari et al. 2019), DailyDialogs (Li et al. 2017), Electoral-Tweets (Mohammad et al. 2015), EmoBank (Buechel and Hahn 2017), EmoInt (Mohammad and Bravo-Márquez 2017), Emotion-Stimulus (Ghazi et al. 2015), fb-valence-arousal (Preoţiuc-Pietro et al. 2016), Grounded-Emotions (Lei et al. 2014), ISEAR (International Survey on Emotion Antecedents and Reactions) (Scherer and Wallbott 1994), SSEC (Stance Sentiment Emotion Dataset) (Schuff et al. 2017), Tales (Alm et al. 2005), and TEC (Twitter Emotion Corpus) (Mohammad 2012).* The datasets have varied properties and were gathered from various sources and domains. There are 2,33,665 sentences in the Unified dataset, and each statement has an associated emotion label. It has a capacity of eleven emotion labels. Since it combines numerous datasets, the samples have many different emotion labels. Table 3.3 shows the detailed description of all fourteen

Table 3.3 Statistics and detail of the Unified dataset

Dataset	Annotation	Size	Topic
AffectiveText Strapparava and Mihalcea [2007]	anger, disgust, fear, joy, sadness, surprise, valence	1,250	news
Blogs Aman and Szpakowicz [2007]	anger, disgust, fear, joy, sadness, surprise, neutral, mixed emotion	5,025	blogs
CrowdFlower Seyeditabari et al. [2019]	anger, disgust, fear, joy, sadness, surprise, enthusiasm, fun, hate, neutral, love, boredom, relief, empty	40,000	general
DailyDialogs Li et al. [2017]	anger, disgust, fear,joy, sadness, surprise	13,118	multiple
Electoral-Tweets Mohammad et al. [2015]	anger, disgust, fear, joy, sadness, surprise, trust, anticipation	4,058	elections
EmoBank Buechel and Hahn [2017]	dominance,valance, arousal	10,548	multiple
EmoInt Mohammad and Bravo-Márquez [2017]	anger, fear, joy, sadness,	7,097	general
Emotion-Stimulus Ghazi et al. [2015]	anger, disgust, fear, joy, sadness, surprise, shame	2,414	general
fb-valence-arousal Preoţiuc-Pietro et al. [2016]	valence, arousal	2,895	questionnaire
Grounded-Emotions Lei et al. [2014]	happy, sad	2,585	weather/events
ISEAR Scherer and Wallbott [1994]	anger, disgust, fear, joy, sadness, surprise, shame, guilt	7,665	events
Tales Alm et al. [2005]	anger, disgust, fear, joy, sadness, surprise	15,302	fairytales
SSEC Schuff et al. [2017]	anger, disgust, fear, joy, sadness, surprise, trust, anticipation	4,868	general
TEC Mohammad [2012]	anger, disgust, fear, joy, sadness, surprise, positive surprise, negative surprise	21,051	general
Unified Klinger et al. [2018]	anticipation, anger, confusion, fear, disgust, love, joy, no emo, sadness, surprise, trust	233,665	general

Unified datasets. Table 3.4 depicts the grouping of different emotion labels for the mapping into eleven Unified emotion labels.

The total data distribution for all of the datasets covered above is shown in Table 3.5.

All the experiments during the model implementation are performed in a Python environment. Initially, the dataset is partitioned into 80% train and 20% test sets. The training set is divided into 90% train and 10% validation set. All the results are reported only on the test set. Traditional metrics such as precision, recall, F-score, and accuracy are computed to evaluate the misinformation detection performance. The model is also assessed using the weighted accuracy evaluation metric on the ByteDance dataset. The weight assigned by the ByteDance competition to agreed and disagreeing samples is 1/15 and 1/5, respectively. The final step in the mis-

Table 3.4 Mapping of different emotion labels into Unified emotion labels

Unified Label	Original Labels
joy	joy, happy, happiness, serenity, calmness, joyful, elation, hp, fun, enthusiasm, relief
noemo	noemo, BLANK, neutral, ne
fear	fear, panic, apprehension, terror, fr, worry
sadness	sadness, sad, Grieg, gloominess, sorrow, shame, sd, guilt
disgust	disgust, dg, dislike, hate, boredom, indifference, disappointment
anger	anger, angry, annoyance, hostility, fury, ag, hate
love	love
confusion	confusion, indecision
anticipation	anticipation, vigilance, expectancy, interest
trust	trust, acceptance, like, admiration
surprise	surprise, uncertainty, amazement, su+, su-

Table 3.5 It depicts the detailed statistics of the various datasets we use to perform all the experiments for this work. FND, fake news detection; N, neutral

Dataset	Type	Source	Size	labels
QQP [Imtiaz et al., 2020]	Novelty	Quora	404,290	3
Unified [Klinger et al., 2018]	Emotion	various	233,665	10+N
ByteDance [Xiaoye, 2019]	FND	ByteDance	400,893	3
FNC [Hanselowski et al., 2018]	FND	FNC	49,972	4
Covid-Stance [Mutlu et al., 2020]	FND	Twitter	14,374	3

information detection process uses scaffold labeling and produced representations after the novelty and emotion models have been individually trained on the datasets. For homogeneity with the ByteDance dataset, the classes of the FNC dataset (agree and disagree) are converted to agreed and disagreed, respectively. Additionally, the Covid-Stance dataset's *against* class is reported as disagreed, and the *favor* class is reported as agreed for consistency with the other labels.

3.6.3   Baseline Models

To validate the performance of the developed model, some baseline models have been implemented which are as follows.

3.6.3.1   Siamese LSTM Network

This baseline model utilizes shared weights for generating source and target representations of the misinformation datasets. An LSTM layer with a fully connected layer and softmax function is used for the ByteDance and Covid-Stance datasets. The stacking of two bidirectional LSTMs is implemented for the FNC dataset. In this model, the original features are concatenated with the features obtained from the second LSTM. This concatenated feature is then passed to a fully connected layer for classification.

3.6.3.2 Multichannel CNN

A multichannel CNN is implemented as a second baseline model. This CNN model has two channels with filter sizes 2 and 3, respectively. The first filter is applied to the premise, while the second filter is applied to the hypothesis. After that, a max-pool operation is performed, and pooled outputs from both channels are obtained. The results are then concatenated and passed through a fully connected layer with a softmax classifier for the final classification.

3.6.4 Results and Analysis

The evaluation outcomes of the proposed model, baselines, and ablation studies on three distinct datasets are displayed in Table 3.6. The model's accuracy, precision, recall, and f-score are shown in the result table for both the agreed and disagreed classes. The newly developed method outperforms the baseline models, according to the results. The model with novelty and emotion information performs better than the other models.

3.6.4.1 Ablation Study

The ablation studies are carried out using all of the datasets, which aids in creating a reliable misinformation detection model. The results of these ablation studies are also displayed in Table 3.6.

(a) Novelty (ESIM) + Emotion (KlingBin)
For textual entailment, this model extracts the novelty representation from the ESIM (Chen et al. 2018) model. The BERT-based model trained on the Klinger binary dataset provides the emotion representations for this model. Based on both datasets, the observation shows that this model provides an accuracy that is comparable with the best models (the model covered in Sect. 3.6). On the disagreed class, which is inferior in the datasets, the best model exhibits higher recall and F-score values.

(b) Novelty (Quora) + Emotion (KlingBin)
The final proposed model and this model are developed in the same manner. But instead of using samples from the ByteDance, Covid-Stance, or FNC datasets, the novelty model is trained solely on the QQP dataset. It is noted that the accuracy is comparable. For the underrepresented, disagreed class, however, the best (final) model produces superior results.

Table 3.6 Results of baselines, ablation studies, and proposed model

Dataset	Model	Agreed			Disagreed			
		Prec	Rec	F-Score	Prec	Rec	F-Score	Acc
Baselines								
ByteDance	Siamese LSTM	0.89	0.98	0.93	0.74	0.34	0.46	87.83
FNC	Siamese BiLSTM	0.74	0.85	0.79	0.33	0.21	0.25	67.5
Covid-Stance	Siamese LSTM	0.85	0.89	0.87	0.82	0.77	0.79	83.92
ByteDance	Multi-Channel CNN	0.89	0.98	0.94	0.81	0.35	0.49	88.57
FNC	Multi-Channel CNN	0.74	0.95	0.83	0.44	0.11	0.18	72.31
Covid-Stance	Multi-Channel CNN	0.86	0.90	0.88	0.84	0.78	0.81	85.16
Ablation Studies								
ByteDance	Novelty (ESIM) + Emotion (KlingBin)	0.91	1.00	0.95	0.99	0.48	0.65	91.81
	Novelty (Quora) + Emotion (KlingBin)	0.91	1.00	0.95	0.96	0.49	0.65	91.74
	Novelty (Quora-BD)	0.95	0.99	0.97	0.92	0.73	0.82	94.83
	Emotion (KlingBin)	0.93	1.00	0.96	1.00	0.61	0.75	93.83
FNC	Novelty (ESIM) + Emotion (KlingBin)	0.89	0.96	0.92	0.89	0.49	0.63	88.19
	Novelty (Quora-FNC)	0.91	1.00	0.95	1.00	0.73	0.84	92.77
	Emotion (KlingBin)	0.86	0.99	0.92	0.96	0.54	0.69	87.19
Covid-Stance	Novelty (Quora) + Emotion (KlingBin)	0.90	0.90	0.90	0.85	0.85	0.85	87.49
	Novelty (Quora-CS)	0.86	0.86	0.86	0.80	0.79	0.79	83.44
	Emotion (KlingBin)	0.78	0.98	0.87	0.96	0.58	0.72	82.18
Developed Model (Discussed in Section 3.6								
ByteDance	Fake-News (QuoraBD+KlingBin)	0.96	0.99	0.98	0.95	0.79	0.86	**96.11**
FNC	Fake-News (Quora-FNC+KlingBin)	0.93	1.00	0.97	1.00	0.80	0.89	**94.73**
Covid-Stance	Fake-News (Quora-CS+KlingBin)	0.95	0.96	0.95	0.93	0.92	0.93	**94.14**

(c) Novelty (Quora with respective datasets)

To conduct this ablation study, all the datasets, *viz.*, ByteDance, FNC, and Covid-Stance, are first mixed with the Quora question pair dataset individually. Then, a novelty detection model is trained on the resultant three datasets. In this method, the misinformation detection model only takes novelty representations and does not consider emotion representation. This model provides comparable results to the final model without using emotional representation.

(d) Emotion (KlingBin)

Similar to the novelty component, the accuracy of the emotion model developed on the ByteDance, FNC, and Covid-Stance datasets is comparable to that of the model trained on the (Klinger et al. 2018) dataset. This model's performance is similar to that of the novelty-only model and the outcomes of the final model generation. The disagreed class, however, demonstrates the need for development.

In this case, the first and second models in the ablation study, which integrated novelty and emotion features, perform worse than the condition in which the models are utilized independently of each other. This could be explained by the fact that the model is still learning the features of the ByteDance dataset. The combined model used in the ablation study employs solely the Quora dataset for its novelty component, while the independent results of the novelty model are on the Quora-BD dataset. The combined model performs below the level of the independent novelty model on Quora-BD, which is aware of the features of the Quora dataset because it has not learned the characteristics of the ByteDance dataset. For the ByteDance dataset, the constructed model outperforms the novelty and emotion models separately, according to the result analysis section. It is discovered during these ablation investigations that an improvement in performance concerning all the evaluation metrics is attained on both the agreed and disagreed classes of all the datasets after integrating the best novelty and emotion models in the final model.

Training and validation learning curves display the model's accuracy and loss for each epoch. The learning curves of the final model for the ByteDance dataset are shown in Figs. 3.4 and 3.5. The learning curves of the final model for the FNC dataset are shown in Figs. 3.6 and 3.7. These graphs display the model's accuracy as well as its loss during training and validation. The model behaves consistently in the turns during training and validation. The loss and accuracy are continuously tuned to a state of equilibrium where overfitting is prevented, and the model learns correctly.

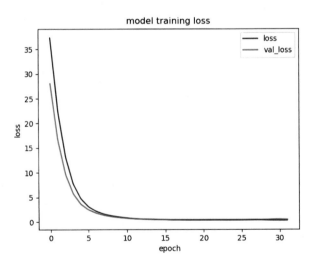

Fig. 3.4 Loss learning curve for ByteDance dataset

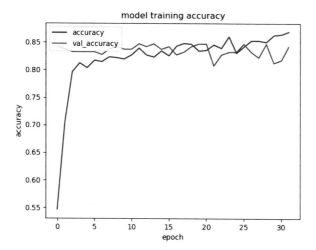

Fig. 3.5   Accuracy learning curve for ByteDance dataset

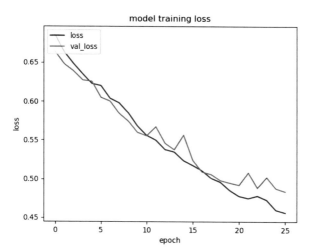

Fig. 3.6   Loss learning curve for FNC dataset

3.6.4.2   Error Analysis

For justifying the model performance, an error analysis is carried out for the classification results achieved for each dataset. For this purpose, the receiver operating characteristics (ROC) curve (Bradley 1997) is plotted, and the value of area under the curve (AUC) (Bradley 1997) is calculated for the obtained corresponding ROC graph. The AUC value is obtained as 0.98 (shown in Fig. 3.8), 0.99 (shown in Fig. 3.9), and 0.99 (shown in Fig. 3.10), respectively, on the ByteDance, FNC, and the Covid-Stance datasets. This suggests that the generated model has good

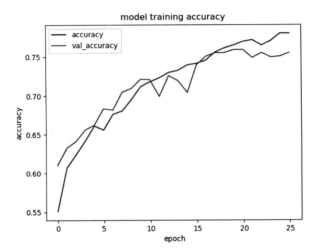

Fig. 3.7 Accuracy learning curve for FNC dataset

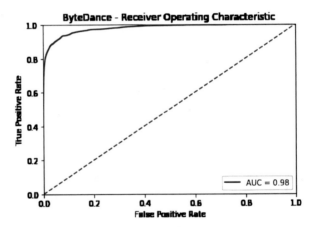

Fig. 3.8 ByteDance ROC curve

performance across all three datasets. Qualitative and quantitative analyses are also done on the datasets to strengthen this justification.

Quantitative Analysis The outputs of the classifiers are closely analyzed using the co-occurrence matrices, which gives better insights. This analysis is shown in Table 3.7. These matrices are generated, considering the co-occurrence of the predicted classes by the novelty and emotion model with the original labels. Here, a(True, True), b(True, False), c(False, True), and d(False, False) are the various combinations of predicted emotion labels on the source and the target. To see if these co-occurrence matrices support the novelty and emotion hypothesis, an analysis is conducted. In order to increase the model's final accuracy based on these findings, scaffold labels are added to the representations. The majority of samples

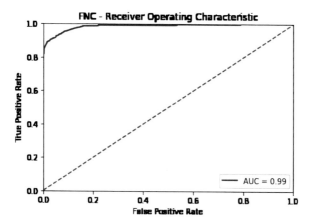

Fig. 3.9 FNC ROC curve

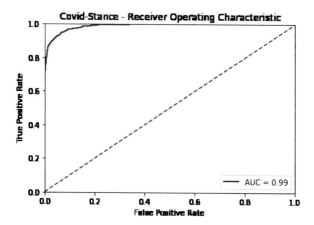

Fig. 3.10 Covid-Stance ROC curve

are primarily categorized as duplicates in the novelty co-occurrence matrices for ByteDance, FNC, and Covid-Stance datasets. On the other hand, the samples of the disagreed class are primarily classified as novel.

The emotion co-occurrence matrix displays the distribution of the actual misinformation labels of the dataset with the *emotion false* and *emotion true* predicted labels. It can be seen that more agreed samples are classified as *emotion false-emotion false* and *emotion true-emotion true* for the Bytedance and FNC dataset. Whereas more disagreed samples are classified as *emotion false-emotion true* and *emotion true-emotion false*. Since the premise is considered false, it is expected that the *favor* class be majorly represented as *emotion false* for the Covid-Stance dataset. As per the expectation, it is seen that the agreed samples (*favor*) are mostly classified as *emotion false* and the disagreed samples (*against*) are significantly classified as *emotion true*.

Table 3.7 The table shows the co-occurrence matrices for the test set of ByteDance, FNC, and Covid-Stance datasets. Emo_True represents emotion true, and Emo_False represents emotion false

Quora_Labels BD_Labels	Duplicate	Novel
Agreed	26710	365
Disagreed	430	1241

BD-Novelty-Quora Co-occurrence Matrix

Quora_Labels Stance	Novel	Duplicate
Agreed	477	1426
Disagreed	497	200

FNC-Novelty-Quora Co-occurrence Matrix

Combined_Results BD_Labels	a	b	c	d
Agreed	7839	5070	5435	8731
Disagreed	313	331	347	680

BD-Emotion Premise Hypothesis Co-occurrence Matrix

Combined_Results Stance	a	b	c	d
Agreed	377	475	408	643
Disagreed	102	210	168	217

FNC-Emotion Premise Hypothesis Co-occurrence Matrix

Quora_Labels Stance	Novel	Duplicate
Against	683	324
For	137	1350

CS-Novelty Co-occurrence Matrix

Emo_Labels Stance	Emo_True	Emo_False
Against	434	573
For	472	1015

CS-Novelty Co-occurrence Matrix

Qualitative Analysis The analysis provided in Sect. 3.6 demonstrates how the model works as a type of *transfer learning* from emotion and novelty recognition to misinformation detection. It is also examined that in the final misinformation detection, FNC novelty matters more than emotion. This is possible because the FNC data consists of a compilation of news story texts that are low in emotion and have a lot of text. Additionally, novelty is more significant in the Covid-Stance dataset than emotion. The emotion model might not do a good job of capturing the emotion in some extensive and semantically complex datasets.

The precision and recall for the agreed class are good, according to the final classification results. However, the model also performs well in precision and recall in the disagreed class, demonstrating that the model may be successfully learned in underrepresented classes. The created architecture is able to accurately represent the entailment relationship between the sources and targets of both datasets. Because of this, the model does well on the disagreed class of the FNC dataset, which provides crucial information on misleading information.

Results are compared with the SOTA models on the ByteDance, FNC, and Covid-Stance datasets to demonstrate the efficacy of the model. The created model outperforms these models in terms of accuracy by significant amounts. It beats the current models for the ByteDance, FNC, and Covid-Stance datasets by 8, 1.54, and

Table 3.8 The table displays a comparison between the proposed model and the existing SOTA models

Model	ByteDance dataset						
	Agreed			Disagreed			Accuracy
	Prec	Rec	F-Score	Prec	Rec	F-Score	
Pham [2019]	–	–	–	–	–	–	88.28
Liu et al. [2019a]	–	–	–	–	–	–	88.15
Yang et al. [2019a]	–	–	–	–	–	–	88.06
Developed Model	0.96	0.99	0.98	0.95	0.79	0.86	**96.11**
FNC Dtataset							
Attardi and Slovikovskaya [2020]	–	–	0.53	–	–	0.31	93.19
Chaudhry et al. [2017]	0.89	0.89	0.89	0.89	0.78	0.83	**95.3**
Developed Model	0.93	1.00	0.97	1.00	0.80	0.89	94.73
Covid-Stance Dataset							
Mutlu et al. [2020]	–	–	–	–	–	–	76.83
Developed Model	0.95	0.96	0.95	0.93	0.92	0.93	**94.14**

17.31 points, respectively. The comparative study of the model with the current SOTA models utilizing various datasets is shown in Table 3.8.

For the Chinese source and target pairs, all of the prior SOTA results are available on ByteDance. The outcomes for the matching English pair included in the original dataset are presented in this work. The ByteDance dataset was used to test the SOTA model (Pham 2019), which proposed a combined prediction model of 18 neural networks, nine tree-based models, and a logistic regression model. In comparison to them, the created model obtains an 8.82% increase in weighted accuracy. Comparable increases in weighted accuracy are observed compared to Liu et al. (2019a) and Yang et al. (2019a). The outcomes have been contrasted with Attardi and Slovikovskaya (2020), which models the FNC misinformation detection task using transfer learning and the FNC dataset. On the FNC dataset, there is a noticeable increase in accuracy of 1.54% overall with respect to their best model. Additionally, it is noted that the constructed model outperforms the agreed and disagreed classes by considerable amounts. The model is able to increase the F-Score by 8 and 6 points for the agreed and disagreed classes, respectively. The model also achieves comparable performance with Chaudhry et al. (2017) by obtaining an 8- and 11-point accuracy increase for the agreed class and the disagreed class, respectively. The findings are compared with the models given in the dataset publication (Mutlu et al. 2020) for the Covid-Stance dataset. When comparing the final model to their best model, which employs LR as the classification model and TF-IDF (Zhang et al. 2011) features, there is a 17.31% improvement.

3.7   Summary

In this chapter, it is discussed how and why novelty and emotion are important attributes for misinformation detection and prevention of spread. A deep learning and machine learning architecture that uses news headline body pairs as input to determine whether the news contains false content has also been covered in this chapter. It uses representations of the news pair that are sensitive to emotion and novelty to identify false information. Pre-trained models are also employed to extract novelty and emotion-aware representations. All the representations are combined with the scaffold labels for the final classification task and fed into the logistic regression model. Comprehensive tests have also been carried out using four existing datasets. Experimental results display that extracting novelty and emotion features helps in misinformation detection. Though this chapter effectively captures the novelty and emotional information for misinformation detection, it does not fill the entire gap in this domain. Numerous alternatives exist for further exploration and development of this work. Future studies could go in one of two directions: (a) a multitask approach can be implemented for misinformation detection where novelty and emotion recognition tasks will be the supporting task and fake news detection will be the main task; (b) these days, a lot of news articles include pictures, music, and videos. Therefore, these modalities for disinformation detection could be included in a potential extension. In this book, Chap. 4 explores the importance of multitasking in misinformation detection. Chapters 5 and 6 explain the importance and role of multimodality in misinformation detection.

Chapter 4
Multitasking for Misinformation Detection

Generally, in the context of machine learning, people used to solve only one task at a time. Regardless of the task, its type, and its nature, the problem is formulated as using data to solve only one task or to perform a single metric optimization at a time. Although the model performs well, this method does not always give high performance due to the dataset size or the ability of the model to learn meaningful representations from it. To tackle this problem, multitasking has been introduced. The concept of multitask learning was first given by researchers *Rich Caruana* in 1997 (Caruana 1997). This chapter first briefly discusses multitask learning and subsequently discusses the utilization and performance of multitask learning in the context of misinformation detection.

4.1 Multitask Learning

Multitask learning is a machine learning approach that solves multiple tasks simultaneously. It improves the generalization of the model by using the standard features contained in the training data of related tasks. In this approach, the model tries to learn how to solve multiple tasks together. It optimizes various loss functions at once. This approach allows training a single model to solve several related tasks rather than training independent models for each task. In the multitask process, the model uses entire data across the different tasks to learn generalized representations of the data useful in multiple contexts. Literature reveals the widespread usage of multitask approaches across various domains, such as computer vision, natural language processing, and recommendation systems. Nowadays, it is commonly leveraged in multiple industries, such as Google, Microsoft, etc., due to its ability to leverage large amounts of data to solve related tasks effectively.

Before going deeper into the implementation of the multitask learning model, it is essential to understand the situations in which the use of multitask learning is

© The Author(s), under exclusive license to Springer Nature Switzerland AG 2024
A. Ekbal, R. Kumari, *Dive into Misinformation Detection*, The Information
Retrieval Series 30, https://doi.org/10.1007/978-3-031-54834-5_4

Fig. 4.1 Multitask model
view

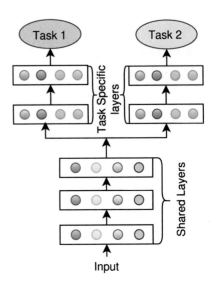

appropriate or inappropriate. Multitask learning is useful if the tasks have some level of correlation. This type of learning improves performance when some underlying information principles are common in different tasks. For instance, two tasks, general image classification and animal image classification, are correlated as both tasks involve learning to detect some patterns like pixels, colors, etc. Multitask learning does not always guarantee the best performance. Training a model for many tasks sometimes results in harmful feature sharing between tasks. In this case, the model for a stand-alone task performs better than a multitask model. This generally happens when the different tasks are unrelated, and the learned representation in one task contradicts the learned representation in another task.

As per the discussion, it can be concluded that the success of the multitask model depends on the nature and behavior of learned features or parameters, which are shared between different tasks. Figure 4.1 shows the fundamental multitask model.

Since neural networks are the most common and efficient models used in multitask learning, this image has been designed by focusing on a neural network architecture. The first three layers represent the common features shared among all the tasks. The third features extracted by the third layer are passed to the task-specific layers separately to solve the specific tasks (i.e., task1 and task2). In the multitask learning approach, one task is considered the main task, and the other are auxiliary tasks. If task1 is the main task, task2 will become the auxiliary task. Like the models designed for solving stand-alone tasks, multitask models also optimize the loss function for all the tasks separately and aggregate those functions into a single loss function to get the final loss function for the model. The following section briefly discusses the loss function for the multitask model in the context of misinformation detection.

4.2 Multitask Learning in Context of Misinformation Detection (A Case Study)

Chapter 3 justifies that novelty and emotion are important components for misinformation detection. However, Chap. 3 discusses a method that first trains the novelty and emotion models to get the novelty and emotion features, and later, the misinformation detection model uses these features to detect false content. Continuing the misinformation detection method discussed in Chap. 3, this chapter introduces a framework that jointly learns the emotion and novelty from the target text, making a convincing argument for fake news detection. Despite the pipeline approach (the pipeline approach first extracts the novelty and emotion-aware features and passes these features to the misinformation detection model), this chapter presents a deep multitask learning architecture that jointly implements emotion recognition, novelty detection, and fake news detection. The multitask model improves the performance over the single-task model. It yields that *textual novelty* and *emotion* are the two important components to consider while implementing an automatic misinformation detection framework. It is discussed in Chap. 3 that false information contains measurably more novel content and has a high intensity of *moral emotion*. False information is also influenced by increased negative emotional language. The brain's analytical capacity is surpassed by the unique and emotional conviction of false information and how these qualities combine with the structure of human memories (Barr 2019) motivated the researchers to explore the role of *textual novelty* and *emotion* for automatic misinformation detection. This analysis also shows that all three tasks are highly correlated, and a multitask approach can be best suited to solve the misinformation detection problem along with novelty detection and emotion recognition.

Analysis in Table 4.1 justifies that emotion recognition, novelty detection, and misinformation detection tasks are interrelated. The study described in (Crawshaw 2020) depicts that the learning of multiple interrelated tasks together exploits the neural network model to learn common semantic representations, which increases

Table 4.1 Table depicts an example of misinformation. It also explores the importance of novelty and emotion for misinformation detection

Premise	Hypothesis	Remarks	
		Novelty	Emotion
Use of a surgical mask reduced the proportion of droplets and aerosols with detectable virus among children and adults with confirmed seasonal coronavirus and seasonal influenza infection.	Facemasks are dirty, dehumanizing and ineffective. Standford univ study: "The data suggests that both medical and non-medical facemasks are ineffective to block human-to-human transmission of infectious Covid-19 disease"	In this news premise explains the effectiveness of face masks whereas hypothesis describes its ineffectiveness. This shows that the hypothesis is novel concerning the premise	The premise shows the "trust" emotion category. In contrast, the hypothesis shows the "disgust" and "sadness" emotion category

the generalization proficiency of the model. Inspired by this advantage, this chapter explores a multitask learning model that jointly learns novelty and emotion patterns in the data to boost misinformation detection performance. The model adopts a two-phase process since misinformation datasets do not have emotion labels for training the multitask model directly. In the first phase, novelty labels are attached to the dataset using a framework similar to Yang et al. (2019b). This also follows the same approach of novelty labels association discussed in Sect. 3.6.1.1 of Chap. 3. The emotion labels for the misinformation datasets are computed using BERT-based architecture. After getting the novelty and emotion labels, a multitask model is developed for misinformation detection in the second phase.

In conclusion, the entire framework is developed in two stages. To automatically generate actual novelty and emotion labels for the misinformation datasets, the first phase uses *novelty detection and emotion recognition*. The *implementation of the developed multitask model* constitutes the second phase. Below are descriptions of each of these phases.

4.2.1 Novelty Detection and Emotion Recognition

Initially, the misinformation datasets lack both novelty and emotion labels. But those labels are crucial to resolving a multitasking framework hypothesis. In order to produce novelty- and emotion-labeled misleading instances, the individual models are trained for novelty and emotion tasks. The process of acquiring novelty and emotion ground-truth labels for the misinformation datasets is the initial phase, and it is covered in this section.

This task is further broken down into two smaller stages. The unique novelty and emotion datasets from the first sub-phase are used to train the novelty and emotion models. The novelty model is first trained using the Quora Question Pair (QQP) dataset. This dataset has been briefly discussed in Sect. 3.6.2 of Chap. 3. For the emotion model, the Klinger dataset and GoEmotion dataset are used. Section 4.2.3 discusses both the emotion datasets in detail. Using the trained novelty and emotion models from the first sub-phase, ground truth novelty and emotion labels are produced for the misinformation datasets.

Novelty Ground-Truth Labels Generation Novelty detection is implemented using a similar framework as Yang et al. (2019b). The first 20% instances of the training set of fake news datasets are appended with the QQP dataset for training the novelty model. The novelty model is further trained using the combined data. The trained model determines whether the hypothesis is duplicate or novel concerning the premise.[1] This trained novelty model predicts novelty labels, i.e., duplicate or novel, on the remaining 80% of the train set and the entire test set of the fake news

---

[1] In this work, source and premise carry the same meaning. Similarly, target and hypothesis also mean the same, and these terminologies are used interchangeably.

datasets. Therefore, this is how the final ground-truth novelty labels for the datasets of misinformation are produced.

Algorithm 1: Generating emotion ground-truth labels

Data: Binary Classed (*emotion true* and *emotion false*) Klinger Dataset and GoEmotion Dataset

Result: Emotion Ground-Truth Labels

1 Train the BERT based, *emotion model 1* on the Binary Classed Klinger Dataset ;

2 From model trained in the previous step, get the emotion labels, *emotion true* and *emotion false* for premise and hypothesis of the Misinformation Dataset ;

3 Construct a single emotion label, *emotion labels 1* by combining the emotion labels of the premise and hypothesis into *emo1* if both are same or *emo2* if both are different ;

4 Train the LSTM based, *emotion model 2* on the Binary Classed GoEmotion Dataset ;

5 Repeat steps 2 and 3 using the *emotion model 2* to obtain *emotion labels 2* ;

6 **for** *sample in the Misinformation Dataset* **do**

7   **if** *sample*.emotion_label_1 == *sample*.emotion_label_2 **then**

8   sample.ground_truth_emotion = sample.*emotion_label_1*;

9   **else**

10   **if** *sample*.fake_news_label == *agreed* **then**

11   sample.ground_truth_emotion = *emo1*;

12   **else**

13   sample.ground_truth_emotion = *emo2*;

14   **end**

15   **end**

16 **end**

Emotion Ground Truth Labels Generation The process of generating ground-truth emotion labels is shown in Algorithm 1. This work introduces two different models for finding the emotion labels for the premise and hypothesis of the fake news datasets. The pre-trained develop the first model, (*emotion model 1*). This model creates a 768-dimensional contextual embedding from a sentence. The obtained embedding is passed into a fully connected layer followed by softmax to predict the emotion classes. Klinger Dataset (Klinger et al. 2018) is used with some label modifications to train this model. This dataset has eight emotion labels: anticipation, sadness, joy, trust, anger, fear, disgust, and surprise. As per the initial hypothesis, sadness, anticipation, trust, and joy emotion labels are mapped as *emotion true*, and fear, anger, surprise, and disgust emotion classes are mapped as *emotion false*.

The previously stated BERT-based model receives the premise of the misinformation dataset as input and outputs a prediction of either *emotion true* or *emotion false*. The emotion labels for the hypothesis in the misinformation dataset are obtained using the same process. It assigns an emotion label to the hypothesis that fits into one of the two emotion classifications. As will be explained later, a single label is created for both the hypothesis and the premise once the emotion labels for each are received independently.

If both the hypothesis and the premise predict the same emotions or if both are either *emotion true* or *emotion false*, then they are combined into a single category, *emo1*. This means that samples where the predicted emotion for the premise and hypothesis is *agree* are given the label *emo1*. In an alternative scenario, when the predicted emotion labels are different, i.e., labels for the premise and hypothesis *disagree* with each other, a different category is designated, say *emo2* as the combined label for the premise and hypothesis. Thus, from the *emotion model 1*, the emotion labels are obtained as *emo1* or *emo2*. After collecting the same from the second emotion model (described next), these emotion labels of *emo1* and *emo2* serve as the intermediate labels utilized to construct the final ground-truth emotion labels for the misinformation datasets.

The LSTM is the foundation for the second emotion recognition model, *emotion model 2*. To find the word vectors, this model uses the pre-trained Glove embedding. The LSTM layer receives these word vectors in order to determine the hidden representation of the words. For the final emotion categorization, a dense layer is put on top of it and run through a Softmax function. The GoEmotion dataset (Demszky et al. 2020) is used to train this model, with some label adjustments made, as will be explained later. According to the first hypothesis, emotion labels for joy and sadness are mapped as *emotion true*, whereas emotion classes for fear, anger, surprise, and disgust are mapped as *emotion false*.

For the fake news datasets, the emotion labels are produced by this trained LSTM model. The labels *emotion true* or *emotion false* are derived for both the premise and the hypothesis, as explained in the process for the *emotion model 1* (i.e., the BERT-based model). As explained in the process for the *emotion model 1*, the same steps are taken to combine the labels of the premise and hypothesis into a single label, either *emo1* or *emo2*. The intermediate *emotion labels 2* are derived from the *emotion model 2*. The final ground-truth emotion labels are derived from these labels and the intermediate emotion labels, which are derived from the *emotion model 1*.

The process described below is used to get the final ground-truth labels, *emo1* and *emo2*, from the intermediate labels gained from the *emotion model 1* and *emotion model 2*.

The final ground-truth emotion label for a given sample is determined by comparing the intermediate emotion labels, *emotion labels 1* and *emotion labels 2*, derived from both emotion models, *emotion model 1* and *emotion model 2*, respectively. However, if the intermediate emotion labels derived from the two emotion models vary, assume *emo1* from *emotion model 1* and *emo2* from *emotion model 2*, the final label is computed according to the following process. For the instance of the fake news dataset with the fake news label *agreed*, the *emo1* label becomes the final ground-truth emotion label. The final ground-truth emotion label for the misinformation dataset instance labeled as *disagreed* is *emo2*. This follows the original hypothesis that if the emotion labels predicted for the premise and hypothesis match, *emo1* is constructed. Put another way, if the emotion labels obtained from the premise and hypothesis *agree* with each other, then the label *emo1* is originally assigned. Therefore, for the agreed samples of the misinformation dataset, *emo1* is regarded as the final ground-truth label. As previously stated, *emo2*

Table 4.2 The table displays the statistics of several datasets used to train the multitask model in the second phase and refine the novelty detection model in the first phase

		Emotion	Novelty	Multitask Model
Phase1	Train	Klinger and GoEmotion dataset	QQP+20% of training set of misinformation data	NA
	Test	Training and test set of misinformation data	Remaining 80% training set of misinformation data	NA
Phase2	Train	NA	NA	Remaining 80% training set of misinformation data
	Test	NA	NA	Test set of misinformation data

is created for the intermediate predicted emotion labels where the predicted emotion class for both the hypothesis and the premise *disagree*, meaning they are not the same. Therefore, for the disagreeing sample of the misinformation dataset, *emo2* is regarded as the final emotion ground-truth label.

In this manner, the final ground-truth emotion labels are retrieved for all instances of the misinformation datasets. Table 4.2 shows the entire dataset statistics used for training and fine-tuning the emotion and novelty models and getting the final ground truth emotion and novelty labels for the misinformation datasets in the first phase. It also displays the dataset statistics for training and testing the final proposed multitask model in the second phase. The train and test sets are completely distinct in both phases, as evidenced by this data.

4.2.2 Proposed Multitask Misinformation Detection Model

Once the novelty and emotion labels have been obtained, the dataset is prepared for multitask learning since all of the ground-truth labels for the supporting and primary tasks are available. Figure 4.2 shows the complete framework of the developed multitask model. *viz.*, **Encoder**, **Novelty Detection Model**, **Emotion recognition Model**, and **Fake News detection model** are its four modules. Each of these modules is discussed below:

Encoder For all three tasks, the encoder is made up of shared layers. For every word of the hypothesis ($H_{W_1}, .., H_{W_n}$) and premise ($P_{W_1}, .., P_{W_n}$), a pre-trained Glove embedding of 300-dimensions is taken into consideration. To create a sentence embedding, all of the word embeddings are concatenated. The pair consisting of the premise and hypothesis is transmitted to distinct embedding layers, which provide distinct sentence embeddings in the form of a size vector (sentence length, 300). Moreover, the hidden representations of the premise and hypothesis words

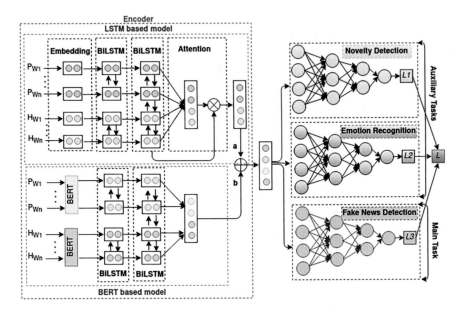

Fig. 4.2 Proposed multitask misinformation detection model. Here, the input representations using pre-trained glove embedding and BERT-based embedding are denoted by *a* and *b*, respectively. *L1*, *L2*, and *L3* represent the loss for individual tasks, and *L* is the aggregated loss

are obtained using a different BiLSTM layer. Equations 4.1 and 4.2 mathematically describe the above discussion.

$$\overrightarrow{h_{Pf_{x,i}}} = LSTM_{pf}(w_{x,i}, \overrightarrow{h_{Pf_{x,i-1}}})$$

$$\overleftarrow{h_{Pb_{x,i}}} = LSTM_{pb}(w_{x,i}, \overleftarrow{h_{Pb_{x,i}}}) \qquad (4.1)$$

$$h_{P_{x,i}} = [\overrightarrow{h_{Pf_{x,i}}}, \overleftarrow{h_{Pb_{x,i}}}]$$

Here, the Bi-LSTM layer's forward and backward hidden representations for each word in the premise sentence are produced by $h_{Pf_{x,i}}$ and $h_{Pb_{x,i}}$. $h_{P_{x,i}}$ indicates the hidden representation of the premise sentence. The hidden representations of the hypothesis sentence are computed similarly using Eq. 4.2.

$$h_{H_{x,i}} = [\overrightarrow{h_{Hf_{x,i}}}, \overleftarrow{h_{Hb_{x,i}}}] \qquad (4.2)$$

The hidden representations of premise and hypothesis are concatenated to obtain a unified representation (shown in Eq. 4.3). A BiLSTM layer is again employed to obtain the systematic semantic representation of hypothesis-premise pairs. The

result of this BiLSTM layer is calculated similarly to 4.1 and 4.2. The outcome of
the second LSTM is computed using Eq. 4.4.

$$Rph = [h_{P_{x,i}}, h_{H_{x,i}}] \qquad (4.3)$$

$$CRph = [\overrightarrow{h_{Rphf_{x,i}}}, \overleftarrow{h_{Rphb_{x,i}}}] \qquad (4.4)$$

The forward and backward directions are shown by f and b, respectively.
Following the second BiLSTM layer, CRph represents the premise hypothesis's
combined representation. The forward and backward hidden representations of the
combined representation are denoted by $h_{Rphf_{x,i}}$ and $h_{Rphb_{x,i}}$, respectively. Not
every word adds the same amount to the meaningful representation of the text.
The final text representation vector, similar to Yang et al. (2016), is formed by
aggregating the representation of those informative words and applying an attention
mechanism over the hidden representation derived from the second BiLSTM layer
to extract significant words. Equations 4.5, 4.6, and 4.7 are used to formulate this
attention mechanism.

$$h_{it} = tanh((W * CRph) + b) \qquad (4.5)$$

$$\alpha_{it} = \frac{exp((h_{it}^T h_w))}{\Sigma_t exp((h_{it}^T h_w))} \qquad (4.6)$$

$$s_i = \Sigma_t \alpha_{it} h_{it} \qquad (4.7)$$

To be more precise, the hidden representation (h_{it}) of a word is generated by
a fully connected layer receiving the output of the second BiLSTM layer (CRph).
The word's importance is determined by passing this hidden representation through
a softmax function, which yields a normalized importance weight (α_{it}). In the end,
the attended textual feature representation is obtained by adding the weighted sum
(s_i) of the word representation. In this case, the randomly initialized vectors W,
b, and h_w learn together during the training phase. In Fig. 4.2, "a" stands for it
and provides a consistent form with meaningful interaction between premise and
hypothesis.

Glove embedding obtains the semantic representation of the words in the context
window only, which may result in a less qualitative sentence representation. The
BERT model (Devlin et al. 2019) is utilized to capture best the semantic and
contextual meaning of the words and sentences in order to get over this limitation. To
compute the BERT-based hidden representation, a BiLSTM layer is employed over
the premise sentence embedding. In a similar manner, the hidden representation of
the hypothesis is calculated. The premise and hypothesis's hidden representations
are combined to create a single representation, which is then covered by another
BiLSTM layer. A common representation with semantic interaction between the
hypothesis and premise is produced as a result of this BiLSTM layer. Lastly, the

word and sentence-based semantic interaction of the premise and hypothesis is obtained by concatenating different combinations of the hidden representations.

Concatenation Layer This layer is implemented to combine the embedding obtained from both models. The concatenation is performed using Eq. 4.8. Here, CR represents the common representation. It is the resultant vector obtained by concatenating the addition, subtraction, and multiplication results of both the embeddings.

$$CR = [(a+b), (a-b), (a*b)] \qquad (4.8)$$

Novelty Detection Model One of the supporting tasks associated with the proposed approach is carried out by this part, which is novelty detection. A feed-forward neural network with two hidden layers and an output layer with a softmax classification function is used in the novelty detection model. This feed-forward network receives the encoder results as input, and the softmax classifier function determines if the hypothesis is new or redundant with respect to the premise.

Emotion Recognition This component of the developed model completes the emotion recognition task, one of the supporting tasks. The emotion recognition model is a feed-forward neural network model with two hidden layers and one output layer, just like the novelty detection model. There is a softmax classifier function in the output layer. This neural network receives the encoder results as input, and the softmax classifier determines if the dataset instance is of type emo1 or emo2.

Fake News Detection Model This model is implemented similarly to models for emotion recognition and novelty detection. It is also a feed-forward neural network model, having two hidden layers and one output layer with a softmax function. The softmax classifier function determines whether the hypothesis and the premise agree or disagree in this instance as well, using the encoder outcomes as input to the network. The features of the dataset also have a role in this decision-making. Since the premise for ByteDance and Covid-Stance is always wrong, the information in the hypothesis is false if it matches with the premise. The information in the hypothesis is true if it conflicts with the premise. For the FNC dataset, the idea is the opposite, as the premise is true in every case. The label itself is true or false for the FNID dataset, so there is no need for mapping.

For each of the three distinct task models in this developed multitask learning framework, the objective function is defined as the cross-entropy loss between the original and predicted labels. Equation 4.9 is used to compute the loss for the novelty detection task, which is expressed as L_N. Similar computations yield L_E and L_F, representing the loss functions for emotion and misinformation detection, respectively.

$$L_N = -\Sigma[y_n \log p_n + (1 - y_n)\log(1 - p_n)] \qquad (4.9)$$

Equation 4.10 illustrates how the final loss is calculated as the weighted sum of all three losses in order to train the model in a multitasking manner.

$$L = \alpha * L_N + \beta * L_E + \gamma * L_F \tag{4.10}$$

Here, y and p represent the original and the predicted class label of the news post.

4.2.3 Datasets

The details of the various data sets that were utilized to train the novelty, emotion, and misinformation detection models are presented in this section. The designed model is trained using real-world benchmark datasets that are publicly accessible. In this chapter, the same datasets discussed in the previous chapter are used. The Quora question pair dataset (Imtiaz et al. 2020) is used to train the novelty model. GoEmotion dataset (Demszky et al. 2020) and Unified dataset (Klinger et al. 2018) are used to train the emotion model. Finally, the misinformation detection model is trained using Fake News Challenge (FNC) (Hanselowski et al. 2018), ByteDance dataset (Xiaoye 2019), Fake News Inference Dataset (FNID) (Sadeghi et al. 2022), and Covid-Stance Dataset (Mutlu et al. 2020). These datasets are the group of news articles collected from various sources and domains. Each dataset has a distinct size. All the datasets have been briefly described in Chap. 3 except the GoEmotion and APR datasets. The below paragraphs provide a brief description of GoEmotion and APR datasets. Table 4.3 shows the statistics of APR dataset and Table 4.4 depicts the data distribution for all the datasets.

Table 4.3 Domain-wise statistics of the Amazon product review (APR) dataset

Category	Users	Items	Reviews	Edges
Men's Clothing	1.25M	371K	8.20M	8.22M
Women's clothing	1.82M	838K	14.5M	17.5M
Music	1.13M	557K	6.40M	7.98M
Movies	2.11M	208K	6.17M	4.96M
Electronics	4.25M	498K	11.4M	7.87M
Books	8.20M	2.37M	25.9M	50.0M
All	**21.0M**	**9.35M**	**144M**	**237M**

Table 4.4 Table showing the distribution of datasets used in the first phase to fine-tune the model and in the second phase to train and test the proposed multitask model

Dataset	Source	Type	Size	labels
QQP	Quora	Novelty	404,290	3
Unified	Various	Emotion	233,665	10+N
GoEmotion	Reddit	Emotion	58,000	27+N
APR	Various	Sentiment	82 Million	2
ByteDance	ByteDance	FND	400,893	3
FNC	FNC	FND	49,972	4
Covid Stance	Twitter	FND	14,374	3
FNID	IEEEDataPort	FND	17,324	2

GoEmotion Dataset The largest manually annotated dataset for textual emotion recognition is called GoEmotions. It has 58k English Reddit comments, along with labels for the relevant emotions. In addition to the neutral category, there are a total of 27 emotion classifications. The emotion labels are *admiration, amusement, approval, desire, caring, gratitude, excitement, love, joy, optimism, relief, pride, annoyance, anger, disapproval, disappointment, embarrassment, disgust, grief, fear, nervousness, remorse, sadness, confusion, curiosity, realization, surprise, and neutral.*

Amazon Product Review (APR) Dataset This dataset is the collection of Amazon Product Reviews from May 1996 to July 2014. This dataset consists of the reviews from six domains, *viz.*, men's clothing, women's clothing, music, movies, electronics, and books. It consists of millions of product reviews in total. This dataset consists of reviews (text, ratings, helpfulness votes), product metadata (descriptions, category information, price, brand, and image features), and links (also viewed/also bought graphs). Table 4.3 depicts the domain-wise statistics of the APR dataset.

4.2.3.1 Experimental Setup

The embedding mechanism, text pre-processing, several hyper-parameters, and implementation specifics are covered in this section. The tests are carried out using the Python libraries Keras, Numpy, Pandas, NLTK, and Sklearn. The accuracy and class-wise F1-score of the system are used to assess its performance. For text cleaning, punctuation, special characters, digits, and short words are eliminated. This model makes use of pre-trained 300-dimension glove embedding and pre-trained BERT-based embedding. For both of the BiLSTMs in the encoder, the unit size of 150 is taken into account. In task-specific layers, the hidden and output layers consider the unit sizes 64 and 2. For each of the three challenges, the classifier function is Softmax. There are 31,744,195 parameters in total for the proposed model. The model is optimized for each task using the Adam optimizer, with cross-entropy as the loss function. The model has 256 batch sizes, an early-stopping callback, and 50 training epochs. Numerous tests are conducted utilizing varying values of alpha, beta, and gamma. Various combinations of alpha, beta, and gamma (0.2, 0.5, and 1) are selected. Following the experiments, it was shown that decreasing the weight assigned to any one of the three tasks resulted in a decline in total performance. This investigation demonstrates that emotion and novelty work together to aid in the identification of disinformation, producing the greatest results in the least amount of search area. As a result, tasks involving the detection of novelty, emotions, and misinformation are given equal weights. Thus, the value of α, β, and γ are determined as 1,1 and 1, respectively.

4.2.4 Baseline Models

To validate the performance of the developed model, some baseline models have been implemented which are as follows:

Siamese LSTM Network This baseline model utilizes shared weights for generating source and target representations of the misinformation datasets. A simple LSTM followed by a fully connected layer and softmax function is used for the ByteDance, Covid-Stance, and FNID datasets. Two stacked Bi-directional LSTMs are implemented for the FNC dataset. In this model, the original features are concatenated with the features obtained from the second LSTM. This concatenated feature is then passed to a fully connected layer for classification.

Multichannel CNN A multichannel CNN is implemented as a second baseline model. This CNN model has two channels with filter sizes 2 and 3, respectively. The first filter is applied to the premise, while the second filter is applied to the hypothesis. After that, a max-pool operation is performed, and pooled outputs from both channels are obtained. The results are then concatenated and passed through a fully connected layer with a softmax classifier for the final classification.

4.2.5 Results and Analysis

Table 4.5 presents the comparative analysis of the baseline models and the proposed model on four different datasets. It shows the accuracy of emotion, novelty, and misinformation detection. It also explores class-wise F1-score for the misinformation detection task achieved from the proposed model and the baseline models. In the two task models, misinformation detection is regarded as the primary task and emotion recognition or novelty detection as the auxiliary task. In the single-task model, the model is trained without any additional tasks. The weighted accuracy is presented for easier comparison with previous efforts, specifically for the ByteDance dataset with the weights determined by the ByteDance competition. The ByteDance dataset's agreed and disagreed samples have weights of 1/15 and 1/5, respectively. The outcomes demonstrate that the performance of our proposed method outperforms that of the baseline models. Since the datasets in this proposed model are a collection of news stories and do not contain much emotional information, the novelty performs better than the emotion model. The ablation research section investigates the specific contributions of novelty and emotion for misinformation detection while the model is trained using a multitask learning approach. Only the novelty detection model is considered as an auxiliary task, and the suggested model results are displayed. As an additional task, it displays the outcome when the emotion prediction model is the sole factor considered. The trained model's results are displayed without any additional tasks. The *Fake News Accuracy*, *Novelty Accuracy*, and *Emotion Accuracy* are represented by *FNA*, *NA*,

Table 4.5 The table shows the evaluation results of the S-LSTM and MC-CNN baseline models, single-task model, the models with two auxiliary tasks, and the proposed multitask model

Model / Dataset		S-LSTM	MC-CNN	FND	N+FND	E+FND	PMTM
FNC	FNA	66.5	62.31	73.26	94.88	94.88	**96.87**
	NA	-	-	43.88	87.11	24.88	87.13
	EA	-	-	61.42	37.57	91.46	93.92
	AF1	0.79	0.83	0.84	0.96	0.96	0.98
	DF1	0.25	0.18	0.19	0.92	0.92	0.94
ByteDance	FNA	87.83	88.57	88.21	97.25	96.74	**98.19**
	NA	-	-	24.89	95.4	52.46	97.4
	EA	-	-	54.83	21.6	66.5	77.54
	AF1	0.93	0.91	0.93	0.98	0.97	0.98
	DF1	0.46	0.49	0.48	0.95	0.97	0.97
FNID	FNA	74.38	79.79	83.2	95.53	96.86	**98.86**
	NA	-	-	74.19	81.4	52.46	80.92
	EA	-	-	61.57	62.99	66.5	64.7
	AF1	0.74	0.79	0.82	0.95	0.97	0.98
	DF1	0.75	0.81	0.84	0.96	0.97	0.96
Covid Stance	FNA	83.92	85.16	84.36	95.03	94.23	**96.07**
	NA	-	-	22.57	83.84	79.59	85.88
	EA	-	-	41.82	62.02	73.01	73.85
	AF1	0.87	0.88	0.86	0.95	0.95	0.97
	DF1	0.97	0.81	0.81	0.94	0.93	0.95

and *EA* in Table 4.5, respectively. The *Agreed F1* (F1 score for agreed class), *Disagreed F1 (F1 score for disagreed class)*, *Fake F1* (F1 score for fake class), and *Real F1* (F1 score for real class) are represented by the textitAF1, DF1, FF1, and *RF1*. The baseline models for the *Siamese LSTM* and *Multichannel convolution neural network* are denoted by *S-LSTM* and *MC-CNN*, respectively. The single task model is called *FND (fake news detection)*, and the two auxiliary tasks are part of the (proposed multitask model) called *PMTM*. The two-task models are *N+FND* and *E+FND*. The accuracy is displayed in percentage terms in the result table (Table 4.5), and it ranges from 1 to 100. The F1-score ranges from 0 to 1 for the agreed and disagreed classes.

4.2.5.1 Error Analysis

The results of the classifiers are carefully examined to get better insights. Table 4.6 shows the real samples from the fake news datasets. The single-task model is the misinformation detection model without any auxiliary tasks in the subsequent discussions. The two-task model is the misinformation detection model with only one auxiliary task (novelty detection or emotion recognition). The three-task model is the proposed model, which gives better performance than the two-task model and shows incorrectly classified examples.

Table 4.6 Table showing error analysis, where the two-task model performs better than the three-task model. GTS, PS1, and PS2 represent the ground-truth stance, predicted stance with only one auxiliary task, and predicted stance with two auxiliary tasks, respectively

Dataset	Premise	Hypothesis	GTS	PS1	PS2
ByteDance	Sheeni Inins is the only one in the family who is happy. The only one in the family is Wu Xin.	Xena's Morning Sun photo only lacks Wuxin and Wu Xin's side of the rumor. Friendship has come to an end	agreed	disagreed (novelty)	agreed
ByteDance	Xena's twin girls have been exposed in front of their face! For their daughter, a ration of food has been prepared, and the time to make a comeback is definite!	Is it true that Sheena's comeback is real?	disagreed	disagreed (emotion)	agreed
Covid-Stance	Cholorquine and Hydroxychloroquine are the cure for the novel coronavirus	Just chill Dan, take some hydroxychloroquine and before you know it this whole coronavirus hoax will just go away; like magic.	against	for (novelty)	against
Covid-Stance	Chloroquine and Hydroxychloroquine are cures for the novel coronavirus	Since the FDA APPROVED THE USE OF Hydroxychloroquine to treat COVID-19, which I still believe is a bullshit virus, I guess President Trump was not selling snake oil after all! Only the fecal matter media and social media platforms alike need the numbers for the fear to continue!!!	for	for (emotion)	against
FNID	With Washington bracing for President Barack Obama to announce his next Supreme Court nominee, Sen. Arlen Specter, a leading Democrat on his chamber's Judiciary Committee, has been sharing his views on the upcoming debate.	Congress can tell the Supreme Court which cases they ought to hear. We have that authority.	real	fake (emotion)	real
FNID	It is not true that Democrat Doug Jones got more than 5,000 votes in a town of less than 3,000 people in the Alabama Senate race. Unofficial results from the Dec. 12 special election show that overall, Jones beat his Republican contender Roy Moore by 1.5 percentage points or about 20,000 more votes.	"UPDATE: Thousands voted for Doug Jones in Alabama town with a population of 2,256"	fake	fake (novelty)	real
FNC	The man behind the world-famous 50ft Crabzilla spotted lurking beneath the waters in Whitstable has described the furor caused by the colossal crustacean as bit off.	Mystery of 50ft giant crab caught on camera yards from British harbor	disagree	agree (novelty)	agree

The first and the second samples are taken from the ByteDance dataset. In the first example, the proposed approach outperforms the two-task novelty model. The example lacks specific novel content, and the three-task model's emotion compensates for the novelty. In the second case, since the premise is emotion-rich and the novelty component confuses the three-task model, the two-task model of emotion outperforms the proposed three tasks. The Covid-stance dataset contains the third and fourth examples. It can be shown that in the third example, the proposed framework outperforms the two-task novelty model. The theory lacks particular novelty content and is heavily emotional. The two-task emotion model outperforms the developed model in the fourth example. The novelty, which is less obvious in the hypothesis than the emotion, confuses the three-task model. The FNID dataset contains the fifth and sixth examples. In the sixth case, the two-task emotion model fails to classify the sentence as real, but the proposed three-task model does. This is because the sentences lack emotion and the three-task model's novelty improves classification. It is noted that the novelty-added two-task model outperforms the proposed three-task model in the sixth example. This is due to the unclear emotions in the sentence, which makes the emotion portion of the three-task model confusing. The final example, where the sentence's semantics are unclear, is drawn from the FNC dataset. This is why both the two-task and three-task models misclassify it.

4.3   Summary

This chapter presents a unified approach for comprehensively identifying misinformation. The chapter starts with the introduction of multitask learning and concludes with the effectiveness of multitask learning in the misinformation detection context. For misinformation detection, it introduces a model that simultaneously performs novelty detection, emotion recognition, and misinformation detection. It determines whether the hypothesis about the premise is true or not by using the premise and hypothesis from a dataset of misinformation as input. This proposed multitask model is designed in two different stages. The novelty and emotion labels are extracted using pre-trained deep learning-based architecture in the first phase. In the second phase, the proposed multitask model is implemented. The proposed models identify emotions, detect novelty, and detect false information simultaneously. Detailed experiments have been conducted on publicly available fake news datasets. The developed model outperforms the current approaches in terms of misinformation detection, according to experimental results.

Chapter 5
Multimodality in Misinformation Detection

In earlier days, generally, in the context of machine learning, artificial intelligence and natural language processing researchers used text data to solve different tasks. As the performance of ML, AI, and NLP models highly depends on the characteristics and quality of the datasets, with the change in time, people have introduced advanced datasets that contain additional information along with text information. This advancement has introduced the concept of multimodality in the research community. This chapter sheds light on multimodality. It starts with a brief introduction to multimodality and continues with its importance, application, challenges, and applicability in the context of misinformation detection.

5.1 Multimodality

In the current era, there has been phenomenal growth in multimodal content that appears through various sources, such as YouTube videos, memes, blogs, Facebook, Instagram, etc. The approach to multimodality described here originated from linguistics. Multimodality introduces the variety of conversational symbols in oral or written communication (Dai 2013). Multimodality theory is one of the famous language theories that explore various modes that people use to communicate with each other and to express themselves. This theory is given by Jewitt and Kress in (2003), in which modes represent the means of communication. According to the language theory, visual, aural, spatial, gestures, and linguistics are the five modes of communication (Jewitt et al. 2016). The term *multimodality* was coined in 1998 based on an article published by Charles Goodwin. This article also depicts that humans use different modes to interact. For instance, gestures, which are very important for communication, are a combination of facial expressions, body language, and hand gestures. Even though multimodality has evolved in the field of language and the context of human communication, in recent years, it has been

A. Ekbal, R. Kumari, *Dive into Misinformation Detection*, The Information Retrieval Series 30, https://doi.org/10.1007/978-3-031-54834-5_5

highly demanded for solving various real-world problems by applying ML, NLP, and AI concepts. As the name suggests, multimodal datasets and models involve the combination of various types of information, such as text, images, speech, and videos, to enhance the performance of the target tasks. As the current era is the digital era, most of the information is processed in forms of multimodal information (i.e., the combination of text, image, audio, or video), which enables the machines to better understand human communication and activities by taking into account additional contextual information beyond just one source of information, such as text. It combines multiple modes or types of information to create more precise determination, draw intuitive conclusion, or make accurate predictions about real-world problems. For instance, multimodality can be used to improve sentiment analysis by incorporating facial expressions and tone of voice along with textual data. In recent years, multimodal AI and NLP has become an emerging field of study and is expected to become increasingly significant as more data becomes available across multiple modalities. This chapter explores in the context of ML, NLP, and AI, specifically for misinformation detection.

5.1.1 Unimodal and Multimodal

Section 1.4 of Chap. 1 discusses the modalities in details. The terms *unimodal* and *multimodal* are frequently used to characterize the number of modes or sources of input or output that are involved in a system or process in a variety of disciplines, such as artificial intelligence, perception, and communication. Here is a description of each:

Unimodal   A system or process that only uses one source or mode of input or output is called a unimodal system. This means it only concentrates on a single type of data or information. For instance, a unimodal system in computer vision may exclusively interpret visual data, such as photos or videos, to carry out operations like image categorization or object detection. It may evaluate audio input when doing speech recognition to convert spoken words into text. It may work with text-based data in natural language processing for tasks like sentiment analysis or language translation. Even most of the AI available models are unimodal only. These models work with one type of data exclusively, and they use algorithms tailored to that modality. ChatGPT is also an unimodal AI system that uses NLP algorithms to understand and extract meaning from the textual contents. It produces the output only in text format. Figure 5.1 shows an example of unimodal information related to the coronavirus. This information is unimodal because it only includes textual content. Figure 5.2 shows the basic building block of the unimodal models.

Multimodal   Multimodal is a system that incorporates multiple sources or modes of input or output. The multimodal system can integrate and handle different types of data or information parallelly to enhance its understanding and performance. For instance, in autonomous vehicles, a multimodal system combines data from

Fig. 5.1 Example of unimodal information

Fig. 5.2 Example of unimodal model

numerous sensors such as radar, LiDAR, cameras, and GPS to perceive the environment extensively and make informed driving decisions. A multimodal system uses a combination of gesture recognition, speech recognition, and touch input to create an intuitive user interface in human-computer interaction. The multimodal approach can also be proved efficient in the healthcare domain, where it integrates data from patient history, different medical imaging techniques, and laboratory tests to make accurate diagnoses. Nowadays, the concept of multimodality is broadly used for solving various NLP tasks, such as emotion recognition, sentiment prediction, language translation, misinformation detection, and many more. Figure 5.3 shows some examples of multimodal information, and Fig. 5.4 represents the basic building blocks of the multimodal systems.

5.2 Importance of Multimodality

The multimodal systems exploit the complementary nature of various data types, which lead to more accurate results. The combination of information from different sources overcomes the limitations present in individual modalities and provides a deeper understanding of the task at hand. In linguistics, multimodality is important because it enhances understanding, expression, and communication by aggregating multiple modes of information input. These modes consist of text, images, audio,

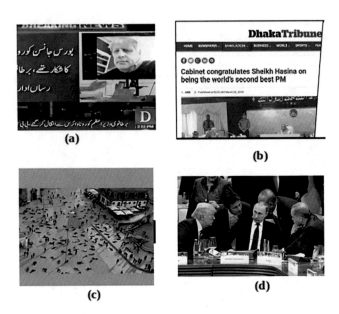

Fig. 5.3 Example of multimodal information. (**a**) British Prime Minister #BorishJohnson passed away due to #Covid_19. (**b**) Prime Minister Sheikh Hasina has been selected the world's second best prime minister by an internationally reputed research organization. (**c**) "Satellite photo in China. More people are drying, the antidote has not been discovered, no soldiers from any troops who are able to prevent this virus. Is this a punishment?". (**d**) US President Donald Trump had met his Russian Counterpart Vladimir Putin on the sidelines of the G20 Summit in Germany

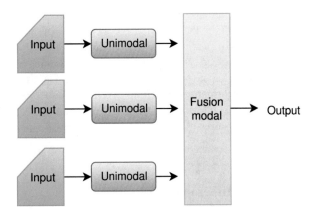

Fig. 5.4 Example of multimodal model

video, gestures, and more. The following points show the significance of multi-modality:

Enhanced Communication Incorporating multiple modes of communication allows individuals to convey their ideas more effectively. For example, the visuals, along with spoken words, attract a larger audience in a presentation. Visuals can help in clarifying the complex concepts easily.

Improved Comprehension Different persons have different learning preferences, and multimodality attracts a large audience. Some people may learn more effectively with visual aids, while others may learn more effectively through aural or hands-on learning. Educators and communicators can reach a wide spectrum of learners by using a variety of modalities.

Redundancy and Robustness Redundancy can be achieved by using different informational formats, which reduces the likelihood of missing crucial information or misinterpreting the message. When one modality is imprecise or unavailable, the other might fill in the gaps.

Expression of Complex Ideas It can be difficult to explain ideas or feelings using one form of communication fully. For instance, describing stunning scenery could fall short compared to displaying the real view in a photo or video along with descriptive prose.

Cognitive Engagement Combining several modalities can enhance memory retention and stimulate cognitive processes. The brain forms more connections when information is given in different ways, making it simpler to recall later.

Cross-Cultural Communication Due to the added context and comprehension-enhancing clues that multimodal information offers, it can help people across cultural and linguistic divides. This is especially useful in today's multicultural, worldwide environment.

Assistive Technologies When creating assistive technologies for those with disabilities, multimodality is essential. For instance, screen readers translating text to speech make written content accessible to people with visual impairments.

Creativity and Expression Multimodal tools and platforms support several modes of expression to foster creativity. People can make artwork, presentations, or other types of content that mix several media, producing more dynamic and interesting results.

Real-World Applications Multimodal processing is necessary for many real-world tasks, like driving, where decisions must be made while combining visual, aural, and spatial input.

Overall, multimodality enriches human communication, expression, and learning, which makes it a valuable aspect of various fields, including media, education, technology, and everyday interactions. Apart from communication, multimodality is essential in natural language processing (NLP) because it allows models to understand and process the information from multiple modalities or sources of data. Traditionally, NLP tasks have primarily focused on text-based data, but the real world is rich with diverse forms of information, such as images, audio, videos, and other sensor data. By incorporating multiple modalities, NLP models can gain a more comprehensive understanding of real-world problems and can solve more complex tasks that go beyond just processing text. The below paragraphs explore some reasons why multimodality is important in NLP:

Enhanced Understanding   The combination of multiple modalities generates a more holistic and deeper understanding of the underlying content. For instance, in an image captioning task, the model generates more accurate and informative captions when analyzing textual and visual information. Thus, multimodality improves the performance of the model by achieving higher accuracy and better generalization.

Robustness and Adaptability   Multimodal models are more robust when handling incomplete and noisy data. Multimodality enables the model to handle fault tolerance if one modality is ambiguous or missing. The model can still rely on other modalities to make predictions.

Contextual Understanding   In some NLP problems, the context provided by one modality can aid the interpretation of another. For instance, in a video analysis task, an audio track provides additional context to understand some visual events better.

Cross-Modal Transfer Learning   Large datasets with a variety of modalities can be used for multimodal pre-training, which enables models to take advantage of transfer learning and perform better on particular tasks even with a limited amount of training data.

Human-Like Communication   Multimodal NLP can assist in bridging the gap between human communication (which frequently encompasses numerous modalities) and machine understanding for more natural and human-like interactions with AI systems.

Multimodality has become an increasingly active area of research in NLP and artificial intelligence. As technology advances, multimodal models are likely to become even more prevalent, enabling more sophisticated applications across various domains, including healthcare, robotics, autonomous vehicles, and virtual reality, among others. However, designing and implementing multimodal systems can be more complex than unimodal systems due to the need for data fusion and synchronization across different sources.

5.3   Application of Multimodality

Nowadays, multimodality has various applications in numerous fields. Researchers are also applying the concept of multimodality to solve various NLP tasks broadly. This section briefly discusses these applications in the context of NLP.

5.3.1 Emotion Recognition

Emotion plays a pivotal role, both in general human experience and in psychiatric illnesses. Emotions seem very helpful in diagnosing and treating pathological and psychiatric disorders, such as depressive and bipolar disorders. Numerous studies also prove that emotion recognition helps in solving opinion mining, misinformation detection, and various other tasks. Therefore, it becomes important to recognize the emotions. Emotion recognition is basically a technique to recognize human emotions. It is more popular in recognizing the emotion from human faces. Nowadays, researchers are also identifying the emotions from speech and written text in addition to images. Theories about basic emotions originated in ancient Greece and China.

The studies presented in Darwin and Prodger (1998) and Ekman (2006) have given the theory of basic emotions. According to basic emotion theory, human beings have a limited number of emotions, viz., fear, joy, anger, and sadness. Further, Ekman has extended his study and introduced six basic emotions, viz., joy, fear, sadness, anger, disgust, and surprise. Further, many researchers have extended this study, which introduced some fine-grained categories of emotions. As per the change in time, the emotion recognition task is performed for solving various other tasks such as opinion mining, misinformation detection (Kumari et al. 2023), social media analysis (Imran et al. 2020), mental health analysis (Bhagat et al. 2023), deception detection (Curtis 2021), dialogue generation (Ma et al. 2023), and many more. Although various models, applications, and algorithms are available for emotion recognition, multimodality has attracted much in this dimension. Multimodal emotion recognition aims to include text inputs, images, sound, and video. Researchers have proposed various multimodal emotion recognition models, such as Soleymani et al. (2011), Abdullah et al. (2021), Garcia-Garcia et al. (2023), and Mocanu et al. (2023) using recent deep learning techniques.

5.3.2 Sentiment Analysis

Sentiment analysis is the technique to classify a block of text as *positive, negative, or neutral*. The main purpose of this task is to analyze people's opinions regarding some news or topic. For instance, if a company wants to analyze whether a product satisfies customer requirements or if there is any need for a product in the market, the company applies sentiment analysis to monitor that product's reviews. This task is also efficient to use for the classification of a large set of unstructured data. Net promoter score (NPS) surveys are used extensively to learn how a customer perceives a product or service. Sentiment analysis also gained popularity due to its feature to process large volumes of NPS responses and obtain consistent results quickly. Researchers have started analyzing the sentiment for textual data, and in current days, it has been extended for the multimodal data. The work presented in

Zhu et al. (2022), Ye et al. (2022), Das and Singh (2023), Ghorbanali et al. (2022), etc. are popular studies for multimodal sentiment analysis.

5.3.3 Visual Question Answering

Visual question answering is a task in which the system has to answer some questions by seeing the images or videos. As this task involves images and/or videos, multimodality is broadly applied to solve any problem in this domain. The studies explored in Ben Abacha et al. (2019), Zheng et al. (2021), Yu et al. (2019), Fukui et al. (2016), and Kafle and Kanan (2017) are the popular visual question answering tasks that have been carried out in recent days.

5.3.4 Image-to-Text and Text-to-Image Generation

Images can be generated from text, and text can also be generated from images. The task basically aggregates the information from one modality and generates another modality based on that information. This task is very much popular and effective in the medical domain for disease diagnosis. For instance, the detailed description can be extracted in textual format from MRI and ultrasound images. Researchers have performed various works in this direction. The studies presented in Yu et al. (2022), Xu et al. (2022), Zhou et al. (2022), Ruiz et al. (2023), etc. are some popular works in this domain.

5.4 Challenges in Multimodality

As this chapter discusses earlier, multimodality refers to combining various types of data, such as text, audio, images, and video, to understand better and generate human languages. While it is significantly well for various applications, it also poses numerous challenges. The following subsections briefly discuss all these challenges.

5.4.1 Data Integration

It is very complex to integrate and align the data from multiple modalities. It is also challenging to ensure that the information from different sources is essential to contribute to effective multimodal processing and understanding correctly. Heterogeneity of the data is also a considerable challenge in multimodality because each modality has its unique data formats, characteristics, and its own processing and representation requirements.

5.4.2 Large-Scale Data and Model Scalability

Large-scale multimodal dataset requires a large amount of resources as well. Collection, processing, and managing large-scale multimodal datasets are resource-intensive. It creates a big computational challenge during storing, accessing, and efficiently processing such data with the availability of the present infrastructure. After data preparation, multimodal systems are developed to solve various NLP tasks. As multimodal models become more complex, they also demand significant computational resources for training and inference. Thus, scaling up multimodal systems while maintaining efficiency also becomes a considerable challenge in this domain. The deployment of such multimodal systems in resource-constrained environments, such as mobile devices, becomes challenging due to limitations in processing power and memory.

5.4.3 Intermodal Alignment

It is a crucial task to ensure that the information from different modalities semantically aligns with each other. For instance, it is very difficult to develop a system that correctly links a description in text to specific objects in an image. Although people have developed various systems for it, this area of research is still under-explored.

5.4.4 Data Annotation

The multimodal data annotation is expensive and time-consuming. It also requires different experts to annotate the same instance of the dataset. For example, if one annotator is an expert in text analysis but not in image analysis, she/he cannot annotate the multimodal data instance. Therefore, labeled data creation and annotation for training multimodal models is a bottleneck in developing such systems.

5.4.5 Privacy and Ethical Concerns

As most of the multimodal systems involve audio and video data, they can raise privacy and ethical concerns. It is very challenging to handle sensitive information responsibly. The multimodal models can inherit biases present in data from each modality, and combining biased information can amplify these biases further, which may lead to ethical and fairness challenges.

5.4.6   Cross-Modal Generalization

It is very difficult to ensure that the developed models generalize well across various combinations of modalities. Models trained on specific multimodal data may not perform well for another type of novel data. Transfer learning and adaption are also challenging in multimodal domains. This is because the transfer learning mechanism that works well in a unimodal setup may or may not work well in a multimodal setup. The multimodal system developed for a domain may not work well in other domains. For instance, the image data of the medical domain will be different from the image data of the education domain. Extending the multimodality for various languages is also challenging due to diverse cultural and linguistic contexts.

5.4.7   Interpretability

As multimodal models combine images and videos, they become more complex. In complex models, it is difficult to understand how the models internally make decisions and generate outputs. It does not become clear which modality is contributing more to the decision. Thus, it is challenging to visualize the model interpretability for applications requiring accountability and transparency.

It is essential to develop various techniques to address these challenges in multimodal NLP to realize the full potential of this field and to develop applications that can effectively understand and generate human language in a multimodal context. Practitioners and researchers are actively working on these challenges to advance the state of the art in multimodal NLP.

5.5   Multimodality in the Context of Misinformation Detection (A Case Study)

This section presents the importance of multimodality as a case study in the context of misinformation detection. As discussed many times in the previous chapter, misinformation is the stories or information intentionally created to mislead or deceive the readers. In the recent era, social media is full of multimedia news and information, and false information creators take advantage of it. Therefore, developing a powerful multimedia misinformation detection system is in high demand. This section explores a multimodal misinformation detection system that takes text and image contents as input and classifies the news as fake or real. The prime objective of this case study is to show the importance of multimodality, which mainly focuses on the fusion of text and image modalities to obtain an efficient multimodal feature that ultimately helps in multimedia misinformation detection. It employs a bidirectional long short-term memory (Bi-LSTM) for textual feature extraction and a multichannel convolutional neural network (CNN) for visual feature extraction. Further, the model fuses these features by implementing multimodal factorized bilinear pooling (MFB). The model is trained on publicly available multimodal misinformation datasets.

False information contains manipulated textual or multimedia content to mislead readers. It has created a threat to journalism, democracy, health, and many other social activities and events that indirectly or directly put communities and individuals at high risk. The spread of false information during the US presidential election 2016 is evidence of it. False information was produced during this election to help either of the two candidates. This report has received a lot of credence and has been shared over 37 million times on Facebook (Wang et al. 2018). Researchers have investigated several misinformation detection mechanisms to combat false news, but most of them are unimodal and have been mostly carried out for text only. As multimedia news is getting popular on social media, false news creators have started creating malicious content by manipulating visual content. Therefore, it is quite difficult to identify this kind of news using textual information alone.

Figure 5.3 depicts some examples of multimodal fake news that were recently propagated on different social media platforms. Every news article has text that is related to an image. The first news in Fig. 5.3 has been broadcast on the Dawn news channel of Pakistan, declaring that British Prime Minister Borish Jonson passed away due to COVID-19. It was a false rumor. The second news claims that Prime Minister Sheikh Hasina has been selected as the world's second-best prime minister by Singapore-based research firm Statistic International (an internationally reputed research organization). Later, BDFactCheck[1] has shown that no survey was conducted, and also, there was no organization as "Statistic International." The third image went viral on social media Web sites, showing that many people are dying in China because of the COVID-19 pandemic. In this news, the text is written for a real event. The image is also taken from a real event, but this is misleading information because the picture was taken on March 24, 2014, while people were lying down in a pedestrian zone in remembrance of the 528 victims of the Katzbach Nazi concentration camp in Frankfurt.[2] The image of the last news has been photoshopped. In the original image, Russian President Vladimir Putin was not sitting on the chair. This kind of news has the potential to be false, and its primary dissemination goal is to deceive the public. Misinformation detection can be done with a variety of conventional learning techniques as well as more modern deep learning models. But the text was the main focus, as seen in Castillo et al. (2011). Figure 5.3 provides examples demonstrating how inaccurately identifying false news items cannot be done with just one modality, either text or visual information. It is difficult to determine if this kind of material is authentic or fake based solely on textual content. The idea of multimodal misinformation detection is born from

---

[1] https://en.bdfactcheck.com/.

[2] https://pictures.reuters.com/archive/GERMANY--BM2EA3O1B2X01.html.

the possibility of identifying the information using textual and picture data. Thus, designing a robust multimedia misinformation detection system is in high demand.

A few previous studies, including (Wang et al. 2018; Khattar et al. 2019), have attempted to identify the characteristics that all of the events have in common, as well as the relationship between text and image. These methods give each component of the text and image the same weight, which might not be suitable for combining the data. The author of Singhal et al. (2019) extracts textual features using the pre-trained VGG19 model (Shaha and Pawar 2018) and extracts visual features using bidirectional encoder representations from transformers (BERT) (Kenton and Toutanova 2019). After extraction, the features that did not exhibit a good correlation between the text and image were concatenated. It might not accurately identify false information.

For visual feature extraction, writers in the literature mostly used pre-trained CNNs like VGG19 (Shaha and Pawar 2018). The Imagenet dataset (Deng et al. 2009) was used to train the VGG19, and it is best suited for object detection. Due to a lack of task-relevant information, VGG19 might be unable to identify the domain-specific semantic features of manipulated or false images because the Imagenet dataset is public domain. Therefore, it is a very difficult task to extract the inherent characteristics of bogus news photos. In addition to feature extraction, feature fusion is an extremely important operation. In previous investigations, authors have obtained a joint multimodal feature representation by simply concatenating textual and visual information. These multimodal features have allowed them to categorize the news posts as authentic or fraudulent. The primary purpose of fusing different modalities is to learn the effective combinations of their features. Although concatenation is the simplest way for this purpose, it creates a stack of features and does not introduce proper interaction between two modality features. Previous multimodal or textual-feature-based systems are inadequate at learning multimodal (textual + visual) shared representation. In this case study, a multimodal misinformation detection system with suitable multimodal feature fusion has been created in order to overcome these restrictions. The system makes use of information from both text and image and aims to optimize the correlation between them. An effective multimodal shared representation can be obtained with the help of the maximized correlation. Empirical evidence from the results demonstrates that adding text to an image can enhance the model's functionality. Inspired by the deficiency of efficient feature fusion techniques and good feature extraction, a novel deep neural network-based framework is developed for multimodal misinformation detection. The framework known as "attention-based multimodal factorized bilinear pooling (AMFB)" is what this framework is called.

The proposed system contains the following four sub-modules: (i) *attention-based stacked bidirectional long short-term memory (ABS-BiLSTM)*, (ii) *attention-based multilevel convolutional neural network-recurrent neural network (ABM-CNN-RNN)*, (iii) *multimodal factorized bilinear pooling (MFB)*, and *multilayer perceptron (MLP)*. The first component extracts textual features, the second component extracts visual features, the third component performs feature fusion, and the last component performs classification. Thus, as discussed earlier, this case study basically focuses on leveraging information from various sources and fusing them to obtain multimodal information, which ultimately helps in misinformation detection. The experiments are performed using *Twitter and Weibo* datasets. These datasets are publicly available. Both the datasets have been briefly discussed in Sect. 2.1 Section of Chap. 2. The evaluation results demonstrate the effectiveness of the proposed method, outperforming the textual models by a wide margin.

5.5.1 Overall Workflow

In order to enable precise, effective, and quick computation of news item credibility, this part explains an intuition of the theoretical underpinnings and demonstrates how to recast the problem. Results (explained in the paragraph above and illustrated in Fig. 5.3) and the significance of many modalities in misinformation detection provide a theoretical framework for more empirical research on false information. The groundwork for developing a repeatable end-to-end procedure to identify multimodal misleading material disseminated on social media is laid by this work. Scientists, researchers, journalists, and the general public who are misinformed will benefit from these efforts to classify multimedia news items as authentic or fake. This study presents three essential fundamental bases of misinformation detection, viz., (i) multimodal feature extraction, which involves taking the textual and visual elements out of multimedia news articles; (ii) multimodal feature fusion, wherein a single shared representation is obtained by combining the retrieved textual and visual features; and (iii) multimodal misinformation detection, wherein the news post is categorized based on the shared representation. The proposed method is shown in Fig. 5.6. The fundamental theoretical concepts are all covered in detail in this section.

The overall process diagram of the suggested multimodal misinformation detection framework is depicted in Fig. 5.5. This figure shows how the proposed methodology is developed from the raw dataset to the final decision. Below is a detailed discussion of each of these stages one by one.

Misinformation Dataset Twitter and Weibo datasets are considered for this work. These datasets are popular and publicly available for multimodal misinformation detection. These datasets consist of multimedia news of the disaster domain. The dataset consists of news_id, text, related image, context characteristics, and ground-truth labels in each instance.

Feature Selection Using news content, the proposed methodology addresses multimodal false news detection. As a result, features include the text content, related images, and associated ground-truth labels from the dataset as features.

Preparation Both the text and the image are pre-processed in this stage. To create a fully multimodal dataset, the occurrences that only contain text or images are first eliminated. In addition, the sentences undergo tokenization for text data, and stop

Fig. 5.5 The overall workflow of the proposed multimodal misinformation detection model

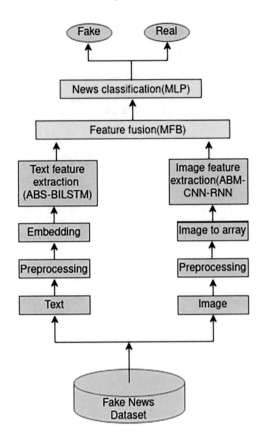

words and punctuation are eliminated. All the images are converted into equal-sized three-dimensional arrays.

Embedding To find word vectors, the 300-dimension pre-trained FastText embedding (Lakmal et al. 2020) is utilized.

Feature Extraction After obtaining word embedding of text, *ABS-BiLSTM* is implemented for the textual feature extraction. For visual feature extraction, *ABM-CNN-RNN* is implemented.

Feature Fusion The shared representation is obtained by implementing the feature fusion process after obtaining the textual and visual feature representations. The methodology section of this study includes a full discussion of the feature fusion mechanism.

News Classification After obtaining the combined representation, the final stage is the news classification. The MLP model is used to detect false information. In the final step, the veracity of the information is determined. A detailed description of the news classification procedure is provided in Sect. 5.5.2.

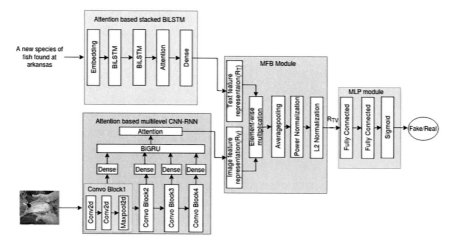

Fig. 5.6 Proposed multimodal misinformation detection model

5.5.2   *Proposed Model*

A deep learning-based method for multimodal misinformation detection is developed in this case study. It determines whether a multimedia news post is authentic or fake by analyzing both textual and visual data. A news post $I_P = \{T,V\}$ is considered as a tuple representing textual (T) and visual (V) modalities of a news post, respectively. For the given instance I_P, the proposed model extracts the textual feature (F_T) and the visual feature (F_V). Figure 5.6 depicts the overall architecture of the proposed model. It consists of four modules: (a) attention-based stacked Bi-LSTM (ABS-BiLSTM); (b) attention-based multilevel CNN-RNN (ABM-CNN-RNN); (c) multimodal factorized bilinear pooling (MFB); and (d) multilayer perceptron (MLP). Each of these modules is discussed below.

5.5.2.1   ABS-BiLSTM

A multimedia news post might have different elements depending on the modality used. The textual elements of the multimedia news posts are extracted in this section of the proposed framework. It effectively captures the word representations with the best contextual and semantic features. This sub-network is formed by stacking two BiLSTM layers together. The second BiLSTM layer receives its input from the first BiLSTM layer's output. Over the collected features, the second BiLSTM layer extracts increasingly complex features and patterns. Mathematically, it is formulated as below:

Given a news post P_x, two stacked BiLSTMs are employed to encode each word into the hidden vectors $h_{P_{x,i}}$. Words are represented by 300-dimensional embedding.

Here, P_x is the xth news post, $w_{x,i}$ is the ith word of xth news post, $w_{x,i}, i \in (1, \ldots, n), x \in (1, \ldots, m)$, and $k \in [1, 2]$. Equation 5.1 explains this discussion mathematically.

$$\overrightarrow{h_F^k} P_{x,i} = LSTM_{p,f}(w_{x,i}, \overrightarrow{h_{P_{x,i-1}}^k})$$
$$\overleftarrow{h_{P_{x,i}}^k} = LSTM_{p,b}(w_{x,i}, \overleftarrow{h_{P_{x,i-1}}^k}) \tag{5.1}$$
$$h_{P_{x,i}} = [\overrightarrow{h_{P_{x,i}}^k}, \overleftarrow{h_{P_{x,i}}^k}]$$

All words may not contribute equally to generate a meaningful text representation. Similar to Yang et al. (2016), attention is focused on the hidden state derived from the second Bi-LSTM layer in order to identify significant words and combine their representations to create the final text representation vector. This attention can be implemented using Eqs. 5.2, 5.3, and 5.4.

$$h_{it} = tanh((W_w h_{P_{x,i}}) + b_w) \tag{5.2}$$

$$\alpha_{it} = \frac{exp((h_{it}^T h_w))}{\Sigma_t exp((h_{it}^T h_w))} \tag{5.3}$$

$$s_i = \Sigma_t \alpha_{it} h_{it} \tag{5.4}$$

The hidden representation (h_{it}) of a word is then produced by a fully connected layer using the output of the second BiLSTM layer ($h_{P_{n,i}}$). The word's importance is determined by passing this hidden representation through a softmax function, which yields a normalized importance weight (α_{it}). Ultimately, the attended textual feature representation is obtained by adding the weighted sum (s_i) of the word representation. In this case, the randomly initialized vectors W_w, b_w, and h_w learn together during the training phase. After passing through a fully connected layer, the output of the attention layer is sent through Eq. 5.5, where R_T provides the attended representation of the text.

$$R_T = relu((W_{s_i} s_i) + b_{s_i}) \tag{5.5}$$

5.5.2.2   Attention-Based Multilevel CNN-RNN (ABM-CNN-RNN)

Because visual content can be captured more quickly and easily than textual content, people are typically more drawn to it. These days, visual content like photos and videos is included in the majority of news articles. Multimedia content advancements increase the production and spread of incorrect information. Therefore, developing a multimodal misinformation detector should heavily rely on an accurate visual feature extraction model. This hypothesis inspired the development of an attention-based multilevel CNN-RNN network for visual feature extraction. Generally, CNN learns high-level features or semantic features through layer-by-layer abstraction. At first, it keeps low-level components like color, form, and line. Subsequently, it picks up high-level features by concentrating on the objects in the picture, their movements and activities, etc. Low-level features have a significant influence on an image's semantic features. In CNN, the intermediate layer provides supplementary data to the top layer. The high-level semantic feature representations frequently hide low-level characteristics, which has a detrimental impact on the model's performance. Existing research on salient object detection (Zhang et al. 2017) and image emotion classification (Yang et al. 2018a) demonstrated that integrating low-level and high-level features produced superior visual feature representations than relying solely on high-level features, which could be used to overcome CNN's limitations.

False information-related visuals also provoke emotions and have some visual effects. This concept inspires the creation of an attention-based multilevel CNN-RNN subnetwork that integrates low- and high-level image characteristics to better capture semantic visual feature representation. First, a CNN network receives the image with the size (224,224) as input. The two two-dimensional convolution layers with a Relu activation function and one two-dimensional max-pooling layer with pool size (2,2) form a CNN block. Each block output results in the addition of a fully connected layer, bringing the feature length down to 32. A bidirectional gated recurrent unit (BiGRU) is now used to detect internal and sequential relationships among the features in both directions, that is, from high level to low level and from low level to high level, using the output of these blocks. An attention mechanism is also constructed over the sequence that is obtained from BiGRU. Since, similar to textual characteristics, the entire set of retrieved visual features cannot be equally significant. After that, this is processed through a fully connected layer to generate the final image representation (R_V). It can be expressed mathematically using Eqs. 5.6 and 5.10:

$$Cb_j = Maxpool(Conv2d(Conv2d(Cb_j - 1)))$$ (5.6)

$$v_j = relu((W_{Cb_j}Cb_j) + b_{Cb_j})$$ (5.7)

$$\overrightarrow{v_f} = \overrightarrow{GRU}(v_j)$$

$$\overleftarrow{v_b} = \overleftarrow{GRU}(v_j)$$ (5.8)

$$v = [\overrightarrow{v_f}, \overleftarrow{v_b}]; \; j \in (1..4)$$

$$s_i = att(v)$$ (5.9)

$$R_V = relu((W_{s_i}s_i) + b_{s_i})$$ (5.10)

Here, W_{Cb_j}, W_{s_i}, b_{Cb_j}, and b_{s_i} are the trainable parameters. The analysis shows that **ABM-CNN-RNN** extracts the multilevel visual features and **ABS-BiLSTM** extracts the high-level implicit textual features. In addition to being unique feature extractors rather than pre-trained techniques, the proposed feature extractors outperform the current feature extraction processes.

5.5.2.3   Multimodal Factorized Bilinear Pooling (MFB)

Features are fused using the MFB module once the final textual (R_T) and visual (R_V) feature representations from both modalities have been obtained. In this case, MFB is favored over conventional concatenation for the following reasons: (a). Determining the boundaries of the retrieved features derived from the various modalities in the usual concatenation is a difficult task (b). It might not find the association between the picture and text feature representations since features are piled one after the other after concatenation.

The MFB module is an effective way to overcome these two issues. The correlation between textual and visual feature representations is maximized by this fusion technique. Let us suppose that the visual feature vector for an image is $(R_V) \in R_n$, while the textual feature vector for text is $(R_T) \in R_m$. Equation 5.11 is then used to define the fundamental multimodal bilinear model:

$$R_{TV} = R_T{}^T W_i R_V \tag{5.11}$$

where a projection matrix is denoted by $W_i \in R^{m*n}$. The bilinear model's output is denoted by R_{TV}. While adding a lot of factors that come with a significant computing cost and overfitting risk, bilinear pooling successfully captures the pairwise interactions between the feature dimensions. W_i in Eq. 5.11 is factorized into two low-rank matrices in order to decrease the number of parameters:

$$R_{TV} = R_T{}^T U_i V_i^T R_V = \sum_{d=1}^{k} R_T{}^T u_d v_d^T R_V \tag{5.12}$$

$$R_{TV} = 1^T (U_i^T R_T \circ V_i^T R_V) \tag{5.13}$$

Here, k is the latent dimensionality of the factorized matrices $U_i = [u_1, \ldots, u_k] \in R^{m*k}$ and $V_i = [v_1, \ldots, v_k] \in R^{n*k}$, $\circ$ is the element-wise multiplication of two vectors, and $1 \in R_k$ is an all-one vector. To obtain the output feature R_T by Eq. 5.13, it requires to learn two three order tensors, $U = [U_1, \ldots . U_o] \in R_{m*k*o}$ and $V = [V_1, \ldots . V_d] \in R_{n*k*o}$ as weights for o output dimension. It can be further reformulated as two dimensional matrices,

$U' \in R^{m*ko}$ and $V' \in R^{n*ko}$, and can be rewritten as follows:

$$R_{TV} = AveragePooling(U'^T R_T \circ V'^T R_V) \tag{5.14}$$

$$R_{TV} = sign(R_{TV})|R_{TV}|^{0.5} \tag{5.15}$$

$$R_{TV} = R_{TV}^T/||R_{TV}|| \tag{5.16}$$

In conclusion, it can be said that the feature fusion mechanism differs from the multimodal feature fusion techniques already in use. In order to obtain the shared representation, the majority of previous efforts concentrated on concatenating textual and visual data, resulting in minimal performance for the detection of fake news. As a result, it is a unique feature fusion process that offers appropriate alignment and optimizes the association between text and image properties.

5.5.2.4 Multilayer Perceptron (MLP)

The feature fusion model is used to create an MLP sub-network with two hidden layers and an output layer with a Sigmoid activation function. The input of this MLP network is fused features. In order to determine the ultimate prediction probability that determines whether a multimedia news post is authentic or fake, it projects them into the target space of two classes. The objective function of the suggested model is the optimization of the binary cross-entropy loss. The mathematical formulation of this can be found in Eq. 5.17:

$$L = -\Sigma[ylogp + (1 - y)log(1 - p)] \tag{5.17}$$

where y is the original class and p is the predicted class of the news post.

Together, the four previously covered elements of the suggested methodology answer the main problem of misinformation detection. ABM-CNN-RNN collects visual features, ABS-BiLSTM extracts textual features, MFB combines these two features, and MLP assesses whether the news is true or fraudulent. This process starts with the model using the text and image of a news article as input.

5.5.2.5 Experimental Setup

The embedding mechanism, pre-processing of text and images, many hyper-parameters, and implementation specifics are covered in this section. Each and every experiment is run in a Python environment. The Python libraries Sklearn, Numpy, Pandas, NLTK, and Keras are used for the experiments. To test the model, the training data is divided into a test set and a validation set at a 90:10 ratio. The effectiveness of the system is assessed using conventional assessment measures,

Table 5.1 The table shows
the list of hyper-parameters
utilized for training the
developed model

Parameters	Weibo	Twitter
Image Size	(224,224,3)	(224,224,3)
Text Length	95	33
Optimizer	Adam(lr=0.00005)	Adam(lr=0.00001)
Batch Size	32	32
Regularizer	L2(0.5)	L2(0.5)
Epochs	100	100
Filter Size	(3,3)	(3,3)
Strides	(1,1)	(1,1)
Dropout	0.2	0.2

including F-score, accuracy, precision, and recall. For Twitter text cleaning, punctuation, digits, special characters, and short words are eliminated. Data segmentation for Weibo data is done using the Jieba Python Module.[3] 300-dimensional FastText pre-trained embeddings are utilized for textual feature extraction. These 300-dimensional vectors are fed into the stacked BiLSTM layer, and the output is fed into the attention layer that comes after the dense layer. The dense layer has 32 units, whereas the first and second BiLSTM layers have 256 and 128 units, respectively.

The collection contains a variety of image sizes. We resize each image to (224,224,3) in order to preserve consistency, and then we feed the images to an attention-based multilevel CNN-RNN network. We employ (1,1) strides, a (3,3) size filter, and 64 units with Conv2d. Each CNN block has one Maxpool 2d layer with a pool size of (2,2) and two CNN layers with Relu activation. Every block's output is routed through a 32-size fully linked layer. The output of all four blocks is then concatenated and passed to a bidirectional GRU layer of size 32. Close attention is paid to this extracted feature. In order to match the size of the textual features, the attended visual features are subsequently transmitted to a fully linked layer of dimension 32 using the Relu activation function. For feature fusion, the MFB module is fed to an MLP with an output layer of size one with a sigmoid activation function and two hidden layers of 32 and 16 with a Relu activation function. In this case, the Adam optimizer and loss function are the binary cross-entropy. The model is trained using early-stopping callbacks and a batch size of 32 for 100 epochs. Table 5.1 enlists all the hyper-parameters used for training the proposed model.

5.5.3 Baselines

To verify the efficacy of the suggested approach, a number of baseline models are put into practice using data from unimodal and multimodal sources.

---

[3] https://pypi.org/project/jieba/.

5.5.3.1 Unimodal Baselines

The following unimodal baselines are implemented for comparisons:

(a) Textual: The pre-trained FastText embedding of 300 dimensions is utilized to obtain the textual feature vector for textual feature-based baseline models, which is then sent to the bidirectional LSTM layers of size 128. The retrieved textual feature representations are once more fed into an MLP with 64 and 32 hidden layers. The news post is classified as real or fake by the output layer using the Sigmoid activation function.

(b) Visual: A pre-trained VGG19 model is used to extract the visual characteristics in order to implement the visual model. The recovered visual feature vectors, which have sizes of 4096, are once more fed into an output layer with a sigmoid activation function for prediction and a fully connected layer with a hidden size of 32.

5.5.3.2 Multimodal Baselines

The following baselines are used for multimodality:

(a) att-RNN: Visual attention is used by att-RNN (Jin et al. 2017) for multimodal misinformation detection. Concatenation was initially employed for the combined text and visual depiction. The combined multimodal feature representation is obtained through element-wise multiplication. Instead of using a word2vec embedding for embedding, a 300-dimensional FastText embedding is used. The same hyper-parameters are used as mentioned in the original att-RNN work.

(b) EANN*: The three parts of the event adversarial neural network (EANN) (Wang et al. 2018) are the fake news detector, event discriminator, and feature extractor. With the aid of an event discriminator, the feature extractor in this model extracts the textual and visual features that are event invariant. Using these attributes, it then categorizes the news posts as real or fake. For the performance comparison, a version of this model with just two parts viz., a feature extractor and a fake news detector, is proposed. This model was trained using the same set of parameters as the original model.

(c) MVAE*: The multimodal variational autoencoder (Khattar et al. 2019) trains three sub-networks to detect fake news. In this case, the goal was to train a variational autoencoder to produce improved joint feature representation for text and image. The classification process also took advantage of the shared latent representation. To provide a fair comparison, the encoder and fake news detecting sections are used to construct this model. The same hyper-parameters that were utilized to train the old model are employed to train the new one.

Table 5.2 Classification results obtained from the existing and proposed model using Weibo and Twitter datasets

Dataset	Model	Real News			Fake News			Accuracy
		Precision	Recall	F-Score	Precision	Recall	F-Score	
Weibo	Textual	0.58	0.69	0.63	0.62	0.50	0.55	0.593
	Visual	0.607	0.611	0.609	0.620	0.604	0.607	0.608
	VQA	0.695	0.838	0.760	0.797	0.634	0.706	0.736
	Neural Talk	0.684	0.840	0.754	0.794	0.713	0.692	0.726
	att-RNN	0.684	0.840	0.754	0.797	0.713	0.692	0.772
	EANN*	0.76	0.86	0.80	0.84	0.72	0.78	0.791
	EANN	NA	NA	NA	NA	NA	NA	0.827
	MVAE*	0.75	0.60	0.67	0.67	0.80	0.73	0.70
	MVAE	0.802	**0.875**	**0.837**	0.854	0.769	0.809	0.824
	Spotfake	0.847	0.656	0.739	**0.902**	**0.964**	**0.932**	**0.892**
	AMFB	**0.85**	0.81	0.83	0.82	0.86	0.84	0.832
Twitter	Textual	0.72	0.43	0.54	0.43	0.71	0.53	0.538
	Visual	0.74	0.68	0.71	0.52	0.59	0.55	0.645
	VQA	0.550	**0.794**	0.650	0.765	0.509	0.611	0.631
	Neural Talk	0.534	0.752	0.625	0.728	0.504	0.595	0.610
	att-RNN	0.589	0.728	0.651	0.749	0.615	0.676	0.664
	EANN*	0.76	0.85	0.81	0.69	0.55	0.61	0.741
	EANN	NA	NA	NA	NA	NA	NA	0.715
	MVAE*	0.79	0.77	0.78	0.62	0.64	0.63	0.724
	MVAE	0.689	0.777	0.730	0.801	0.719	0.758	0.745
	Spotfake	0.832	0.606	0.701	0.751	0.900	0.820	0.777
	AMFB	**0.87**	0.76	**0.81**	**0.89**	**0.95**	**0.92**	**0.883**

5.5.4 Results and Analysis

Table 5.2 compares the proposed model and the current models on two distinct datasets. For both real and fake classes, the table presents the accuracy, precision, recall, and F1-score of the AMFB model. The outcomes demonstrate that the suggested method outperforms the current baseline and SOTA models. It is clear that the visual model outperforms the textual one in terms of performance. This could be the case because textual information sometimes includes noisy and unstructured data, but the visual provides more convincing proof. The results show that adding images to text is advantageous since it performs better than using only images or text alone.

Training and validation learning curves display the accuracy and loss of the proposed (AMFB) model for every epoch. The learning curves of the proposed model for the Twitter and Weibo datasets are shown in Figs. 5.7 and 5.8, respectively. The loss in both curves steadily declines to an equilibrium point, indicating that the model learns correctly. Due to the smaller volume of Weibo validation data compared to Twitter validation data, the validation accuracy curve of the Weibo dataset varies more than that of the Twitter data.

Dimensionality reduction is employed using T-distributed stochastic neighbor embedding (t-SNE) (Zhong et al. 2017) to analyze how the model discriminates real news from fake news. Figures 5.9 and 5.10 display the projected features learned by

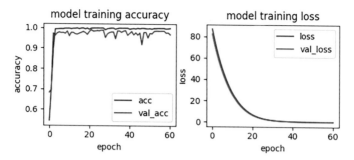

Fig. 5.7 Twitter data learning curves

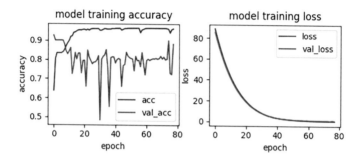

Fig. 5.8 Weibo data learning curves

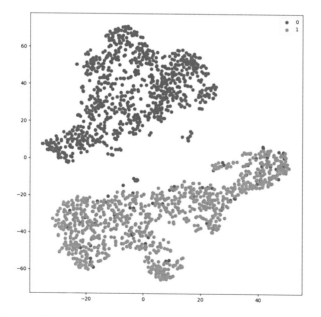

Fig. 5.9 Projection of feature representations for Twitter data

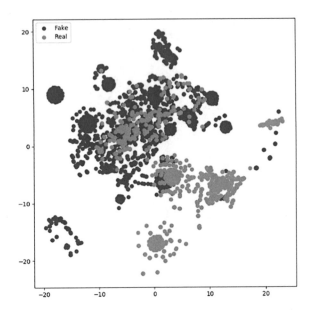

Fig. 5.10 Projection of feature representation for Weibo data

the proposed model in a two-dimensional plane for both Twitter and Weibo datasets. It is to be noted that for both datasets, the model achieves high separability. There are two reasons why the Weibo dataset has more overlapping occurrences than the Twitter dataset: (i) in the Weibo dataset, the majority of images are more involved, and (ii) Weibo is a Chinese dataset, and after segmentation, the length of some sentences becomes larger than that of the Twitter dataset. Long or complicated sentences do not yield better semantic information extracted by the machine.

5.5.4.1 Qualitative Analysis

To gain more understanding, the classifiers' outputs are examined. From the Twitter dataset, two distinct tweets are displayed in Fig. 5.11. The first tweet's text content appears authentic and is categorized as real by the textual model. However, the image has been altered. Both the words and the image in the second tweet are considered real by the textual and visual models. However, contrary to the text, the image in the second tweet was not shot during the earthquake in Nepal. All the tweets shown in Fig. 5.11 are fake, and they are correctly classified as fake by the proposed model. This justifies that the proposed model effectively extracts visual and textual features and determines whether it is fake or real. Some tweets from the Twitter dataset are displayed in Fig. 5.12. While existing models like att-RNN and EANN, as well as baseline models like textual and visual models, produce incorrect predictions, the proposed model properly identified these tweets. Thus,

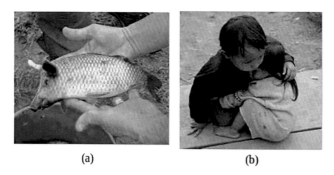

Fig. 5.11 Examples of correctly classified fake tweets by AMFB but misclassified by single modality model. (**a**) New species of fish found at arkansas. (**b**) A 4 year old attempts to protect his sister from the devastation of NepalEarthquake

Fig. 5.12 Examples of correctly classified real tweets by AMFB but misclassified by existing model. (**a**) Great picture thierry legault captures iss transit of the sun during eclipse. (**b**) NepalEarthquake: death toll rises to 758, emergency declared. North, Eastern Indial also hit

the aforementioned observation demonstrates that our proposed model works better than textual, visual, att-RNN, and EANN.

5.5.5   Comparison to the State of the Art (SOTA)

The comparative study between the developed model and the current SOTA (Singhal et al. 2019) is covered in this part. Table 5.2 displays a detailed description of the results. BERT has been applied to textual feature extraction in Spotfake (Singhal et al. 2019), which is certainly an effective method. The proposed model is less difficult since feature extraction is done using attention-based stacked LSTM and FastText embedding rather than the layered encoder of BERT. Sentences in Weibo and Twitter datasets are not syntactically and semantically correct, and the data is noisy. Additionally, the majority of the words in the sentences are incomplete, giving way to the outliers in the lexicon. While BERT does a better job than FastText,

FastText can even handle it more effectively. As the FastText mechanism is less complex, it is used for embedding in this work. Spotfake extracts general image characteristics using the pre-trained VGG19 architecture; it might not extract the invariant image features. The SOTA model concatenates textual and visual features to obtain the joint feature representation that does not correlate well between image and text. Therefore, misleading news (shown in the second example of Fig. 5.3) cannot be classified correctly. The proposed model uses the MFB module to maximize the correlation between textual and visual feature representation. It provides better joint feature representation and helps the model in the correct classification of multimedia posts.

The proposed model performs better by taking appropriate measures to address the problems identified by the Spotfake model. Despite the imbalance in the Twitter dataset, where over 50% of the instances are associated with a single event, the model attains an accuracy increase of almost 9.8%. Spotfake reported high accuracy for the Weibo dataset. Spotfake reports rather low precision, recall, and F1-score for the true class, even for a balanced dataset such as Weibo. Because of the greater complexity of the image in the Weibo dataset, pre-trained VGG19 is unable to capture the high-level domain-specific inherent properties of the images, which leads to a biased outcome. While the model's accuracy is lower than that of the Spotfake model, its precision, recall, and F1-score values for both classes are more evenly distributed. Furthermore, the proposed model is simpler than Spotfake.

5.6 Summary

This chapter briefly discusses the importance of multimodality in solving various NLP tasks. The chapter starts with a discussion of the basic introduction of multimodality, and after that, it discusses various applications and challenges of multimodality. Later, this chapter briefly explores a case study in which it discusses how multimodality is important in misinformation detection. The case study describes an end-to-end deep learning system that determines if a multimedia post is authentic or fake based on its text and image input. The critical point of any multimodal system is to get the efficient and best multimodal features, which is the prime objective of solving misinformation detection in the work of this chapter.

Chapter 6
Novelty and Emotion in Multimodal Misinformation Detection

Chapter 3 presents a brief introduction to novelty and emotion. It deliberates the contribution of emotion and novelty for textual misinformation detection. Chapter 5 briefly explains the concept of multimodality and its importance for misinformation detection. Continuing the novelty and emotion concepts explored in Chap. 3 and the multimodality concept explored in Chap. 5, the current chapter of the book explores the contribution of emotion and novelty for multimodal misinformation detection. More specifically, this chapter presents a case study that investigates a specific category of misinformation in which authentic images are assigned with different related events with new textual information to mislead the readers.

Multimedia news nowadays spreads false information quickly on social media by using the same (non-novel) visuals with different (novel) text in various situations, which misleads the newsreaders. By utilizing an image from a previous posts and altering the words linked with it in the current context, false information can be created. It becomes quite difficult to identify this type of false information because the image appears real and seems relevant to the updated text.

Figure 6.1, published by *The Logical Indian*[1] shows an example of false news in which an image has been shown, and it is claimed that the Ukrainian President *Volodymyr Zelensky* has joined the army to fight against Russia during the Ukraine-Russia war in 2022. However, this image was captured while Ukrainian President Volodymyr Zelensky was visiting the Donetsk region, eastern Ukraine, in 2021. Figure 6.2 depicts the real news. It contends that without background knowledge or previous information about the actual incident during which the image was captured, fake information detection is impossible. In addition to this, *novel and emotional* contents are the potential factors that work as the fuel for the rapid dissemination of false information. The chapter first starts with the introduction of a multimodal misinformation dataset, which includes *background knowledge* of the misleading articles. After that, the chapter continues with the introduction of a

---

[1] https://thelogicalindian.com/fact-check/ukraine-president-joins-defence-troop-34155.

Fig. 6.1 Misleading news claiming that Ukrainian President Volodymyr Zelensky has joined the army to fight against Russia

Fig. 6.2 Original image showing that Ukrainian President Volodymyr visiting the Donetsk region, eastern Ukraine, in 2021

multimodal architecture using *supervised contrastive learning (SCL)-based novelty detection* and *emotion prediction* tasks for misinformation detection. Extensive experiments are also performed to reveal that the developed model gives outstanding performance.

6.1   Contrastive Learning

It is a deep learning technique for unsupervised representation learning. The aim of this technique is to study a representation of data such that similar data samples remain near to each other in the representation space while dissimilar data instances remain far apart, i.e., as the name suggests, samples are contrasted against each other. The contrastive learning mechanism is useful in the case of solving a task of domains in which data annotation is difficult, such as the biomedical imaging domain. In this domain, expert doctors are required to annotate the data, which is time-consuming and expensive. Therefore, the recent research in deep learning focuses on reducing the requirement for supervised model training. For this, a good number of methodologies have been proposed, such as unsupervised learning, semi-supervised learning, and self-supervised learning. In unsupervised learning, the model is trained on the unlabeled dataset. In semi-supervised learning, the model is trained on a few labeled data samples along with a huge amount of unlabeled data samples. In self-supervised learning, the model itself labels the data, and labels predicted with high confidence are used as ground truths in future iterations of the model training.

Contrastive learning is also a type of self-supervised learning. In recent era, the contrastive learning has attracted many researchers and proved to be effective in numerous natural language processing (NLP) and computer vision (CV) tasks, including image retrieval, cross-modal retrieval, and zero-shot learning. In these tasks, the learned representations can be used as features for downstream tasks such as classification and clustering. Now, it is frequently being used in supervised and semi-supervised settings.

Figure 6.3 shows the basic working principle of the contrastive learning models. The fundamental contrastive learning model selects a data sample, called *anchor*; a data point that belongs to the same distribution as the anchor, called the *positive sample*; and another data point that belongs to a different distribution called the *negative sample*. The contrastive learning model tries to minimize the distance between the anchor and positive samples in the latent space and, at the same time, maximize the distance between the anchor and the negative samples.

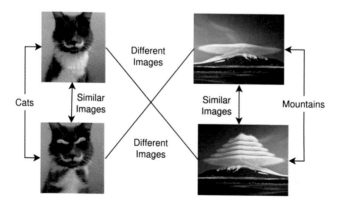

Fig. 6.3 This figure shows basic framework of contrastive learning

6.1.1   Applications of Contrastive Learning

Contrastive learning has broad applications in computer vision and natural language processing. The following subsections explore various applications:

6.1.1.1   Video Sequence Prediction

The VideoMoCo (Pan et al. 2021) is a model developed for predicting video sequences. This model uses contrastive learning methodology for unsupervised image representation learning. In this study, the model takes a video sequence as an input sample, and it tries to improve the temporal feature representations.

6.1.1.2   Object Detection

The DetCo (Xie et al. 2021) is a robust methodology that uses the contrastive self-supervised approach for object detection. It applies the contrastive learning between the global image and local patches. It also applies the multilevel supervision to intermediate representations, which facilitate consistent and discriminative local and global representation at each level of the feature pyramid. It ultimately improves detection and classification simultaneously.

6.1.1.3   Semantic Segmentation

Contrastive learning has also been applied broadly for the segmentation of natural images. A study presented in (Zhao et al. 2021) uses a supervised contrastive loss for pre-training a model and uses the traditional cross-entropy for fine-tuning. This approach increases intra-class compactness and inter-class separability, thereby resulting in a better pixel classifier.

6.1.1.4   Remote Sensing

The study presented in (Li et al. 2022) develops a model named *GLCNet*, which utilizes a supervised fine-tuning and a self-supervised pre-training approach for the segmentation of remote sensing image data. The authors exploit both the local regions and global image-level representations using a local features matching contrastive learning module and a global style contrastive learning module. Thus, contrastive learning helps in robust feature extraction in this task.

6.1.1.5   Perceptual Audio Similarity

Apart from the NLP and vision-related tasks, contrastive learning has also been explored in speech processing for finding the audio similarity. The study presented in CDPAM (Manocha et al. 2021) utilizes an unsupervised contrastive learning-based approach for classifying audio samples based on their perceptual similarity. The authors fine-tune the model by collecting human judgments on triplet comparisons to improve generalization to a broader range of audio perturbations.

6.1.1.6   Embedding Space Learning

Embedding is very important to solve any kind of NLP task, and contrastive learning plays a vital role in it. A popular study (Gao et al. 2021) applies the contrastive learning approach to learn the embedding space in which similar sentences remain close to each other, while dissimilar ones remain far apart.

6.2   Dataset Description

Important sources for researching the multimodal misinformation detection problem include Weibo (Jin et al. 2017), Twitter (Boididou et al. 2015), TI-CNN (Yang et al. 2018b), Fakeddit (Nakamura et al. 2020), Fauxtography (Zlatkova et al. 2019), and NewsBag (Jindal et al. 2020). During the COVID-19 infodemic, people have also created some multimodal misinformation datasets, which helped prevent misinformation related to COVID-19. Some popular COVID-19 misinformation datasets include MM-COVID (Li et al. 2020a), CHECKED (Yang et al. 2021), ArCOV-19 (Haouari et al. 2021), ReCOVery (Zhou et al. 2020a), and MMCoVaR (Chen et al. 2021).

The quality of the datasets that are now available is good, but none of them contain the background or source information of the news stories that are essential for this task. Therefore, this chapter first explains a multimodal misinformation dataset that contains both source and context information. This dataset includes 4950 fake samples and 6816 real samples. Each dataset instance is represented as a source-target pair. The multimodal samples of the three existing multimodal fake news datasets, Fauxtography, ReCOVery, and TI-CNN, are combined to generate the target sample. The source is the related background information extracted from different Web sites corresponding to that target.

6.2.1 Data Collection

TI-CNN, Fauxtography, and ReCOVery datasets are approximately balanced. These datasets also include good-quality images. Therefore, the new dataset is prepared using the abovementioned datasets. A set of target instances is formed by combining the multimodal samples of each dataset with their class labels. This set contains text and the URL of the image in every instance. Each sample is also assigned a label as fake or real. In the set of target samples, the metadata (background information) is gathered for the multimodal occurrences in the following three steps.

1. **Source Information Extraction:** For source information extraction, Google Reverse Image Search[2] is performed using the target image URL. Further, the URLs of all the sources containing text or image information related to the target image are extracted. After that, a get request is sent to the URLs of all sources and text and pictures present on a particular source are extracted. The target instance with missing source information and unimodal source-target pair is removed. To get reliable background information, the source itself must be credible. So, the source credibility is computed in the next step.

2. **Credible Source and Data Selection:** The news source credibility is checked using Mediabias.[3] A maximum of four reliable sources are considered from the list of all sources returned by reverse image search, and the data is extracted from these four sources only. During source information extraction, it is analyzed that, on average, there are four sources for every target instance. This analysis reached a decision to consider only four sources. The information obtained from less reliable sources is discarded. Thus, the textual information is extracted from credible sources, and all the images present in these sources are saved. In this way, there are up to four sources for each instance, each of which has a collection of images along with some text. The text is regarded as the source text.

3. **Source Image Selection:** Initially, all the images having a dimension less than 50×50 are removed from the list of images corresponding to each source. Further, unimodal source information is removed again. Since this work explores a misinformation detection problem containing novel text and non-novel images, only one source image is extracted, which is almost similar to the target image. For this purpose, a 4096-dimensional vector representation is computed for all the target and source images using VGG16 (Tammina 2019) pre-trained model. After that, cosine similarity is calculated between the vector representations of all the source images and the target image. Finally, only one image is kept per source, which is most similar to the target image. This highly similar image is the final source image.

---

[2] https://www.google.com/imghp?hl=en.
[3] https://mediabiasfactcheck.com/.

6.2.2 Data Annotation

As this dataset is created using existing datasets, each sample is already associated with fake or real labels. The data samples are annotated to decide whether the extracted background information from various sources is relevant to the corresponding target instance or not. The main purpose of this annotation is to keep the sample if the obtained metadata is relevant to the target or, otherwise, to remove it. In this way, *yes* or *no* labels are assigned for each sample. This annotation is completely based on the textual information of the target and source data sample. The automatic annotation is performed for all the data samples. To check the automatic data annotation quality, human annotation is performed for the 100 data samples. Figure 6.4 depicts the complete data preparation process, and subsequent paragraphs briefly explain the annotation schema.

Automatic Annotation In automatic annotation, two types of annotations are performed for each source-target pair of the dataset: (i) *yes* label is assigned to each sample if the source is relevant to the target; otherwise, *No* label is assigned. These labels are obtained using a threshold value. Named entity recognition (NER) on both the source text (S) and the target text (T) is used in order to determine the threshold value. The threshold is determined by dividing the total number of entities in the target text by the ratio of *the number of common entities present in source and target text*. Equation 6.1 defines the threshold where R denotes the ratio or threshold.

$$R = \frac{|S \cap T|}{|T|} \tag{6.1}$$

A label *Yes* is assigned for a maximum R-value, and a label *No* is assigned for the remaining samples. (ii) Fake or real labels are assigned for each sample in the second type of annotation. The real label is assigned to the source-target pair instance if the target data label is real, and the fake label is assigned if the target label is fake. As such, it is fully automatic and dependent only on the target data label.

Human Annotation Hundred (100) samples from the dataset are randomly selected, and human annotation is performed to cross-verify the quality of automatic annotation. Each instance includes *target_text, target image URL, and source information*. Source information contains *source text, source URL, source reliability, and source image URL*. The selected samples are provided to one well-qualified human annotator with post-graduation in English literature. It is also ensured that the annotator is expert in speaking, reading, and writing English. For the annotation, below mentioned guidelines are provided to the annotator:

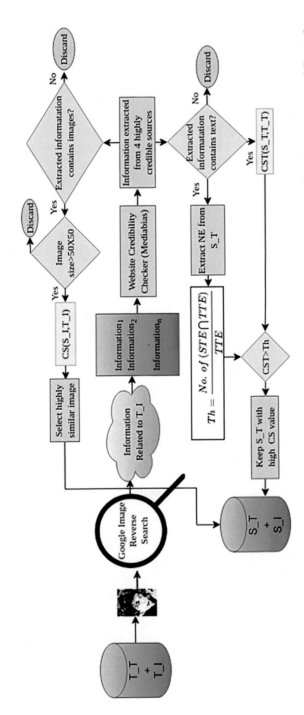

Fig. 6.4 Overall workflow of dataset development. Here, S_T, T_T, S_I, and T_I represent the *Source_Text*, *Target_Text*, *Source_Image*, and *Target_Image*, respectively. CS and CST represent the cosine similarity for image and text, respectively. STE and TTE depict *Source Text Entity* and *Target Text Entity*, respectively. *Th* represents threshold

Table 6.1 Table depicting the statistics of TI-CNN, Fauxtography, ReCOVery, and developed dataset

Dataset->		Fauxtography	ReCOVery	TI-CNN	Developed Dataset
Train	Real	1113	1309	3031	5453
	Fake	992	360	2608	3960
Test	Real	278	327	758	1363
	Fake	248	90	652	990

1. Open target image URL in the browser;
2. Go through every source text and assign the label as *No* if the text is not in English,
3. Otherwise, read the source text and check the following things: (a) source text is discussing the image; (b) source text gives some relevant information about the image; (c) the source text provides any prior information about the image. If any of the above criteria is fulfilled, assign the label as *Yes* for that source.

6.2.3 Data Statistics

To prepare the dataset, the data instances from TI-CNN, Fauxtography, and ReCOVery are considered. The developed corpus contains 11,766 instances, out of which 6,816 samples are real, and 4950 samples are fake. The data is split in an 80:20 ratio to form the train and test set with a consistent random state to reproduce the results. Table 6.1 shows the dataset statistics and distribution briefly.

6.2.4 Data Pre-processing

For pre-processing the text, all the punctuations are removed, and the text is converted into lowercase. The length of each text is limited to a maximum of 300 words. Non-English text is translated to English using Python's deep-translator[4] library using the Google Translator mode. For the images part of the dataset, each image is encoded with 224*224 dimensions with red-green-blue color channels. Figure 6.5 depicts two more examples from the dataset in which the "Source Text" is the textual information of the extracted background knowledge. It is observed that the information provided in the source text is important for fake news detection.

---

[4] https://deep-translator.readthedocs.io/en/latest/.

Image	Target Text	Source Text	Label
	several male students at baraboo high school were photographed performing the nazi sieg heil salute	a wisconsin school district has launched an investigation after a photo of what appears to be a group of mostly white male students holding up a nazi salute went viral. in the image about students from baraboo high school in baraboo wisconsin dressed in suits are seen smiling with their right arms extended straight in the air reminiscent of the infamous sieg heil salute. some students also appear to be giving the okay sign white power salute in the photo. baraboo school district superintendent lori mueller released a statement on monday condemning the group photo. if the gesture is what it appears to be the district will pursue any and all available and appropriate actions including legal to address the issue mueller said in a letter sent to parents monday morning.	Real
	fifteen homeless people in chicago were found dead on the street because of record low temperatures that hit the city in late january	When the devastating winter storm swept through Chicago in late January, perhaps concerned social media users were mistaken with a meme that inflated the storm's toll on the city. the post that originated on twitter on january said chicago homeless are frozen to death. while the tweet was viewed multiple times with more than one likes, the accompanying photo of a homeless man sleeping on a snowy street was actually taken in January and published in the Canadian national post newspaper. I also suspect people were found frozen dead on the street. snopes contacted chicago police for more information but as of the time of publication, only seven deaths in various states had been linked to the extreme cold in the midwest. According to the snopes website, none of the reported victims were listed as homeless although three people were found dead outdoors in Michigan and iowa. The only fatality reported in Chicago during the storm involves an unidentified man hit by a snowplow.	Fake

Fig. 6.5 Image shows two examples from the developed dataset. The source text gives more information about the event, which helps in misinformation detection

6.3 Misinformation Detection Model (A Case Study)

6.3.1 Proposed Model

This section presents a case study that proposes a multimodal misinformation detection method. It consists of three modules: *the novelty detection module, the image emotion recognition module, and the misinformation detection module.* Figure 6.6 shows the overall structure of the proposed model. Subsequent sections describe every component in detail.

6.3.1.1 Novelty Detection Module

A novelty detection task is performed using SCL. It finds high-level semantic relationships between target and source multimedia news pairs to extract the novelty-aware multimodal feature from these news pairs. The multimodal encoder takes the multimodal source and target as input, as will be covered in more detail below.

Multimodal Encoder There are two distinct approaches to developing the encoder, viz., (i) the text data is encoded using a pre-trained BERT model in the first method. It extracts the 768-dimensional textual feature representations. The fixed-length word sequence *(w = w_1,..w_n)* is given as input to the BERT model. Here, n is the sequence length. Visual feature representation is encoded using pre-trained ResNet18 (He et al. 2016) model. Further, the multimodal feature is obtained by concatenating the textual and visual features. (ii) Multimodal data is encoded using the VisualBert model (Li et al. 2019) to obtain the multimodal feature in the second method. After that, source and target data are projected in 128-dimensional feature space by employing two fully connected layers. These features are represented by MS and MT, respectively. After obtaining both features, the proposed model is trained using contrastive learning. According to the property of contrastive learning, the target representation attracts the source representation if both are semantically similar; otherwise, both repeal each other. This separation makes one class novel or different from the other. In this manner, appropriate novelty learning with contrastive learning identifies more meaningful interactions between the various modalities and recognizes intricate semantic relations between the source and target. The contrastive loss function is optimized to train the novelty model. Equation 6.2 defines the loss function, which is similar to Khosla et al. (2020). Here, I is the set of indices of the one modality, P is the set of another modality, and τ is a scalar parameter. z_i and z_p represent the final projected vector of the modalities in the embedding space. A is the set of different representations of the modalities.

$$L_{SCL} = \sum_{i \in I} \frac{-1}{|P(i)|} \sum_{p \in P(i)} log \frac{exp(\frac{z_i \cdot z_p}{\tau})}{\sum_{a \in A(i)} exp(\frac{z_i \cdot z_p}{\tau})} \tag{6.2}$$

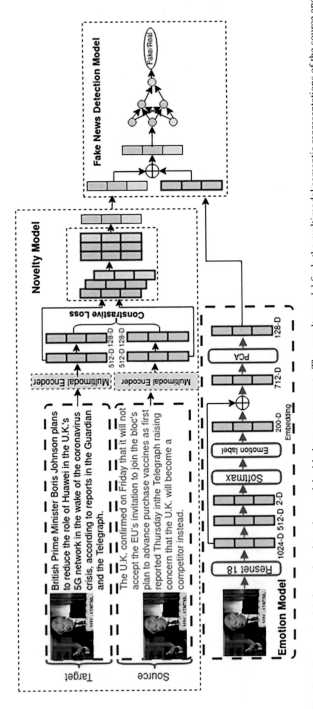

Fig. 6.6 Proposed misinformation detection model with three components. The novelty model finds the multimodal semantic representations of the source and target pair using SCL. The emotion model extracts emotion-aware visual representation, and finally, the misinformation detection model classifies the news as fake or real

6.3.1.2   Image Emotion Prediction

Emotion-aware visual feature representation is obtained using a neural network-based emotion classification model. The combined form of ArtPhoto (Machajdik and Hanbury 2010) and UnbiasedEmo (Panda et al. 2018) image emotion datasets is used to pre-train this network. The combined dataset includes love, joy, fear, sadness, surprise, and anger labels. Only two emotion labels, viz., *emotion true* and *emotion false*, are considered to perform the experiments. *Emotion true* label is formed by combining love, joy, and sadness labels, whereas *emotion false* label is formed by the combination of surprise, fear, and anger. A pre-trained ResNet18 model is used for image encoding. Further, the obtained image representation is given as input to an MLP network consisting of two hidden layers and one output layer with a softmax activation function. Since the number of data samples in each emotion class is imbalanced, the weighted cross-entropy loss is optimized during training. Later, this trained emotion model predicts the emotion labels for the images present in the developed dataset. Equation 6.3 defines the image emotion model.

$$IR_i = ResNet18(I_i) \tag{6.3}$$

IR_i represents the encoded representation of each image I_i, which is obtained from ResNet18. This representation is projected in 1024 and 512-dimensional feature space, respectively, following Eq. 6.4.

$$IR1_i = tanh(W_{IR_i} * IR_i + b_{IR_i})$$
$$IR2_i = tanh(W_{IR1_i} * IR1_i + b_{IR1_i}) \tag{6.4}$$
$$I_out = Softmax(W_{IR2_i} * IR2_i + b_{IR2_i})$$

6.3.1.3   Misinformation Detection

Following Eq. 6.5, the 512-dimensional feature representations for the source (N_{SR}) and target (N_{TR}) are obtained after pre-training the novelty model. These features are then merged to generate the multimodal representation (N_{MR}).

$$a = N_{TR} + N_{SR}; b = N_{TR} - N_{SR}$$
$$c = N_{TR} * N_{SR}; N_{MR} = Concat(a, |b|, c) \tag{6.5}$$

Ultimately, the misinformation detection model is developed by projecting these fused representations into 512-dimensional feature space and using them as a novelty-aware multimodal feature representation. Additionally, from a pre-trained image emotion model, the 512-dimensional emotion-aware visual feature representations are retrieved, and scaffolding is carried out by concatenating a 200-dimensional representation of predicted emotion labels to it. In this manner, an emotion-aware visual feature representation with 712 (512 + 200) dimensions is created. Furthermore, the 128-dimensional emotion-aware feature representations of images are obtained by applying the principle component analysis (PCA) (Bro and Smilde 2014).

After obtaining emotion-aware visual and novelty-aware multimodal feature representations, both features are concatenated. This concatenated feature is passed to the MLP model containing two hidden layers and an output layer with a softmax classifier function to classify the news as fake or real. The proposed misinformation detection model is trained using cross-entropy loss optimization.

6.3.2 Experiments and Results

This section presents the experimental details, the baseline model's performance, and a detailed explanation of the experimental results. It also provides the error analysis for some real examples where the proposed model does not give the correct solution.

6.3.2.1 Experimental Setup

Experiments are carried out with a single Nvidia GeForce RTX GPU with 10GB of RAM and the Pytorch library. The accuracy and class-wise F1-score of the system are used to evaluate its performance. The baseline models are trained using the Adam optimizer (Kingma and Ba 2015). These models are trained for 100 epochs with a batch size of 128. Using the Layer-wise Adaptive Rate Scaling (LARS) optimizer (You et al. 2017), the contrastive learning framework is pre-trained for 1,000 epochs. Additionally, it is pre-trained with a batch size of 512 using Stochastic Gradient Descent (SGD) (Bottou 2012) for 1,000 epochs. The emotion model undergoes 100 epochs of pre-training with a batch size of 128 using the Adam optimizer. The final suggested model is trained with a batch size of 128 across 100 epochs. The Adam optimizer is used to maximize the loss. The train and test sets of the dataset are divided into an 80:20 ratio initially. Additionally, the train set is split into the train and validation sets at a 90:10 ratio. On the test set, the outcomes are reported. The total number of parameters is 17,533,985 in this proposed model.

6.3.2.2 Baselines and Comparing Systems

A few of the models are designed, and some existing models are implemented as baselines to validate the proposed model performance. Table 6.2 shows the results of all the baseline models.

Table 6.2 The table shows results of the model with/without background information. Here, WBG means *with background knowledge*; W/O BG means *without background knowledge*; FF1 and RF1 represent F1 score for fake and real class, respectively; Acc is the accuracy; MA is the micro-average; and WA is the weighted average

Model	Dataset	WBG					W/O BG				
		FF1	RF1	Acc	MA	WA	FF1	RF1	Acc	MA	WA
BERT+ResNet	TICNN	94.02	94.59	94.32	94.31	94.32	79.07	80.97	80.07	80.02	80.06
	Fauxtography	85.77	88.46	87.26	87.12	87.25	69.13	76.01	73.00	72.57	72.92
	Recovery	61.84	91.49	86.09	76.66	84.66	31.25	87.53	78.89	59.39	74.57
	Developed Dataset	85.92	89.04	87.68	87.48	87.67	85.53	88.94	87.46	87.23	87.45
VisualBERT	TICNN	88.62	89.75	89.21	89.19	89.21	79.76	80.36	80.07	80.06	80.07
	Fauxtography	88.12	89.36	88.78	88.74	88.81	68.78	74.69	72.05	71.74	72.04
	Recovery	64.39	83.50	77.45	73.95	79.10	52.73	74.53	66.90	63.63	69.52
	Developed Dataset	80.44	84.97	83.00	82.71	82.99	76.33	83.04	80.24	79.69	80.10
BERT (Text Only)	Developed Dataset	80	83.04	81.64	81.52	81.71	–	–	–	–	–
ResNet (Image Only)	Developed Dataset	–	–	–	–	–	44.47	70.90	61.81	57.68	59.32
SAFE	Developed Dataset	95.17	96.40	95.87	95.78	95.86	–	–	–	–	–
EANN	Developed Dataset	–	–	–	–	–	81.31	87.07	84.72	84.19	84.65

1. **ResNet18 and BERT:** The textual information is encoded using the pre-trained BERT (Devlin et al. 2019), while the visual information is encoded using the pre-trained ResNet18 model (He et al. 2016). Multimodal representations for the source and target are created by concatenating the textual and visual representations. After that, an MLP network with two hidden layers and one output layer with a softmax function takes this multimodal representation as input. The MLP model classifies the news as fake or real. This baseline model is implemented in two different ways: one with background knowledge (using source-target pair) and the other without it (using only target data).

2. **BERT (Text only):** This baseline model only considers source and target text for misinformation detection. It first extracts the 768-dimensional source and target text representations using a pre-trained BERT model. Both source and target features are concatenated and then passed through a feed-forward neural network having two feed-forward layers and *tanh* activation function. Features obtained from the second layer are again passed to an output layer with two neurons and a softmax activation function.

3. **ResNet18 (Image only):** In this baseline model, only the target image is used for misinformation detection. It is basically implemented as one of the ablation studies. The pre-trained ResNet-18 model yields the 512-dimensional representation of every target image. Similar to the Text-only model, the representations are passed via two feed-forward layers, each with 512 and 128 units with *tanh* activation function, before being transmitted to the output layer, which has two units with softmax activation for classification.

4. **VisualBERT:** In this model, the multimodal (image and text) information is encoded using pre-trained VisualBERT (Li et al. 2019) model. An MLP model is employed over the representation obtained from VisualBERT. The MLP model

is the same as the previous baseline model. Two variations are implemented for this model also. One model is implemented with background knowledge, and the other model is implemented without background knowledge.

5. **SAFE:** The SAFE (Zhou et al. 2020b) model is also implemented as a baseline. This model takes the news headline, body, and image as input to find their similarity for fake news detection. The target text of the developed data is used as the headline, the source text is used as the body, and the target image is used as image input for this model. Since the dataset developed for this work assigns fake and real labels according to the agreement of the source and the target text, it can be believed that SAFE will work as one of the strong baselines. The ablation study is not performed only using textual or visual information because the hypothesis proves the importance of background information for misinformation detection. Evaluation results demonstrate that background knowledge improves the model performance.

6. **EANN:** Event Adversarial Neural Networks (Wang et al. 2018) is also implemented as one of the baselines. Using an adversarial setting for multimodal misinformation detection, this model can effectively identify event-invariant characteristics and perform well on unseen events. Since event-specific labels are not explicitly included in the developed dataset, a method is developed to get the event labels. The CLIP (Radford et al. 2021) model is initially used to extract the multimodal features of the target data, which consists of text and images. After that, K-means++ clustering (Arthur and Vassilvitskii 2006) is employed on the retrieved features for ten clusters, which is the EANN framework's default number of clusters. These sample cluster labels are considered the event labels. The EANN framework is subsequently trained for 100 epochs using these event labels, the target image, and text.

6.3.2.3 Results and Discussion

The comparison of the baseline models with and without background information is displayed in Table 6.2. The outcomes of both the Visual BERT and BERT+ResNet models are presented. Every base dataset that comprises the generated dataset also has the findings reported on it. The table's results demonstrate how well both models perform on all four datasets using background information. Accuracy gains of 16.06 points with BERT+ResNet and 9.9 points with Visual BERT are observed on the developed dataset. The above results justify that background information helps in misinformation detection effectively. It is also observed that the SAFE model with background knowledge yields the best performance among all the baselines. The BERT+Resnet model obtains richer textual embeddings using BERT compared to the EANN model. Therefore, it performs better than the EANN model. The EANN model outperforms the VisualBERT model due to the absence of discrete objects in some images. Since the BERT+ResNet and VisualBERT models employ multimodal information rather than just text, it is to be predicted that their accuracy is higher than that of the text-only results produced by the BERT-based model.

Table 6.3 Table shows the results of proposed model. It can be observed that the model with novelty, emotion, and background knowledge performs better. Here, *B+R* and *VB* represent *BERT+ResNet* and VisualBert models, respectively

Model	Dataset	Proposed Model with Novelty					Proposed Model with Novelty and Emotion				
		FF1	RF1	Acc	MA	WA	FF1	RF1	Acc	MA	WA
B+R	TICNN	94.75	95.16	94.96	94.95	94.96	99.03	99.11	99.07	99.07	99.07
	Fauxtography	89.21	91.19	90.30	90.20	90.30	96.77	97.44	97.14	97.10	97.14
	Recovery	75.28	93.29	89.44	84.28	89.14	93.04	97.99	96.88	95.51	96.85
	Developed Dataset	89.32	91.75	90.69	90.54	90.69	**97.47**	**98.03**	**97.79**	**97.75**	**97.79**
VB	TICNN	88.95	89.60	89.29	89.28	89.29	97.92	98.09	98.01	98.01	98.01
	Fauxtography	83.19	85.46	84.41	84.32	84.44	96.66	97.20	96.95	96.93	96.96
	Recovery	62.59	82.86	76.49	72.73	78.20	95.43	98.58	97.84	97.00	97.86
	Developed Dataset	81.29	86.12	84.06	83.71	84.01	**97.27**	**97.88**	**97.62**	**97.58**	**97.62**

Additionally, among all the experiments, the target image alone produces the lowest accuracy. The reason for this is that, in the absence of any other information, classifying news as authentic or fake can be challenging when relying solely on the original image stored in the dataset.

Evaluation results of the proposed model using only novelty and both novelty and emotion are shown in Table 6.3 for both the BERT+ResNet and Visual BERT with all four data split configurations as mentioned above. It can be seen that 2.76 and 1.35 points accuracy improvements are obtained using only novelty compared to the background knowledge framework of BERT+ResNet and Visual BERT, respectively. This justifies that the contrastive learning approach helps in misinformation detection. The final proposed model obtains 9.86 and 14.91 points improvement in accuracy over the baselines of the background knowledge model using BERT+ResNet and Visual BERT, respectively. Hence, it can be concluded that the final proposed framework using novelty and emotion produces the best result.

Training and validation learning curves display the accuracy and loss of the proposed model for each epoch. Figure 6.7 depicts the learning curves of the model for the created dataset. This curve displays the model's accuracy as well as its loss during training and validation. It is observed that the model behaves consistently both in training and validation. Continuous optimization of the loss and accuracy leads to an equilibrium position where the model learns adequately and does not introduce overfitting.

6.3.3 Case Studies

A detailed analysis is performed to show the effectiveness of the proposed method. Figure 6.8 depicts an instance of the ReCOVery dataset. It shows the UK's prime minister, which was originally labeled as fake. While the novelty-only model predicts it to be real, the final proposed model with BERT+ResNet forecasts it to be phony. Here, the emotions of the target image are a major factor in identifying it as a fake. The picture expresses anger, surprise, and disgust emotions that belong

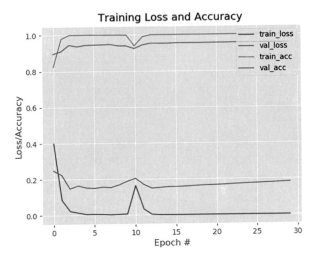

Fig. 6.7 Loss and accuracy curves for developed dataset

Target Image	Target Text	Source Text	GTL	MME	Model1 Output	Model2 Output
	British Prime Minister Boris Johnson plans to reduce the role of Huawei in the U.K.'s 5G network in the wake of the coronavirus crisis, according to reports in the Guardian and the Telegraph.	The U.K. confirmed on Friday that it will not accept the EU's invitation to join the bloc's plan to advance purchase vaccines as first reported Thursday inthe Telegraph raising concern that the U.K. will become a competitor instead.	Fake	Resnet18 + BERT	Novelty + Emotion -> Fake	Novelty Only -> Real

Fig. 6.8 This figure shows correctly classified examples by the proposed model. Here, GTL represents ground-truth label, and MME represents multimodal encoder

to the fake emotion class. Therefore, the final model that incorporates both novelty and emotion outperforms the novelty-only model.

6.3.4 Error Analysis

Figure 6.9 depicts two instances from the developed dataset. Since the emotions shown in the first example are disgust and fear, which belong to the false class, the novelty+emotion model performs better. Also, the content of the source and the target text are from different contexts, although they mention both President Trump's and Israel's prime ministers' names. The contrastive learning model captures this better than the SAFE framework. The novelty-only paradigm outperforms the novelty and emotion combined approach in the second example. Since the original photo was taken in the 1980s and the source text makes it clear that this picture is manipulated, the novelty detection model can identify this news as phony.

Target Image	Target Text	Source Text	GTL	MME	Model1 Output	Model2 Output
	Just two days after his stunning election victory, President-elect Donald Trump delivered a message to Israel, describing his personal affection for the Jewish state and hopes that his administration will be able to strengthen ties strained by eight years of tense relations between Israel and the Obama administration.	Israeli Prime Minister Benjamin Netanyahu addressed an enthusiastic crowd at AIPAC in Washington on Tuesday, while facing deep political and possibly criminal problems back at home. Before speaking Monday to the most powerful pro-Israel lobby in the country, the American Israel Public Affairs Committee (or AIPAC), presidential candidate Donald Trump -- who famously says heals his own best adviser -- sought counsel from Jewish friends	Fake	Visual BERT	Novelty+Emotion -> **Fake**	SAFE -> Real
	A photograph shows Queen singer Freddie Mercury applying intricate face makeup	An image purportedly showing musician Freddie Mercury applying intricate make-up to his face has been circulating online for several years: This image was most likely created by Deviant Art poster QueenAnatolia, who originally shared the picture in 2009. The original photograph was taken by Neal Preston before a Queen concert circa 1980	Fake	Visual BERT	Novelty only-> **Fake**	Novelty+Emotion -> Real
	Tanks are seen in the government-held industrial town of Avdiyivka, Ukraine	Major fighting around the industrial city in Ukraine has everyone asking if Putin is up to something big, or just testing the resolve of a new Trump administration. Why is the war in Ukraine suddenly going from frozen conflict to scorcher? Is this Vladimir PutinÂ¢Â€Â™s way of testing Donald Trump, not two full weeks into his job as U.S. president, or is it just another provocation designed to keep Kiev weak and insecure after three years of invasion, annexation and occupation?	Real	Resnet18+BERT	Without Background Knowledge -> **Real**	With Background Knowledge -> Fake

Fig. 6.9 Figure shows some examples incorrectly classified by the proposed model

Still, it is evident that the picture captures the emotion of sadness that characterizes real news in general. Therefore, the novelty and emotion model becomes confused, leading it to predict the data as real. In the third instance, the model with prior information is not performing as well as without background knowledge. The target text and image both express that tanks are observed in a certain location without the need for a previous knowledge model. When we utilize the background knowledge model, we find that adding details about Trump and Putin confuses the model and detracts from the tanks' primary topic. Therefore, this image is accurately classified as real by the model without any prior knowledge, whereas it is classified as fake by the model with prior knowledge.

6.4 Summary

The significance of novelty and emotion in identifying multimodal disinformation is covered in this book chapter. It presents a case study of a novel issue and suggests an effective solution for false information detection. False multimedia news contains non-novel images but novel text information. This type of misinformation detection requires a new multimodal misinformation dataset containing the background information for each instance. Thus, the chapter starts by developing a dataset using the TI-CNN, Fauxtography, and ReCOVery datasets and complementing them with the background information. The studies and examples demonstrate the importance of background knowledge in appropriate misinformation detection, which supports the creation of a new dataset. This chapter also looks into the impacts of novelty and emotion since these are the key components that lead to the dissemination of misleading information. The novelty and emotion-aware multimodal feature representations are extracted by using the pre-trained visual emotion and novelty models that are trained separately using SCL. The multimodal properties are then encoded into an MLP network in order to detect false information. Therefore, the main goal of this chapter is to examine how emotion and novelty play an important role in a multimodal setup.

Chapter 7
Multilinguality in Misinformation Detection

Most of the prior studies in the NLP community so far have a precise focus on solving English language-based tasks only. As per the current status, there are over 7,100 languages worldwide, and it is extremely challenging to develop the NLP methodologies for all of them. The rapid growth of multilingual Web and social media content in low-resource languages has become an emerging domain of research to solve various NLP tasks. Thus, there is an increasing need for NLP solutions for other languages. In light of this need, this chapter briefly introduces multilinguality, its importance, application, and challenges. For better understanding, it also discusses a case study that explores the multilinguality in the context of misinformation detection.

7.1 Multilinguality

Multilinguality is a method that integrates linguistics of different languages to process and analyze substantial information of different natural human languages to solve various generic problems of NLP. In other words, multilinguality is just using multiple languages simultaneously for a specific purpose. For example, different languages can be used to design a chatbot that can communicate the preferences of users. Recently, various popular NLP models, such as mBERT, XLM, XLM Roberta, etc., are available for solving multilingual problems. Further subsections briefly discuss this concept.

© The Author(s), under exclusive license to Springer Nature Switzerland AG 2024
A. Ekbal, R. Kumari, *Dive into Misinformation Detection*, The Information
Retrieval Series 30, https://doi.org/10.1007/978-3-031-54834-5_7

7.2   Importance of Multilinguality

In the current time, the people in the world speak approximately 7,000 different languages. Around 400 languages are spoken by more than 1M speakers, and approximately 1,200 languages are spoken by more than 100k people (van Esch et al. 2022). The need for language independence was first highlighted by Bender (2011) in 2011. A study (Ruder et al. 2022) published in ACL 2021 depicts that almost 70% of the work is being done only using the English language. Several languages in Asia, Africa, and the Americas that are spoken by tens of millions of people have received little research attention. There is a large linguistic diversity in continents such as Africa, where around 2,000 languages are spoken, and in individual countries such as Indonesia, where around 700 languages are spoken.

Different languages have different rules, and some languages work completely differently. For instance, Spanish, French, and Italian are very similar, but they utilize different ideographs or symbols from some Asian languages like Japanese and Chinese. The research and technology are still underexplored for such low-resource languages. Designing the NLP model for each and every language is almost impossible due to resource unavailability and other challenges. Therefore, it is important to develop a language-independent model that is efficient in solving the tasks of multiple languages.

7.3   Applications of Multilinguality in NLP

Multilinguality in natural language processing (NLP) focuses on processing and understanding multiple human languages simultaneously. It has an extensive application across numerous domains due to its capability of handling diverse linguistic data. The below paragraphs briefly discuss some key applications of multilingual NLP.

7.3.1   Machine Translation

Machine translation is a popular task of NLP, which translates the text from one language to the other language. Multilingual NLP has taken a sharp turn to solve this task and is broadly used in machine translation systems like Google Translate nowadays. The concept of multilingual has made cross-language communication easier. It has brought the machine learning task to a different turn. The study presented in Aharoni et al. (2019), Zhang et al. (2021a), Das et al. (2023), etc. are the popular machine translation tasks that have explored the importance of multilingual features.

7.3.2 Cross-Lingual Information Retrieval

Multilingual NLP is also very effective for information extraction in different languages. It is basically a sub-field of information retrieval that retrieves information written in a language other than the query language. For instance, if the user asks the query in English, cross-lingual information retrieval extracts the information in Hindi, Bangla, Urdu, etc. People have given various synonyms for the term *cross-language information retrieval* such as trans-lingual information retrieval, multilingual information retrieval, etc. The term cross-lingual and multilingual information retrieval also performs well if users write a query in various languages. It actually takes the query in mixed languages and extracts the information in the user's language. To perform such types of information extraction, cross-lingual information techniques take the help of multilingual dictionaries, parallel corpora, comparable corpora, and machine translation. The study presented in Jiang et al. (2020), Nasharuddin and Abdullah (2010), Ogundepo et al. (2022), etc. are some popular works to explore the importance of multilinguality in information extraction. Multilingual NLP is also very useful for the information extraction from medical records written in different languages, which can improve patient care and healthcare research in multilingual regions.

7.3.3 Sentiment Analysis

In recent years, sentiment analysis has gained huge popularity in the NLP research community. It is a process to extract the emotions, subjective opinions, and attitudes expressed in speech or text. It extracts these attributes in either positive, negative, and neutral forms. This task has been proven very effective in multilingual content analysis. This task is majorly performed for social media analysis, global information analysis, monitoring brand sentiment, and customer feedback analysis in global markets. The investigations explored in Goel et al. (2018), Câmara et al. (2022), Mamta et al. (2022), and Patwa et al. (2022) are some popular work for multilingual sentiment analysis.

7.3.4 Chatbots and Virtual Assistants

As we have discussed at the beginning of this chapter, there is a large variety of languages in the world. Therefore, it is very difficult to design a chatbot or virtual assistant for each and every domain in each individual language. To reduce this effort, researchers are applying the concept of multilingual information processing to develop multilingual chatbots and virtual assistants. These chatbots and assistants can communicate with users in their preferred language, which results in making them more user-friendly and accessible to diverse audiences. In this way, incorporating multilinguality also reduces the developer's cost and efficiency. The studies presented in Kasinathan et al. (2021), Badlani et al. (2021), and Anastasiou et al. (2022) are the popular studies of this domain.

7.3.5 Multilingual Content Analysis and Classification

Various NLP models can categorize content, such as social media posts, news articles, and other documents, into predefined topics or categories. The multilingual classification model classifies the text content regardless of the language the content is written in. This is valuable for content recommendation and news aggregation platforms. The study presented in Velankar et al. (2022), Ghosh et al. (2022b), etc. are the popular study for multilingual text classification. Compliance departments and law firms can use multilingual NLP to analyze legal documents and contracts written in different languages.

7.3.6 Multilingual Speech Recognition

Multilingual NLP systems can also be used to transcribe and analyze spoken language in multiple languages. It is important for applications like transcription services and voice assistants. The studies presented in Pham et al. (2022), Zhang et al. (2022), Lugosch et al. (2022), etc. have better explored the role of multilinguality for speech recognition.

7.3.7 Cross-Lingual Document Summarization

Summarization is a technique to analyze the text and extract the most important sentences from the text content. Nowadays, this technique is applied for news summarization, social media content analysis related to a particular topic, document summarization, etc. As the text is not limited to the English language only, multilingual or cross-lingual automatic document summarization techniques are highly demanded. These techniques create concise summaries of documents in different languages, which make it easier to understand and process large volumes of information. Researchers have explored the importance and role of multilingual content analysis for document summarization tasks in various studies like Gangathimmappa et al. (2023), Taunk and Varma (2023), Pant and Chopra (2022), Grashchenkov et al. (2022), etc.

7.3.8 Language Learning and Teaching

Multilingual NLP tools and systems can assist language learners by providing translation, synonyms, antonyms, paraphrases, pronunciation feedback, and language exercises for multiple languages. These multilingual applications can simultaneously be used to teach learners with different language diversity.

7.3.9 Fake News Detection

After the transformation from traditional news sources to social media platforms, misinformation has become a challenging part of life. In the current era, misinformation detection is an emerging problem in the NLP domain. Since social media users belong to local and global communities both, their language also has a large variety. And fake news creators create false content as per their preference and expertise in the language. Therefore, it is important to develop multilingual misinformation and fake news detection techniques. Various popular studies such as Mohawesh et al. (2023a), Hammouchi and Ghogho (2022), Mohawesh et al. (2023b), Ahuja and Kumar (2023), etc. have explored the multilingual content for misinformation detection. Multilingual content analysis can also be used for fraud detection by processing financial news and documents.

7.3.10 Multilingual Content Generation

Content generation techniques are used to create text, articles, or reports. Multilingual content generation tools can benefit content marketing and global branding efforts for generating content in various languages.

In essence, incorporating multilingual concepts in NLP enhances the accessibility of information and communication in our multilingual and multicultural world, which offers significant advantages across industries and applications.

7.4 Challenges in Multilinguality

Multilinguality, or the ability to work with multiple languages, presents various challenges across different domains, including machine learning, natural language processing, communication, and international business. The below subsections describe some of the key challenges in multilinguality.

7.4.1 Language Diversity

As this chapter discusses, there are thousands of languages spoken around the world. Each language has its vocabulary, linguistic rules, unique grammar, and cultural nuances. For instance, there are some similarities among Italian, Spanish, and French. On the other hand, these languages are completely different from specific Asian language groups, i.e., Japanese, Chinese, and Korean, which share similar ideographs and symbols. Thus, building techniques and tools to handle this diversity is a significant challenge for the NLP research community.

7.4.2 Data Availability

Even a large number of people speak different languages other than English. However, researchers are still facing the problem of resources as these languages have limited publicly available digital content and resources. The unavailability of resources for regional languages such as Hindi, Bangla, Telugu, etc., makes it difficult to train and develop models for the low-resource languages. There is a lack of large-scale, high-quality data for many languages. It creates a problem in building language translation and language understanding systems for language pairs that are not commonly encountered (low-resource languages), which can be especially challenging due to the lack of parallel data for training. Thus, the lack of resources is also a considerable challenge in solving the multilingual NLP tasks.

7.4.3 Resource Intensity

Various significant computational resources are required to train multilingual models. However, designing, constructing, purchasing, and maintaining these resources is very expensive, which becomes difficult for smaller organizations and researchers. It also limits the exploration of problems in the multilingual domain.

7.4.4 Cross-Lingual Transfer

As there is a large variety of languages, it is difficult to develop the systems for each and every language. To overcome this situation, the system can be designed for one language, and it can be utilized for another language. But due to diversity in linguistic features among various languages, what works well in one language might not work as effectively in another language. People also use a mix of multiple languages during communication. Therefore, transferring the knowledge acquired from one language to another language and learning the knowledge from mixed languages are very big challenges for researchers.

7.4.5 Cultural Sensitivity

It is also a big challenge observed while solving multilingual problems. In different cultures, the same word may have different meanings. Therefore, to avoid misunderstanding and biases across various cultures, the language models need to be culturally sensitive, which demands cultural knowledge in addition to linguistic knowledge. Thus, it limits the research to low-resource and regional languages, which is also a considerable obstacle in a multilingual domain.

7.4.6 Domain Adaptation

The linguistic features are also domain-dependent. The words, ascents, and languages vary significantly across different domains such as medical, legal, technical, education, agriculture, etc. Therefore, similar to cultural sensitivity, domain adaption is also a challenging task for multilingual models.

7.4.7 Ethical Concerns and Legal and Regulatory Issues

As multilingual models become more widely used, concerns about bias, fairness, and privacy become increasingly important. It is crucial to ensure that these models do not perpetuate stereotypes or harm culture and underrepresented languages. Different countries may have different regulations regarding data collection, data handling, and language processing, which can create legal challenges for multilingual applications that are operated across borders.

Addressing these challenges in multilinguality requires a multidisciplinary approach that combines expertise in linguistics, cultural studies, machine learning, and international collaboration. Researchers and developers must work together to create inclusive and effective multilingual systems that benefit a diverse global population.

7.5   Benefits of Multilinguality

As this chapter discusses from the beginning, multilinguality refers to the ability of NLP systems to understand, process, and generate text in multiple languages. There are various benefits to incorporating multilinguality in NLP:

7.5.1   Global Accessibility

NLP systems that support many languages can serve users from various linguistic backgrounds and reach a larger audience. This is crucial in a multilingual, international society where communication takes place in many languages. Due to language independence, the same system can be used by various people of different language backgrounds. It can also be expensive to create distinct models for each language. Since they can manage many languages with a single model and don't require redundant infrastructure, multilingual models can be more effective. Therefore, it can reduce the system development cost and improve its effectiveness.

7.5.2   Cross-Lingual Information Retrieval

The multilinguality is beneficial for cross-lingual information retrieval. It helps the users find information despite language obstacles. For instance, a user who is an expert in English can also search and access the information in Hindi and still get relevant results. Multilingual models also help in automated translation tasks. It has been proved very efficient for low-resource and regional languages also. It also supports the pre-training of multilingual models, which can further be adjusted for certain language-specific tasks, eliminating the need for laborious data collecting and unique training for each language.

7.5.3   Cross-Lingual Sentiment Analysis

In recent days, various companies and organizations are taking benefit of multilingual NLP systems for developing their businesses. They usually utilize this system for sentiment analysis of the clients across languages, which helps them understand client or customer sentiment in different markets. According to the result, they changed their policies for higher profits.

7.5.4 Enhanced Language Understanding

In order to improve language interpretation and creation across all supported languages, multilingual models can learn universal linguistic properties. This can be beneficial for tasks like text summarization and language modeling, machine translations, etc. Multilingual NLP models can more effectively comprehend and process mixed-language material in areas where individuals frequently code-switch between languages in conversation, such as Spanglish. Multilingual NLP models can also facilitate the dissemination of knowledge across languages by transferring knowledge, information, and facts.

7.5.5 Multilingual Customer Support

Multilinguality can also be beneficial in developing various chatbots and virtual assistants. Various companies and organizations can take the benefit of these chatbots and assistants for providing customer support in various languages, which can improve user experiences.

7.5.6 Enhanced Research Opportunities

Apart from the various application benefits, multilinguality also provides benefits to researchers in conducting cross-lingual studies, analyzing language evolution, and studying linguistic phenomena across different languages. Thus, it can broaden the research area for solving various unresolved tasks.

While there are many advantages to multilingualism in NLP, it's crucial to remember that in order to fully exploit these benefits, issues like discrepancies in language resource availability, data biases, and dialect variances must also be resolved. Nevertheless, multilingual NLP offers significant potential for removing language barriers and expanding the inclusiveness and accessibility of NLP applications to a global audience.

7.6 Multilinguality in Context of Misinformation Detection (A Case Study)

In recent years, substantial advancements in automatic misinformation detection have been observed. But the majority of these are aimed at languages with lots of resources, like English. The amount of research on low-resource Indian languages like Hindi, Tamil, and Bengali is still insignificant. The lack of data and other related resources is the reason for this. As online news becomes more bilingual and multimedia, users are being misled by inaccurate information. The image in these news stories appears real and fits in with the updated text. Sometimes, the text is written in different languages, which becomes very challenging to detect. Along with the multilinguality, this case study explores the role of novelty and emotion in misinformation detection.

For example, Fig. 7.1 claimed that one of them in the picture is Swati Kovind, daughter of President Ram Nath Kovind. The claim adds that after Tata Sons found out about Swati, the company transferred her to the airline's Internal Affairs Office. A Facebook page posted the image with this claim in the Hindi language. It garnered more than 7,000 likes at the time of writing.[1] Although Swati Kovind served as an air hostess, background knowledge collected using Google Reverse Image Search shows that none of them in Fig. 7.1 is Swati Kovind and successfully detected it as fake news.

Despite the fact that a great deal of research has been done on many aspects of disinformation detection. Nevertheless, only a small number of systems have concentrated on emotion-aware and unique misinformation detection using prior knowledge of the languages with comparatively low resources. These issues can be resolved by developing significant resources and a functional baseline. For this purpose, a new multilingual, multimodal disinformation dataset has been prepared for Indian languages, including Bengali, Tamil, and Hindi. Each language has unique instances, where an instance is a single assertion that could be true or false. As a result, an instance cannot exist in more than one language. The instances of all three languages are combined to train the model, resulting in a multilingual model. Emotion recognition and novelty detection are performed as supporting tasks in the developed deep learning-based misinformation detection model.

7.6.1　Data Description and Analysis

A few resources, such as CHECKED (Yang et al. 2021) and ArCOV-19 (Haouari et al. 2021), are available in languages other than English. The multilingual multimodal misinformation datasets are FactDRIL (Singhal et al. 2021), MuMiN (Nielsen and McConville 2022), and MM-COVID (Li et al. 2020b). These datasets lack background information about the news articles (where and in what context it was first published), which is essential for identifying false or misleading content. To avoid these limitations, a novel multilingual multimodal misinformation (MMM) dataset is created. This dataset contains 10,473 samples from three different Indian languages, viz., Bengali, Hindi, and Tamil. Every dataset instance is represented as a source-target pair. The combination of multimodal Bengali, Hindi, and Tamil

---

[1] https://www.altnews.in/president-ram-nath-kovind-daughter-swati-kovind-false-claim-duty-changed/.

संस्कार.....🙏

आप में से कितने लोग इस महिला को जानते पहचानते हैं? इनका नाम स्वाति है!! दो महीने पहले तक जिन्होंने एयर इंडिया की फ्लाइट से ऑस्ट्रेलिया की यात्रा की होगी वो पहचान लेंगे, ये एयर इंडिया की बोईंग 777 और 787 में लम्बे समय तक फ्लाइट अटेंडेंट थीं।

हां, आपकी जानकारी के लिए बता दूं, इनके पिता हाई प्रोफाइल व्यक्ति हैं। लेकीन कभी भी इनकी वास्तविक पहचान इन्होंने खुद भी उजागर नही की, चुपचाप अपनी नौकरी पूरी दक्षता से करती रहीं।

दो महीने पहले जब एयर इंडिया का स्वामित्व 'टाटा' को मिला और इनके प्रोफाइल की जानकारी टाटा मैनेजमेंट को हुई, तब इनकी सुरक्षा को ध्यान में रखते हुये चुपचाप इनका ट्रांसफर इंटरनल अफेयर ऑफिस एयर इंडिया में कर दिया गया।

इनका पूरा नाम जानकर आप चौंक जायेंगे, जी हां.... इनका पूरा नाम स्वाति कोविन्द है। वर्तमान राष्ट्रपति महामहिम रामनाथ कोविन्द जी की पुत्री ... स्वाती कोविन्द।
साभार

Fig. 7.1 An image related to Swati Kovind, daughter of President Ram Nath Kovind, has been circulated over social media by claiming that *"after Tata Sons found out about Swati, the company transferred her to the Internal Affairs Office of the airline."* Later, it has been proved that Swati Kovind is not in the viral image

language instances forms the target. The related background information, extracted from different Web sites corresponding to each target, is considered as a source.

7.6.1.1   Data Collection

The developed dataset includes multimedia news spread across the country and mostly focused on politics, other social activities, COVID-19, health, and religion domains. The target instances of the *MMM* dataset are collected using the following steps:

Fake Sample Collection The FactDRIL dataset (Singhal et al. 2021) is considered to prepare fake samples in the developed dataset. FactDRIL is a multilingual multimodal disinformation repository that has been gathered from Indian fact-checking Web sites such as *althindi, boomlive, newschecker, etc.*. In addition to English, the repository contains 13 low-resource Indian languages with instances of claims and their investigations. To generate the new dataset, only multimodal occurrences from the languages *Hindi, Bengali*, and *Tamil* are considered. These occurrences are combined to create a set of target samples that include the false claim and picture URL pair. Each and every sample is given a fake label.

Real Sample Collection The real data instances are collected from two trusted news Web sites: *Abplive* and *News18*. All the pages having general-domain national news are crawled, and all the news article URLs are scraped using the beautifulsoup[2] library of Python. Only Hindi instances are collected from the Abplive Web site. Bengali, Hindi, and Tamil samples are collected from the News18 website. At last, a real label is assigned to each sample. The background information for each multimodal sample of the target sample set is collected in the following steps:

Source Information Extraction Multiple image URLs may be present in the target instance. Multilingual knowledge distillation (MKD) (Reimers and Gurevych 2020) and the OpenAI CLIP Model (Radford et al. 2021) are used to identify the most pertinent image among all the target images. As a result, only one picture URL is kept for every target instance. Next, a Google reverse image search is performed for every target picture URL to obtain the source data, and the URLs of all the sources that include information about the target image are retrieved either in text or image form. Now, a get request is sent to all URLs of the sources, and the text and images present on that particular source are extracted. The target instances for which source information is not available are removed. All the source-target pairs without images are also removed to ensure the complete multimodality of the data. When a source text is written in a language other than the target language, the Googletrans Python Library[3] is used to translate it into the target language. To obtain authentic background information, the source itself needs to be very reliable. Therefore, the next step is to assess the reliability of the source.

Trustworthy Source Selection It is possible for a small section of the news story to have incorrect information rather than the full article having to contain false content. It is presumed that certain Web sites consistently post accurate news. However, some Web sites consistently post misleading information. By assuming this, it is observed that the Web sites that disprove fake news provide a convenient way to access a repository of false information, whereas trusted news Web sites like News18 and Abplive mostly post real news. Although false information can occasionally be found on reliable news Web sites, it is extremely uncommon and inadvertent. To

---

[2] https://pypi.org/project/beautifulsoup4/.

[3] https://pypi.org/project/googletrans/.

gather the background information for each case, a number of Web sites have been visited. As it was said earlier, there is a chance that these Web sites also include false information. Therefore, MediaBias scores of various Web sites are used to remove the information derived from non-trusted Web sites and to consider the source material exclusively from trusted Web sites. Here, the reliability of the Web sites is assessed, and the data is obtained by looking at their MediaBias score. This MediaBias score is not used for the credibility checking of the instance. MediaBias assigns a class among the six classes, viz., very low, low, mixed, primarily factual, high, and very high. Maximum four source information are considered only from *primarily factual, high, and very high class.* The number of sources is limited to four because each target sample has, on average, four multimodal source information. Textual information is extracted from authentic Web sites, and all the images present on these websites are saved. There are up to four sources for each sample, each of which has a collection of images along with some text. The text is regarded as the source text. While cutting the background information down to four is the primary goal of this stage, several target samples are also removed because of the source's poor reliability. By doing so, the textual information from credible source Web sites is extracted, and all the images present on them are saved. In this way, all of the source data that was taken from Web sites with a poor reputation are removed.

Source Image Selection The images with dimensions smaller than 50x50 are eliminated from the list of images associated with each source in this stage, and the unimodal source information is removed once more. Since this research aims to detect fake news using non-novel images and novel text, one source image is preserved, which is roughly identical to the target image but may deviate slightly. To determine the degree of similarity between the target and source images, the VGG16 (Simonyan and Zisserman 2014) model is employed, and cosine similarity is calculated. Finally, only the most similar image is kept from every source.

7.6.1.2 Data Annotation

Since the *MMM* dataset is developed by collecting fake samples from the FactDrill repository and real samples from trusted news sources, the labels are directly assigned as fake and real, respectively. The aim of this annotation is only to keep the source information if it is related and relevant to the corresponding target sample. Otherwise, it is removed. In this way, every sample is labeled with either *yes* or *no*. All samples with *no* labels are removed, and samples with label *yes* only are included in the dataset. It is predicated based on the wording of the source and target examples. To verify the accuracy of the automatic annotation, human annotation is performed further.

Automatic Annotation Two types of annotations are considered for each source-target pair of the MMM dataset:

(i) The label of the source-target pair that is comparable to the target label is assigned in the first type of annotation. The real label is assigned to the source-target pair instance if the target data label is real, and the fake label is assigned if the target label is fake. As such, it is fully automatic and dependent only on the target data label.

(ii) For the second form of annotation, "yes" is assigned to the label if the source is relevant to the target; "no" is assigned in the other cases. The threshold value is the foundation for this annotation. Named entity recognition (NER) on both the source text (S) and the target text (T) is used in order to determine the threshold value. The threshold is determined by dividing the total number of entities in the target text by the ratio of *the number of common entities present in source and target text*. Equation 7.1 defines the threshold where R denotes the ratio or threshold. The threshold value determines the semantic similarity between the source and target texts. For this reason, it is presumed that it might have some semantic resemblance if the threshold value is higher than 0.5. In accordance with this theory, the threshold is set at 0.5. When the highest threshold value of the source is more than 0.5, the instance is assigned the label "yes." Otherwise, the instance is assigned the label "No."

$$R = \frac{|S \cap T|}{|T|} \tag{7.1}$$

Human Annotation The quality of automatic data annotation is assessed by manually annotating 500 instances of each of the languages: Tamil, Bengali, and Hindi. These 500 examples are selected randomly from real and fake classes in equal proportion for each language. Each instance includes an ID, target-image-URL, target-text, source-URL, source-text, source-image-URL, and source reliability. The selected instances of Bengali and Hindi are provided to native Bengali and Hindi speakers who are proficient in speaking, reading, and writing. Initially, 500 Tamil sentences were translated into English due to the unavailability of native Tamil speakers. Three English speakers were then given these translated instances for annotation. The following tasks are expected of each of the three annotators: (i) Open the image in the browser by searching for the target image's URL. (ii) Study the source text and locate. (a) The source text describes the target image or has a connection to it. (b) The source text provides any prior knowledge about the target image. Label the item "yes" if any of the aforementioned points ((a) and (b)) are true; otherwise, label the item "no."

The Cohen's Kappa coefficient (Cohen 1960) is used to compute the agreement score between the automatic and all three human annotations for the 500 instances of each language. It results in 89.5%, 91.27%, and 86.3% agreement on Bengali, Hindi, and Tamil languages, respectively. It indicates that the automatic data annotation quality is high.

Table 7.1 Statistics and distribution of *MMM* dataset

Dataset	Hindi	Bengali	Tamil	**MMM**
Total	7163	1543	1767	10473
Real	3563	1005	1065	5633
Fake	3600	538	702	4840

7.6.1.3   Data Statistics

The *MMM* dataset is the collection of data samples from Bengali, Hindi, and Tamil languages. The developed corpus contains 10,473 samples, including 4840 fake and 5,630 real samples. To build the train and test sets, the data is split in an 80:20 ratio. Table 7.1 shows the data statistics along with the distribution of the MMM dataset.

7.6.2   Proposed Model

This section presents a brief description of the proposed framework. Figure 7.2 shows the overall model. It consists of three modules: *Image emotion prediction, novelty detection, and misinformation detection*. All these three modules are discussed below in detail.

7.6.2.1   Novelty Detection

Supervised contrastive learning (SCL) is used in the novelty detection challenge to extract novelty-aware multimodal feature representations from target and source multimodal news pairings and identify high-level semantic interaction within them. The multimodal source and target are given to the model as input, as will be covered in more detail below. A pre-trained MultilingualBERT model (Devlin et al. 2018) is used to encode the text data, which extracts the 768-dimensional textual feature representations. The visual data is encoded using ResNet18 (He et al. 2016). Afterward, the multimodal feature representations are obtained by concatenating the textual and visual data. To project the encoded source and target representations in a 128-dimensional latent space, two fully connected layers are employed over them. Further, contrastive learning is used to train the model. While using contrastive learning, the target representation attracts the source representation if both are of the same class and, in other cases, both repeals each other. To train the novelty model, the contrastive loss function is optimized similarly to a study presented in Khosla et al. (2020). Equation 7.2 shows the mathematical definition of the loss function. Here, P is the set of positive samples (samples of the same class of anchor), I is the set of indices of the target (anchor), and τ is a scalar parameter.

$$L_{SCL} = \sum_{i \in I} \frac{-1}{|P(i)|} \sum_{p \in P(i)} \log \frac{exp(\frac{z_i \cdot z_p}{\tau})}{\sum_{a \in A(i)} exp(\frac{z_i \cdot z_p}{\tau})} \tag{7.2}$$

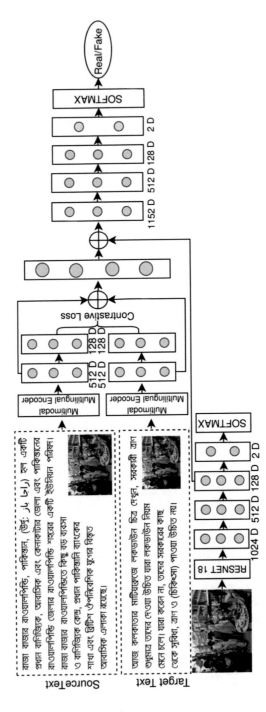

Fig. 7.2 Proposed multilingual multimodal misinformation detection model

7.6.2.2   Image Emotion Prediction

False information spreads inevitably due to the emotional attraction of news material. While textual emotions have been studied in a number of earlier publications
on misinformation detection, visual emotions have not received as much attention.
Visual emotion is far more effective than textual emotion in persuading people to
trust misleading information in the age of multimedia information. Inspired by this,
an emotion-aware visual feature representation is extracted by building a neural
network-based model. The combined form of ArtPhoto (Machajdik and Hanbury
2010) and UnbiasedEmo (Panda et al. 2018) datasets are used for pre-training
this model. The instances of the combined dataset are assigned with one of the
six emotion labels, viz., joy, love, sadness, fear, surprise, and anger. According
to a study by MIT researchers, responses to false rumors typically exhibit more
shock, anxiety, and disgust. The true stories, on the other hand, arouse stronger
feelings of anticipation, sadness, joy, and trust. Influenced by this, surprise, fear,
and disgust are categorized into one category, and sadness, anticipation, joy, and
trust are categorized into another group. These emotions can be categorized based
on the news features that reduce the decision-making distance. Furthermore, there
is a significant imbalance in the dataset, which is used to predict visual emotions.
This is another important factor in the decision to classify the emotion instances
into binary groups. In line with (Kumari et al. 2021), two emotion labels are used
for all the experiments: *emotion false*, which is created by combining the labels for
fear, surprise, and anger, and *emotion true*, which is created by combining the labels
for joy, love, and sadness. Given a set of n images I = (I1, .., In) and their emotion
labels EL = (EL1, .., ELn), each image ELi is encoded using ResNet18 to the model.
Later, this encoded image representation is passed through a multilayer perceptron
(MLP) network that consists of two hidden layers with 1024 and 512 neurons and
one output layer with two neurons and a softmax classifier function. Because each
emotion class has an uneven number of instances, the weighted cross-entropy loss
is optimized during training. After training this emotion model, the emotion labels
of images present in the developed dataset are predicted.

7.6.2.3   Misinformation Detection

After pre-training the novelty model, 512-dimensional feature representations are
extracted for the source (N_{SR}) and target (N_{TR}). Later, both features are concatenated using Eq. 7.3 to obtain a multimodal representation (N_{MR}).

$$a = N_{TR} + N_{SR};$$
$$b = N_{TR} - N_{SR};$$
$$c = N_{TR} * N_{SR}; \tag{7.3}$$
$$N_{MR} = Concat(a, |b|, c)$$

The misinformation detection model is developed by projecting this fused representation into 512-dimensional feature space and using it as a novelty-aware multimodal feature representation. Additionally, pre-trained image emotion models are used to extract 512-dimensional emotion-aware visual feature representations. Finally, emotion-aware representations are combined with novelty.

The obtained emotion-aware visual representation and novelty-aware multimodal representation are concatenated and passed to MLP, containing two hidden layers and an output layer with a softmax function to classify the news as fake or real. The cross-entropy loss is optimized to train the misinformation detection model.

7.6.3   Experiments and Results

This section includes case studies, error analysis, findings, baseline, and experimental setup.

7.6.3.1   Experimental Setup

All the experiments are performed with an NVIDIA GeForce RTX GPU and 11GB of RAM using the Pytorch library. The baseline models are trained for 100 epochs using the Adam optimizer with batch size 128. The contrastive learning framework is pre-trained for 1,000 epochs using the LARS optimizer for Stochastic Gradient Descent (SGD) with 512 batch size, which takes about 10 minutes. The emotion model is pre-trained for 10 minutes using the Adam optimizer with 128 batches and 100 epochs. Finally, the final proposed model is trained for 100 epochs with a batch size of 128 and Adam optimizer in roughly 15 minutes.

7.6.4   Baselines and Comparing Systems

To verify the effectiveness of the proposed approach, a few baseline models are implemented. Table 7.3 displays the results of the baseline and the proposed models. In addition to this, some cutting-edge methods, such as MLBViT and EANN are also implemented for the comparison, feeding the target image and text into a multimodal feature extractor and substituting MultilingualBert for Text-CNN. The results of these comparative systems are displayed in Table 7.2.

MLBERT+ResNet   This model encodes visual and textual content of target using pre-trained ResNet18 (He et al. 2016) and pre-trained MultilingualBERT (Devlin et al. 2018), respectively. The textual and visual representations are concatenated to obtain multimodal representations. This target multimodal representation is passed

Table 7.2 Comparative analysis of different models across different languages. Here, MVEN is the proposed model (*Multilingual + VisualEmo + Novelty*); MLBViT represents *MultiLingualBert + Vision Transformer* model

Model->		MLViT	EANN	MVEN
Hindi	FS	.723	.883	**.939**
	Acc	.735	.822	**.938**
Bengali	FS	.748	.845	**.946**
	Acc	.758	.856	**.945**
Tamil	FS	.743	.870	**.946**
	Acc	.752	.883	**.946**
MMM	FS	.775	.855	**.955**
	Acc	.780	.868	**.956**

to the MLP network, consisting of two hidden layers and one output layer with a softmax function.

MLBERT+ResNet (WBG) The textual and visual information for the source and target are encoded using the same pre-trained model discussed in the previous baseline model. The concatenated source and target multimodal representations are passed to the MLP network consisting of two hidden layers and one output layer with a softmax classifier function. This baseline also considers both source information and the target information.

Unimodal + VisualEmo This model encodes the target text information using MultilingualBERT. It computes the target image emotion using a method similar to the proposed model. The textual representation and emotion-aware visual representation are then passed to the MLP network for the final classification.

Multimodal + VisualEmo In the visualEmo model, the visual emotion is computed similarly to the previous baseline. Later, source multimodal representation and this emotion-aware visual representation are passed to MLP with Softmax classifier function for the final classification.

Multimodal + Novelty This baseline implements the proposed model without an emotion module. It applies SCL between the source and target multimodal representation to compute the novelty-aware representation. Later, only the novelty-aware multimodal representation is passed to the MLP with the Softmax classifier function.

7.6.5 Results and Discussion

Table 7.3 displays the outcomes of the proposed model as well as the baseline models. It presents the results for the Hindi, Bengali, and Tamil language datasets individually, as well as for the created *MMM* dataset. Table 7.3 illustrates that, across all datasets, the *Multilingual + ResNet (WBG)* model outperforms the *Multilingual + ResNet* model, which highlights the significance of background knowledge. The *Multimodal + VisualEmo* model outperforms the *Multilingual + ResNet* model in terms of results. Furthermore, there is a performance difference between the

Table 7.3 This table shows the results of the proposed and the ablation studies models. Here, *Multimodal + VisualEmo + Novelty* represents the proposed model, and F1, ACC, MA, and WA represent F1 score, accuracy, macro-average, and weighted average, respectively

Model	Dataset	Fake F1	Real F1	Acc	WA	Model	Dataset	Fake F1	Real F1	Acc	WA
MLBERT + ResNet	Hindi	0.668	0.722	0.697	0.695	MLBERT + ResNet(WBG)	Hindi	0.876	0.889	0.876	0.883
	Bengali	0.627	0.813	0.751	0.734		Bengali	0.866	0.879	0.867	0.873
	Tamil	0.666	0.812	0.759	0.750		Tamil	0.872	0.885	0.873	0.880
	MMM	0.703	0.765	0.737	0.737		MMM	0.886	0.901	0.886	0.895
Unimodal + VisualEmo	Hindi	0.813	0.837	0.819	0.826	Multimodal + VisualEmo	Hindi	0.861	0.874	0.860	0.868
	Bengali	0.791	0.817	0.799	0.805		Bengali	0.840	0.859	0.848	0.851
	Tamil	0.801	0.826	0.807	0.841		Tamil	0.846	0.836	0.833	0.846
	MMM	0.808	0.851	0.834	0.830		MMM	0.857	0.858	0.857	0.857
Multimodal + Novelty	Hindi	0.919	0.928	0.914	0.925	Multimodal + VisualEmo + Novelty	Hindi	0.934	0.942	0.938	0.939
	Bengali	0.900	0.917	0.904	0.910		Bengali	0.939	0.950	0.945	0.946
	Tamil	0.902	0.911	0.899	0.905		Tamil	0.940	0.951	0.946	0.946
	MMM	0.907	0.926	0.910	0.920		MMM	**0.949**	**0.960**	**0.956**	**0.955**

Multimodal + VisualEmo and *Unimodal + VisualEmo* models. Based on the aforementioned three elements, it can be concluded that multimodality, emotion, and prior knowledge all contribute to the prediction of fake news. *Multimodal + Novelty* model gives a 2.46 accuracy gain over the background knowledge framework. Thus, it can be proved that the contrastive learning methodology helps detect false information. Compared to the *Multilingual + ResNet* baseline model, the final proposed model (*Multimodal + VisualEmo + Novelty*) achieves a 21.77 accuracy improvement. Hence, the final proposed architecture that utilizes novelty and emotion outperforms all of the baselines and produces the most effective results. It also obtains an 8.8 accuracy improvement over the EANN model.

7.6.5.1 Case Studies and Error Analysis

A thorough study is shown in Fig. 7.3 to demonstrate the effectiveness of the background information, novelty, emotion, and multimodality. The first example demonstrates how the model's accuracy in prediction is enhanced by concatenating background knowledge (source text) with target text. In the second example, the source text and target text describe that the location of the target image is Pakistan and Kolkata, respectively. The *Multimodal + Novelty* model, which makes use of supervised contrastive learning, can identify this location mismatch with ease. In the third case, the target image's emotion is joy, which is more likely to be related to actual news. Therefore, the suggested model that combines novelty and emotion correctly predicts it. In the last example, the model's ability to forecast accurately is aided by the visual characteristics of the source and target images along with the source and target text.

Figure 7.4 presents a few cases that are incorrectly classified by the proposed model. In the first case, Avni Chaturvedi is depicted in the target image, but it is incorrectly claimed in the target text that Urvisha Jariwala is shown. The *Multimodal + Novelty* model accurately predicts fake news because it only considers novelty and captures the mismatch between the source and target texts. However, the *Multimodal + VisualEmo + Novelty* model misleads because the emotion associated with this

Target Image	Target Text	Source Text	GTL	Model 1 Output	Model 2 Output
	वायुसेना के एक हेलीकॉप्टर ने प्रवासी मजदूरी पर फूल बरसाए, जो लॉकडाउन के कारण देश के अलग-अलग हिस्सों में फंसे हुए हैं। "बन्ते हैं एक तस्वीर हजार शब्दों से ज्यादा बोलती है। मुझे नहीं मालूम कि ये फोटो कितना सही है (किसी ने इसे फेसबुक पर पोस्ट किया था), लेकिन इस फोटो में 2020 के हर फेसबुक पोस्ट को मात दी है। एयरफोर्स के इस हेलीकॉप्टर ने एक फ्रेम में कैप्चर करने के लिए फोटोग्राफर अवॉर्ड जीतना चाहिए. इतिहास इस जंगी हेलीकॉप्टर से बनता है।"	एक भारतीय वायु सेना (IAF) के हेलीकॉप्टर ने भुवनेश्वर के कलिंगा इंस्टीट्यूट ऑफ मेडिकल साइंसेज (KIMS) अस्पताल के ऊपर फूलों की पंखुड़ियों की वर्षा की KIMS ओडिशा में कोविड -19 रोगियों का इलाज करने वाले प्रमुख अस्पतालों में से एक रहा है। IAF के हेलीकॉप्टर ने वर्षा की पंखुड़ियों को राष्ट्र की ओर से धन्यवाद के रूप में पंखुड़ियों की वर्षा की हेलीकॉप्टर ने आज सुबह 09:45 से 10:30 बजे के बीच दस्तक की पास	Fake	MLBERT + ResNet > **Real**	MLBERT + ResNet (WBG) > **Fake**
	आयुष कलनजलार माहिशासुरनपुज नक्पाट्टिन निऊ माध्युम, निश्चानी ज़ान शुधुयाढ ऊपानर नऊशा पीटिक यारा सरकारुडान निग्रम पोलन चेला। ज़ाला सरकारुडान कढ निग्म श्रीगिया। ज़ान ७ (निक्णा) ५६४८ पीटिक नया	ज़ाला वायुर राज्यानर्विट्टि ऽमाकिलान, (सिट्टु र.उ) बल एककिट श्रीधन वानिज़िक ज़ारासुर राज्यानर्विट्टि ज़नारा ज़ालनामाढ राज्यानर्विट्टि ज़ुनाना राज्यानर्विट्टि ज़नुदसुर किदु वरु वरना ज़ुइ ज़्याानीज़िक वारतकर श्राया यार। ऽभविनिथांक युग्म विभुरुप जावाज़िक ज़माना साबझ़ए।	Fake	MLBERT + ResNet (WBG) > **Real**	Multimodal + Novelty > **Fake**
	தேர்தல் பிரசாரத்தில் ஒரு பகுதியாக பெண்கள் மணிப்பூர் நடனம் ஆடியது இதைவை பார்த்த மதிய அமைமச்சர் பெயிர்புருடன் இரானி அவுருக்குடன் தேர்ந்து மணிப்பூர் நடனம் ஆடினார் இது தொடுர்பான வீடியோவை பலர்ம் பகிர்ந்து வருகின்றனர்	மணிப்பூரி இயல்பாற்குக்கு நடனமாடிய அலைமாச்சர் ஸ்மிருதி இரானி: மணிப்பிர் தேர்தல் பிரசாரத்தில் ஈ(டுபட்(டெனா மதிய பெண்களாக மற்றும் குழுத்தைகள பெம்பாட்(டித் துணை அலைமாச்சர் ஸ்மிருதி இரானி. மணிப்பூர் பெண்களுடன் இணைக்குடிமார் பாரம்பரிய நாட்(டுப்புற நடனத்தில் பங்கேற்(டிமார். மணிப்பைப்புரில் பாரம்பரிய உடைபில் வீடியோ டைனமாக பரவி வையுரவாக பரவி வருகிறது.	Real	Multimodal + Novelty > **Fake**	Multimodal + VisualEmo + Novelty > **Real**
	காஜிரங்கா நேஷனல் பார்க் இல் காண்டா மிக் மந்தி களது எண்ணிக்கை மிகப்பெரிய இதிசில் 864 வர்ஷ் கிமி இல் நிவாசம் வாரே இருக்கை இ 25-28 மார்ச் எரக் கில் காந் நவீனரான எண்ணம் இ 2,413 ஆந் பாரா கார இ 200 ஆந் ஊவடித்து இ இ ஹால் க்கா ஜனாரானா 2018 ஆந் எண்ணம் இ 2,413 இ பண்ணா இ 2,613 ஹீ நடை இ	அஸ்ஸாம் க காஜிரா நேஷனல் உத்யான் இ எக் ஸிங் வாலே காண்டௌ க்கீ ஸங்க்யா இ பிஷ்லே 4 வர்ஷ் இ 200 க்கீ வ்ருத்தி ஹுஈ ஹை இ ஹால் க்கீ ஜனகணனா இ பார்க் இ கல் 2,413 க்காண்டௌ ஹை இ 2018 க்கீ பிஷ்லீ ஜனகணனா இ பார்க் இ கல் ஹா ஹா இ ஸமான்தா ஹுஈ ஜனகணனா க அனுஸார், 903 மாதா ஸவரக்க காண்டா மில் பாயே கயே இ ஆகணவாணீ ஸவாத்தானா க ரிபோர்ட் ஹை கி பார்க் இ 146 ஏடுஷ் பீ ஹை இ	Real	Unimodal + VisualEmo > **Fake**	Multimodal + VisualEmo > **Real**

Fig. 7.3 Some misinformation examples correctly classified by model 2. Here, GTL represents ground-truth label, and Model 1 Output and Model 2 Output are the output obtained by different models shown in that particular column

Target Image	Target Text	Source Text	GTL	Model 1 Output	Model 2 Output
	फेसबुक, ट्विटर और व्हाट्सएप्प पर वायरल एक संदेश का दावा है कि पाकिस्तान के व्हालकोट में हवाई हमले करने वाले भारतीय वायुसेना की पायलट सुरत के अमलका भदन स्कूल से निकली उर्मिला जरीवाला नामक लड़की हैं। राजस्थान की भाजपा नेता रितिलेखा सोनकली यह दावा करती हुई एक सोशल मीडिया पुर्ज़र्स ने फेसबुक वाले लोगों में एक भी कई सोशल मीडिया	फ्लाइड लेफ्टिनेंट अवनी चतुर्वेदी (जन्म 27 अक्टूबर 1993) मध्य प्रदेश के रीवा जिले की एक भारतीय पायलट हैं। उन्हें अपने दो साथियों, मोहना सिंह जीतरवाल और भावना कंठ के साथ पहली महिला लड़ाकू पायलट घोषित किया गया था।[1][2] इन तीनों को जून 2016 में भारतीय वायु सेना के लड़ाकू स्क्वाड्रन में शामिल किया गया था। उन्हें औपचारिक रूप से 18 जून 2016 को तत्कालीन रक्षा मंत्री मनोहर पर्रिकर द्वारा राष्ट्र की सेवा के लिए नियुक्त किया गया था। [3]	Fake	Multimodal + Novelty > **Fake**	Multimodal + VisualEmo + Novelty > **Real**
	प्रधानमंत्री नरेंद्र मोदी ने हाल ही पश्चिम बंगाल में एक राजनीतिक रैली को संबोधित किया। सादा शिट पद्धु मामले में सीधीआई की कार्रवाई से शुरू हुए विवाद के बाद केंद्र और पश्चिम बंगाल सरकार के बीच संबंध खराब हुए हैं। कम भीड़ के कारण सभा रद्द ये तो हुला था पर भारी भीड़ के कारण PM मोदी को बंगाल रैली में अपना भाषण छोटा करना पड़ा	पीएम मोदी के अभियान की कई तस्वीरों में, वह एसी केन्द्रल के साथ दिखाई देती हैं 'नमो चाय की दुकान से लेकर नमो मिष्ठान्न फोन तक, साड़ी की दुकानों से लेकर मिठाई की दुकानों तक और काशी पर नमो-टेग, नैपकिन, प्रिंटन, केप से लेकर सन्न-बोर्ड तक। यह नमो यात्रा। 2014 के अभियान के माध्यम से हर जगह देखा जाता था।"	Fake	Multimodal + VisualEmo + Novelty > **Fake**	MLBERT + ResNet (WBG) > **Real**
	XE ক্রিকিনাথ্যে ভাইরালের উৎপঞ্চা এই ম্যাসেল্টের উৎপাদ্যানে মাধ্য প্রস্তুত, রাথা, গলা ঘুসফুস, কালি এবং গাঁথ, ছাক্কল ভদ্দি এবং বিবর্ণিত, গ্লাস্ট্রন্টোইন্টেস্টিনাল মান্সা	নগনগই উত্তরপ্রদেশ বিধানসভা নির্বাচনের আগে রাজধানী লাখনৌতে কেরানীর ভয়ঙ্কর বিস্ফোরণ ঘটেছে (মৃত্যুই নিঃশ্ব)। একসাথে আঙ্গু 80 জন নিহিত হয়েছে এবং মোল্লন হাসপাতালে পেখা গেছে। সংক্রামিত পাওয়া গেছে। মোল্লু হাসপাতালের 40 জন ক্ষী করোনা পজিটিভ পাওয়া গেছে, এবং এটি ভদ্দির বিষয় যে ভাদের সবাই উপসর্গহীন। এদামোনো পরিস্থিয় ভাদের সবাই করোনায় আক্রান্ত পাওয়া গেছে। হাসপাতালের দিক থেকে সবাই আক্রান্ত হয়েছেন। ও নিচের ভ্রুটি নিয়ে কেলাঙ্কারিইতেন থাকার নির্দেশ॥	Real	Multimodal + VisualEmo + Novelty > **Fake**	Multimodal + VisualEmo > **Real**

Fig. 7.4 Error analysis on some misclassified examples

image is joy, which is a quality of true news. In the second instance, the novelty and emotion-infused model outperforms the background knowledge (WBG) model. Based on the source text gathered, which unambiguously indicates that the original image was an old photo taken in the 2014s, the novelty emotion model has the ability to label this news as fake. Nevertheless, the background knowledge model fails to detect the mismatch between the source and target text, leading to inaccurate predictions. The *Multimodal + VisualEmo* model outperforms the proposed model in the last example. Both the source text and the target text, when it comes to novelty and emotion, provide some information on COVID-19; however, the source text includes extra information regarding the election, while the target text places greater emphasis on symptoms that could mislead the reader.

7.7 Summary

This chapter examines the value of multilingualism and how it can be used to address different NLP issues. A case study of the multilingual multimodal disinformation detection in Tamil, Bengali, and Hindi is also covered in this chapter. The same image is now frequently used to deceive readers by appearing in multiple textual contexts. In order to solve this issue, this chapter first presents a multilingual multimodal misinformation dataset. It then conducts experiments to determine the impact of multilinguality, novelty, emotion, background knowledge, and multimodality. Later in the chapter, a novel framework that outperforms the current models is introduced. It is based on novelty and emotion. Later, the chapter introduces a novel framework based on novelty and emotion, which outperforms the existing models.

Chapter 8
Book Summary

This book has briefly introduced and solved several emerging problems in the broad areas of misinformation detection. It has explored fake and misleading information, the purpose of creating misinformation, the reason behind spreading it, key elements that motivate or compel people to spread the misinformation, why and how the misinformation negatively impacts the individual and society, etc. It has discussed the implementation of various robust misinformation detection systems to answer these questions.

Although the rising interest in misinformation detection in recent years has resulted in various fake news or misinformation detection systems, the prior mechanisms do not explore novelty and emotional factors in this domain. As already revealed, novelty and affect information (emotion and sentiment) are the impelling causes for misinformation that accelerate its dissemination. This book has discussed various mechanisms for affective information and novelty-aware misinformation detection in unimodal and multimodal setups to overcome this limitation. In unimodal setup, this book has explored various mechanisms that detect misinformation having textual content. In multimodal setup, the mechanisms leverage the information from text, image, and audio-video content. The work presented in this book will help the community tackle the misinformation detection problems with high accuracy and efficiency.

The preface of the book has presented the overall background, motivation, objective, and roadmap of this book. The first chapter briefly introduced the misinformation. It started with a concise description of the history of misinformation and continued to the definition, types, modalities, and impact of it. The second chapter briefly described the recent advancements in the misinformation detection domain. This chapter mainly focused on various datasets and methods developed in recent years. In this chapter, we have also included the prior works that leveraged novelty and affective information. The first two chapters are introductory, and from the third chapter onward, this book presents the solution for tackling misinformation detection. The third chapter started with the fundamentals of novelty and emotion, which later continued with the discussion of the role and importance of leveraging the novelty and emotion information using deep learning models for misinformation detection. Chapter 4 explored the importance of multitasking and its application in various domains, including misinformation detection. It exploited novelty and affective information to better understand the textual and visual patterns by proposing a deep learning multitask framework as a case study that simultaneously performs novelty, emotion, and misinformation. It is observed that the multitask architecture outperforms all the existing and baseline approaches by correctly predicting misinformation. This book provides a comprehensive network that concurrently performs all three tasks mentioned above. This chapter also explored a misinformation dataset with novelty, emotion, and sentiment labels.

The latter part of the book introduced multimodality. It discussed how multimodality helps in solving various tasks. The fifth chapter discussed how and why multimodality is essential for misinformation detection. It also described a multimodal misinformation detection system as a case study that uses additional information in the form of images to understand the misinformation better and create more interactive and robust systems. It focused on finding the correlation between text and image content to perform better multimodal fusion. It has devised an attention-based deep learning framework as a case study that demonstrates the joint representation of textual and visual features to detect a multimedia news post as fake or real. This framework has been evaluated on the publicly available multimodal misinformation datasets comprising short text associated with an image.

The sixth chapter focused on the role of novelty and emotion in multimodal setup. It explored a novel task of a specific type of multimodal misleading news as a case study in which authentic images are used in different related contexts with irrelevant texts to mislead the readers. The detection of such types of news is difficult without any prior information. As such datasets are not readily available, the chapter first introduced the misinformation dataset with background knowledge. The existing multimodal misinformation datasets are utilized to create the new dataset. After that, a multimodal deep learning framework has been developed using *supervised contrastive learning (SCL)-based novelty detection* and *emotion prediction* tasks for misinformation detection. Various experiments have also revealed that the proposed model outperforms the existing models.

Finally, following up on the above works on single-modality and multimodality, the seventh chapter concentrates on multilingualism. People like the news in regional languages much compared to the English language. By taking advantage of this, false content creators use different regional languages to create misinformation, which impacts a large number of readers. Chapter 7 briefly discussed an investigation that shows how false multilingual content spreads more rapidly than false content in English. It first discusses the basic introduction of multilingual texts and continues with the importance, applications, challenges, and benefits of multilinguality in the NLP domain. This chapter also introduced a deep learning-based framework that leverages multilingual text content and images to identify misinformation. The evaluation of the proposed system depicts that adding multilingual text in a misinformation detection framework yields better performance than the existing approaches and makes it more convenient for the user.

The last chapter (Chap. 8) summarized the entire contents of the book. Thus, this book explored the misinformation from scratch. It introduced various misinformation detection mechanisms as a case study. It also compared the proposed case study approaches with various existing models. Thus, this book can be handy for academicians and researchers in misinformation detection.

References

Abdul-Mageed, Muhammad, and Lyle Ungar. 2017. Emonet: Fine-grained emotion detection with gated recurrent neural networks. In *Proceedings of the 55th annual meeting of the association for computational linguistics (volume 1: Long papers)*, 718–728.

Abdullah, Sharmeen M. Saleem Abdullah, Siddeeq Y. Ameen Ameen, Mohammed A.M. Sadeeq, and Subhi Zeebaree. 2021. Multimodal emotion recognition using deep learning. *Journal of Applied Science and Technology Trends* 2 (02): 52–58.

Aharoni, Roee, Melvin Johnson, and Orhan Firat. 2019. Massively multilingual neural machine translation. In *Proceedings of the 2019 Conference of the North American Chapter of the Association for Computational Linguistics: Human Language Technologies, Volume 1 (Long and Short Papers)*, 3874–3884.

Ahuja, Nishta, and Shailender Kumar. 2023. Mul-fad: attention based detection of multilingual fake news. *Journal of Ambient Intelligence and Humanized Computing* 14: 1–11.

Ajao, Oluwaseun, Deepayan Bhowmik, and Shahrzad Zargari. 2019. Sentiment aware fake news detection on online social networks. In *ICASSP 2019-2019 IEEE International Conference on Acoustics, Speech and Signal Processing (ICASSP)*, 2507–2511. IEEE.

Akhtar, Md. Shad, Dushyant Singh Chauhan, Deepanway Ghosal, Soujanya Poria, Asif Ekbal, and Pushpak Bhattacharyya. 2019. Multi-task learning for multi-modal emotion recognition and sentiment analysis. In *NAACL-HLT (1)*.

Alm, Cecilia Ovesdotter, Dan Roth, and Richard Sproat. 2005. Emotions from text: Machine learning for text-based emotion prediction. In *Proceedings of Human Language Technology Conference and Conference on Empirical Methods in Natural Language Processing*, 579–586.

Aman, Saima, and Stan Szpakowicz. 2007. Identifying expressions of emotion in text. In *International Conference on Text, Speech and Dialogue*, 196–205. Springer.

Ameur, Mohamed Seghir Hadj, and Hassina Aliane. 2021. Aracovid19-mfh: Arabic COVID-19 multi-label fake news & hate speech detection dataset. *Procedia Computer Science* 189: 232–241.

Amplayo, Reinald Kim, SuLyn Hong, and Min Song. 2018. Network-based approach to detect novelty of scholarly literature. *Information Sciences* 422: 542–557.

An, Xiangdong, Jimmy Xiangji Huang, and Yuqi Wang. 2020. Diversity and novelty in biomedical information retrieval. In *Biomedical Information Technology*, 369–396. Amsterdam: Elsevier.

Anastasiou, Dimitra, Anders Ruge, Radu Ion, Svetlana Segărceanu, George Suciu, Olivier Pedretti, Patrick Gratz, and Hoorieh Afkari. 2022. A machine translation-powered chatbot for public administration. In *Proceedings of the 23rd Annual Conference of the European Association for Machine Translation*, 329–330.

Angioni, Manuela, and Franco Tuveri. 2019. Discovering emotions through the building of a linguistic resource. In *WEBIST*, 351–357.

Antol, Stanislaw, Aishwarya Agrawal, Jiasen Lu, Margaret Mitchell, Dhruv Batra, C. Lawrence Zitnick, and Devi Parikh. 2015. VQA: Visual question answering. In *Proceedings of the IEEE International Conference on Computer Vision*, 2425–2433.

Arthur, David, and Sergei Vassilvitskii. 2006. k-means++: The advantages of careful seeding. Technical Report, Stanford.

Attardi, Giuseppe, and Valeriya Slovikovskaya. 2020. Transfer learning from transformers to fake news challenge stance detection (FNC-1) task. In *Language Resources and Evaluation*. Paris: ELRA.

Badlani, Sagar, Tanvi Aditya, Meet Dave, and Sheetal Chaudhari. 2021. Multilingual healthcare chatbot using machine learning. In *2021 2nd International Conference for Emerging Technology (INCET)*, 1–6. IEEE.

Bappy, Jawadul, Tajuddin Manhar Mohammed, Lakshmanan Nataraj, Arjuna Flenner, Shivkumar Chandrasekaran, Amit Roy-Chowdhury, Jason HBSK Lawrence Peterson, et al. 2017. Detection and localization of image forgeries using resampling features and deep learning. In *Proceedings of the IEEE Conference on Computer Vision and Pattern Recognition Workshops*, 69–77.

Barr, Rachel Anne. 2019. Fake news grabs our attention, produces false memories and appeals to our emotions. https://theconversation.com/fake-news-grabs-our-attention-produces-false-memories-and-appeals-to-our-emotions-124842, November 2019. Accessed 09 Sep 2020.

Becker, Karin, Viviane P. Moreira, and Aline G.L. dos Santos. 2017. Multilingual emotion classification using supervised learning: Comparative experiments. *Information Processing & Management* 53 (3): 684–704.

Ben Abacha, Asma, Sadid A. Hasan, Vivek V. Datla, Dina Demner-Fushman, and Henning Müller. 2019. VQA-med: Overview of the medical visual question answering task at imageclef 2019. In *Proceedings of CLEF (Conference and Labs of the Evaluation Forum) 2019 Working Notes*. 9–12 September 2019.

Bender, Emily M. 2011. On achieving and evaluating language-independence in NLP. *Linguistic Issues in Language Technology* 6 (3).

Bhagat, Dhritesh, Aritra Ray, Adarsh Sarda, Nilanjana Dutta Roy, Mufti Mahmud, and Debashis De. 2023. Improving mental health through multimodal emotion detection from speech and text data using long-short term memory. In *Frontiers of ICT in Healthcare: Proceedings of EAIT 2022*, 13–23. Springer.

Bhutani, Bhavika, Neha Rastogi, Priyanshu Sehgal, and Archana Purwar. 2019. Fake news detection using sentiment analysis. In *2019 Twelfth International Conference on Contemporary Computing (IC3)*, 1–5. IEEE.

Boididou, Christina, Katerina Andreadou, Symeon Papadopoulos, Duc-Tien Dang-Nguyen, Giulia Boato, Michael Riegler, Yiannis Kompatsiaris, et al. 2015. Verifying multimedia use at mediaeval 2015. *MediaEval* 3 (3): 7.

Bottou, Léon. 2012. Stochastic gradient descent tricks. In *Neural networks: Tricks of the trade*, 421–436. Berlin: Springer.

Bradley, Andrew P. 1997. The use of the area under the roc curve in the evaluation of machine learning algorithms. *Pattern Recognition* 30 (7): 1145–1159.

Breja, Manvi. 2015. A novel approach for novelty detection of web documents. *International Journal of Computer Science and Information Technologies* 6: 4257–4262.

Bro, Rasmus, and Age K. Smilde. 2014. Principal component analysis. *Analytical Methods* 6 (9): 2812–2831.

Buechel, Sven, and Udo Hahn. 2017. Emobank: Studying the impact of annotation perspective and representation format on dimensional emotion analysis. In *Proceedings of the 15th Conference of the European Chapter of the Association for Computational Linguistics: Volume 2, Short Papers*, 578–585.

Câmara, António, Nina Taneja, Tamjeed Azad, Emily Allaway, and Richard Zemel. 2022. Mapping the multilingual margins: Intersectional biases of sentiment analysis systems in English, Spanish, and Arabic. In *Proceedings of the Second Workshop on Language Technology for Equality, Diversity and Inclusion*, 90–106.

Caruana, Rich. 1997. Multitask learning. *Machine Learning* 28: 41–75.

Castelo, Sonia, Thais Almeida, Anas Elghafari, Aécio Santos, Kien Pham, Eduardo Nakamura, and Juliana Freire. 2019. A topic-agnostic approach for identifying fake news pages. In *Companion Proceedings of The 2019 World Wide Web Conference*, 975–980.

Castillo, Carlos, Marcelo Mendoza, and Barbara Poblete. 2011. Information credibility on twitter. In *Proceedings of the 20th International Conference on World Wide Web*, 675–684. ACM.

Chaudhry, Ali K., Darren Baker, and Philipp Thun-Hohenstein. 2017. Stance detection for the fake news challenge: identifying textual relationships with deep neural nets. *CS224n: Natural Language Processing with Deep Learning*.

Chauhan, Dushyant Singh, Md. Shad Akhtar, Asif Ekbal, and Pushpak Bhattacharyya. 2019a. Context-aware interactive attention for multi-modal sentiment and emotion analysis. In *Proceedings of the 2019 Conference on Empirical Methods in Natural Language Processing and the 9th International Joint Conference on Natural Language Processing, EMNLP-IJCNLP 2019, Hong Kong, China, November 3–7, 2019*, 5646–5656.

Chauhan, Dushyant Singh, Md. Shad Akhtar, Asif Ekbal, and Pushpak Bhattacharyya. 2019b. Context-aware interactive attention for multi-modal sentiment and emotion analysis. In *Proceedings of the 2019 Conference on Empirical Methods in Natural Language Processing and the 9th International Joint Conference on Natural Language Processing (EMNLP-IJCNLP)*, 5647–5657.

Chauhan, Hardik, Mauajama Firdaus, Asif Ekbal, and Pushpak Bhattacharyya. 2019c. Ordinal and attribute aware response generation in a multimodal dialogue system. In *Proceedings of the 57th Annual Meeting of the Association for Computational Linguistics*, 5437–5447.

Chauhan, Dushyant Singh, S.R. Dhanush, Asif Ekbal, and Pushpak Bhattacharyya. 2020. Sentiment and emotion help sarcasm? A multi-task learning framework for multi-modal sarcasm, sentiment and emotion analysis. In *Proceedings of the 58th Annual Meeting of the Association for Computational Linguistics*, 4351–4360.

Chen, Qian, Xiaodan Zhu, Zhen-Hua Ling, Diana Inkpen, and Si Wei. 2018. Neural natural language inference models enhanced with external knowledge. In *Proceedings of the 56th Annual Meeting of the Association for Computational Linguistics (Volume 1: Long Papers)*, 2406–2417.

Chen, Mingxuan, Xinqiao Chu, and KP Subbalakshmi. 2021. MMCoVAR: Multimodal COVID-19 vaccine focused data repository for fake news detection and a baseline architecture for classification. In *Proceedings of the 2021 IEEE/ACM International Conference on Advances in Social Networks Analysis and Mining*, 31–38.

Chi, Haixiao, and Beishui Liao. 2022. A quantitative argumentation-based automated explainable decision system for fake news detection on social media. *Knowledge-Based Systems* 242: 108378.

Chiang, David, and Min Zhang. 2021. Proceedings of the 59th annual meeting of the association for computational linguistics and the 11th international joint conference on natural language processing: Tutorial abstracts. In *Proceedings of the 59th Annual Meeting of the Association for Computational Linguistics and the 11th International Joint Conference on Natural Language Processing: Tutorial Abstracts*.

Choi, Hyewon, and Youngjoong Ko. 2021. Using topic modeling and adversarial neural networks for fake news video detection. In *Proceedings of the 30th ACM International Conference on Information & Knowledge Management*, 2950–2954.

Choi, Hyewon, and Youngjoong Ko. 2022. Effective fake news video detection using domain knowledge and multimodal data fusion on YouTube. *Pattern Recognition Letters* 154: 44–52.

Cohen, Jacob. 1960. A coefficient of agreement for nominal scales. *Educational and Psychological Measurement* 20 (1): 37–46.

Crawshaw, Michael. 2020. Multi-task learning with deep neural networks: A survey. *CoRR* abs/2009.09796. https://arxiv.org/abs/2009.09796

Cruz, Jan Christian Blaise, Julianne Agatha Tan, and Charibeth Cheng. 2020. Localization of fake news detection via multitask transfer learning. In ed. Nicoletta Calzolari, Frédéric Béchet, Philippe Blache, Khalid Choukri, Christopher Cieri, Thierry Declerck, Sara Goggi, Hitoshi Isahara, Bente Maegaard, Joseph Mariani, Hélène Mazo, Asunción Moreno, Jan Odijk, and Stelios Piperidis, *Proceedings of The 12th Language Resources and Evaluation Conference, LREC 2020, Marseille, France, May 11–16, 2020*, 2596–2604. European Language Resources Association. https://aclanthology.org/2020.lrec-1.316/

Cuan-Baltazar, Jose Yunam, Maria José Muñoz-Perez, Carolina Robledo-Vega, Maria Fernanda Pérez-Zepeda, and Elena Soto-Vega. 2020. Misinformation of COVID-19 on the internet: infodemiology study. *JMIR Public Health and Surveillance* 6 (2): e18444.

Curtis, Drew A. 2021. Deception detection and emotion recognition: Investigating face software. *Psychotherapy Research* 31 (6): 802–816.

Dai, Sin. 2013. The origin and development of multimodal discourse analysis. *Foreign Language Research* 2: 17–23.

Dalgleish, Tim, and Mick Power. 2000. *Handbook of cognition and emotion*. Hoboken: Wiley.

Darwin, Charles, and Phillip Prodger. 1998. *The expression of the emotions in man and animals.* Oxford: Oxford University Press.

Das, Ringki, and Thoudam Doren Singh. 2023. Multimodal sentiment analysis: A survey of methods, trends and challenges. *ACM Computing Surveys* 55 (13s): 1–38.

Das, Sudhansu Bala, Divyajyoti Panda, Tapas Kumar Mishra, Bidyut Kr Patra, and Asif Ekbal. 2023. Multilingual neural machine translation system for Indic to Indic languages. *arXiv preprint arXiv:2306.12693.*

Demszky, Dorottya, Dana Movshovitz-Attias, Jeongwoo Ko, Alan Cowen, Gaurav Nemade, and Sujith Ravi. 2020. Goemotions: A dataset of fine-grained emotions. In *Proceedings of the 58th Annual Meeting of the Association for Computational Linguistics*, 4040–4054.

Deng, Jia, Wei Dong, Richard Socher, Li-Jia Li, Kai Li, and Li Fei-Fei. 2009. ImageNet: A large-scale hierarchical image database. In *2009 IEEE Conference on Computer Vision and Pattern Recognition*, 248–255. IEEE.

Devlin, Jacob, Ming-Wei Chang, Kenton Lee, and Kristina Toutanova. 2018. BERT: Pre-training of deep bidirectional transformers for language understanding. *CoRR* abs/1810.04805. http://arxiv.org/abs/1810.04805

Devlin, Jacob, Ming-Wei Chang, Kenton Lee, and Kristina Toutanova. 2019. Bert: Pre-training of deep bidirectional transformers for language understanding. In *NAACL-HLT (1)*.

Dhawan, Mudit, Shakshi Sharma, Aditya Kadam, Rajesh Sharma, and Ponnurangam Kumaraguru. 2022. Game-on: Graph attention network based multimodal fusion for fake news detection. *arXiv preprint arXiv:2202.12478.*

Ekman, Paul. 2006. *Darwin and facial expression: A century of research in review.* Singapore: Ishk.

Etzioni, Oren, Michele Banko, Stephen Soderland, and Daniel S. Weld. 2008. Open information extraction from the web. *Communications of the ACM* 51 (12): 68–74.

Faustini, Pedro Henrique Arruda, and Thiago Ferreira Covoes. 2020. Fake news detection in multiple platforms and languages. *Expert Systems with Applications* 158: 113503.

Firdaus, Mauajama, Hardik Chauhan, Asif Ekbal, and Pushpak Bhattacharyya. 2020. MEISD: A multimodal multi-label emotion, intensity and sentiment dialogue dataset for emotion recognition and sentiment analysis in conversations. In *Proceedings of the 28th International Conference on Computational Linguistics*, 4441–4453.

Fukui, Akira, Dong Huk Park, Daylen Yang, Anna Rohrbach, Trevor Darrell, and Marcus Rohrbach. 2016. Multimodal compact bilinear pooling for visual question answering and visual grounding. In *Conference on Empirical Methods in Natural Language Processing*, 457–468. ACL.

Gangathimmappa, Mahesh, Neelakandan Subramani, Velmurugan Sambath, Rengaraj Alias Muralidharan Ramanujam, Naresh Sammeta, and Maheswari Marimuthu. 2023.

Deep learning enabled cross-lingual search with metaheuristic web based query optimization model for multi-document summarization. *Concurrency and Computation: Practice and Experience* 35 (2): e7476.

Gao, Tianyu, Xingcheng Yao, and Danqi Chen. 2021. SimCSE: Simple contrastive learning of sentence embeddings. In *Proceedings of the 2021 Conference on Empirical Methods in Natural Language Processing*, 6894–6910.

Garcia-Garcia, Jose Maria, Maria Dolores Lozano, Victor MR Penichet, and Effie Lai-Chong Law. 2023. Building a three-level multimodal emotion recognition framework. *Multimedia Tools and Applications* 82 (1): 239–269.

Ghadiri, Zahra, Milad Ranjbar, Fakhteh Ghanbarnejad, and Sadegh Raeisi. 2022. Automated fake news detection using cross-checking with reliable sources. *CoRR* abs/2201.00083. https://arxiv.org/abs/2201.00083

Ghanem, Bilal, Paolo Rosso, and Francisco Rangel. 2020. An emotional analysis of false information in social media and news articles. *ACM Transactions on Internet Technology (TOIT)* 20 (2): 1–18.

Ghanem, Bilal, Simone Paolo Ponzetto, Paolo Rosso, and Francisco Rangel. 2021. FakeFlow: Fake news detection by modeling the flow of affective information. In *Proceedings of the 16th Conference of the European Chapter of the Association for Computational Linguistics: Main Volume*, 679–689.

Ghazi, Diman, Diana Inkpen, and Stan Szpakowicz. 2015. Detecting emotion stimuli in emotion-bearing sentences. In *International Conference on Intelligent Text Processing and Computational Linguistics*, 152–165. Springer.

Ghorbanali, Alireza, Mohammad Karim Sohrabi, and Farzin Yaghmaee. 2022. Ensemble transfer learning-based multimodal sentiment analysis using weighted convolutional neural networks. *Information Processing & Management* 59 (3): 102929.

Ghosal, Deepanway, Md. Shad Akhtar, Dushyant Chauhan, Soujanya Poria, Asif Ekbal, and Pushpak Bhattacharyya. 2018a. Contextual inter-modal attention for multi-modal sentiment analysis. In *Proceedings of the 2018 Conference on Empirical Methods in Natural Language Processing*, 3454–3466.

Ghosal, Deepanway, Md. Shad Akhtar, Dushyant Singh Chauhan, Soujanya Poria, Asif Ekbal, and Pushpak Bhattacharyya. 2018b. Contextual inter-modal attention for multi-modal sentiment analysis. In *Proceedings of the 2018 Conference on Empirical Methods in Natural Language Processing, Brussels, Belgium, October 31–November 4, 2018*, 3454–3466.

Ghosal, Tirthankar, Vignesh Edithal, Asif Ekbal, Pushpak Bhattacharyya, Srinivasa Chivukula, and George Tsatsaronis. 2020. Is your document novel? Let attention guide you. an attention-based model for document-level novelty detection. *Natural Language Engineering* 1–28. https://doi.org/10.1017/S1351324920000194

Ghosal, Tirthankar, Tanik Saikh, Tameesh Biswas, Asif Ekbal, and Pushpak Bhattacharyya. 2022a. Novelty detection: A perspective from natural language processing. *Computational Linguistics* 48 (1): 77–117.

Ghosh, Samujjwal, Subhadeep Maji, and Maunendra Sankar Desarkar. 2022b. Graph neural network enhanced language models for efficient multilingual text classification. *arXiv preprint arXiv:2203.02912.*

Giachanou, Anastasia, Paolo Rosso, and Fabio Crestani. 2019. Leveraging emotional signals for credibility detection. In *Proceedings of the 42nd International ACM SIGIR Conference on Research and Development in Information Retrieval*, 877–880.

Giachanou, Anastasia, Paolo Rosso, and Fabio Crestani. 2021. The impact of emotional signals on credibility assessment. *Journal of the Association for Information Science and Technology* 72: 1117–1132.

Gilda, Shlok. 2017. Evaluating machine learning algorithms for fake news detection. In *2017 IEEE 15th Student Conference on Research and Development (SCOReD)*, 110–115. IEEE.

Goel, Vikas, Amit Kr Gupta, and Narendra Kumar. 2018. Sentiment analysis of multilingual twitter data using natural language processing. In *2018 8th International Conference on Communication Systems and Network Technologies (CSNT)*, 208–212. IEEE.

Goodfellow, Ian, Jean Pouget-Abadie, Mehdi Mirza, Bing Xu, David Warde-Farley, Sherjil Ozair, Aaron Courville, and Yoshua Bengio. 2014. Generative adversarial nets. In *Advances in Neural Information Processing Systems*, 2672–2680.

Grashchenkov, Kirill, Andrey Grabovoy, and Ildar Khabutdinov. 2022. A method of multilingual summarization for scientific documents. In *2022 Ivannikov Ispras Open Conference (ISPRAS)*, 24–30. IEEE.

Gravanis, Georgios, Athena Vakali, Konstantinos Diamantaras, and Panagiotis Karadais. 2019. Behind the cues: A benchmarking study for fake news detection. *Expert Systems with Applications* 128: 201–213.

Guha, Sreya. 2017. Related fact checks: A tool for combating fake news. *arXiv preprint arXiv:1711.00715*.

Guo, Chuan, Juan Cao, Xueyao Zhang, Kai Shu, and Miao Yu. 2019. Exploiting emotions for fake news detection on social media. *CoRR* abs/1903.01728. http://arxiv.org/abs/1903.01728

Hammouchi, Hicham, and Mounir Ghogho. 2022. Evidence-aware multilingual fake news detection. *IEEE Access* 10: 116808–116818.

Hanselowski, Andreas, P.V.S. Avinesh, Benjamin Schiller, Felix Caspelherr, Debanjan Chaudhuri, Christian M. Meyer, and Iryna Gurevych. 2018. A retrospective analysis of the fake news challenge stance-detection task. In *Proceedings of the 27th International Conference on Computational Linguistics*, 1859–1874.

Haouari, Fatima, Maram Hasanain, Reem Suwaileh, and Tamer Elsayed. 2021. Arcov19-rumors: Arabic COVID-19 Twitter dataset for misinformation detection. In *Proceedings of the Sixth Arabic Natural Language Processing Workshop*, 72–81.

He, Kaiming, Xiangyu Zhang, Shaoqing Ren, and Jian Sun. 2016. Deep residual learning for image recognition. In *Proceedings of the IEEE Conference on Computer Vision and Pattern Recognition*, 770–778.

Hossain, Md. Zobaer, Md. Ashraful Rahman, Md. Saiful Islam, and Sudipta Kar. 2020. BanFake-News: A dataset for detecting fake news in bangla. In ed. Nicoletta Calzolari, Frédéric Béchet, Philippe Blache, Khalid Choukri, Christopher Cieri, Thierry Declerck, Sara Goggi, Hitoshi Isahara, Bente Maegaard, Joseph Mariani, Hélène Mazo, Asunción Moreno, Jan Odijk, and Stelios Piperidis, *Proceedings of The 12th Language Resources and Evaluation Conference, LREC 2020, Marseille, France, May 11–16, 2020*, 2862–2871. European Language Resources Association. https://aclanthology.org/2020.lrec-1.349/

Huang, Yin-Fu, and Po-Hong Chen. 2020. Fake news detection using an ensemble learning model based on self-adaptive harmony search algorithms. *Expert Systems with Applications* 159: 113584.

Huang, Shujun, Nianguang Cai, Pedro Penzuti Pacheco, Shavira Narrandes, Yang Wang, and Wayne Xu. 2018. Applications of support vector machine (SVM) learning in cancer genomics. *Cancer Genomics-Proteomics* 15 (1): 41–51.

Imran, Ali Shariq, Sher Muhammad Daudpota, Zenun Kastrati, and Rakhi Batra. 2020. Cross-cultural polarity and emotion detection using sentiment analysis and deep learning on COVID-19 related tweets. *IEEE Access* 8: 181074–181090.

Imtiaz, Zainab, Muhammad Umer, Muhammad Ahmad, Saleem Ullah, Gyu Sang Choi, and Arif Mehmood. 2020. Duplicate questions pair detection using Siamese MaLSTM. *IEEE Access* 8: 21932–21942.

Jewitt, C., and GJIAP Kress. 2003. *Multimodal literacy (new literacies and digital epistemologies) peter lang inc*. Lausanne: International Academic Publishers.

Jewitt, Carey, Jeff Bezemer, and Kay O'Halloran. 2016. *Introducing multimodality*. Milton Park: Routledge.

Jiang, Zhuolin, Amro El-Jaroudi, William Hartmann, Damianos Karakos, and Lingjun Zhao. 2020. Cross-lingual information retrieval with BERT. In *LREC 2020 Language Resources and Evaluation Conference 11–16 May 2020*, 26.

Jin, Zhiwei, Juan Cao, Yu-Gang Jiang, and Yongdong Zhang. 2014. News credibility evaluation on microblog with a hierarchical propagation model. In *2014 IEEE International Conference on Data Mining*, 230–239. IEEE.

Jin, Zhiwei, Juan Cao, Yongdong Zhang, and Jiebo Luo. 2016a. News verification by exploiting conflicting social viewpoints in microblogs. In *Proceedings of the AAAI Conference on Artificial Intelligence*, vol. 30.

Jin, Zhiwei, Juan Cao, Yongdong Zhang, Jianshe Zhou, and Qi Tian. 2016b. Novel visual and statistical image features for microblogs news verification. *IEEE Transactions on Multimedia* 19 (3): 598–608.

Jin, Zhiwei, Juan Cao, Han Guo, Yongdong Zhang, and Jiebo Luo. 2017. Multimodal fusion with recurrent neural networks for rumor detection on microblogs. In *Proceedings of the 25th ACM International Conference on Multimedia*, 795–816.

Jindal, Sarthak, Raghav Sood, Richa Singh, Mayank Vatsa, and Tanmoy Chakraborty. 2020. NewsBag: A benchmark multimodal dataset for fake news detection. In ed. Huáscar Espinoza, José Hernández-Orallo, Xin Cynthia Chen, Seán S. ÓhÉigeartaigh, Xiaowei Huang, Mauricio Castillo-Effen, Richard Mallah, and John McDermid, *Proceedings of the Workshop on Artificial Intelligence Safety, co-located with 34th AAAI Conference on Artificial Intelligence, SafeAI@AAAI 2020, New York City, NY, USA, February 7, 2020*. CEUR Workshop Proceedings, vol. 2560, 138–145. CEUR-WS.org. http://ceur-ws.org/Vol-2560/paper27.pdf

Jose, Saucedo-Dorantes Juan, Jaen-Cuellar Arturo Yosimar, and Elvira-Ortiz David Alejandro. 2020. Smart monitoring based on novelty detection and artificial intelligence applied to the condition assessment of rotating machinery in the industry 4.0. In *New Trends in the Use of Artificial Intelligence for the Industry 4.0*. IntechOpen.

Kaelbling, Leslie Pack, Michael L. Littman, and Andrew W. Moore. 1996. Reinforcement learning: A survey. *Journal of Artificial Intelligence Research* 4: 237–285.

Kafle, Kushal, and Christopher Kanan. 2017. Visual question answering: Datasets, algorithms, and future challenges. *Computer Vision and Image Understanding* 163: 3–20.

Kajava, Kaisla, Emily Öhman, Piao Hui, Jörg Tiedemann, et al. 2020. Emotion preservation in translation: Evaluating datasets for annotation projection. In *Proceedings of Digital Humanities in Nordic Countries (DHN 2020)*.

Karimi, Hamid, Proteek Roy, Sari Saba-Sadiya, and Jiliang Tang. 2018. Multi-source multi-class fake news detection. In *Proceedings of the 27th International Conference on Computational Linguistics*, 1546–1557.

Karpathy, Andrej, and Li Fei-Fei. 2015. Deep visual-semantic alignments for generating image descriptions. In *Proceedings of the IEEE Conference on Computer Vision and Pattern Recognition*, 3128–3137.

Kasinathan, Vinothini, Aida Mustapha, and Chow Khai Bin. 2021. A customizable multilingual chatbot system for customer support. *Annals of Emerging Technologies in Computing (AETiC)* 5 (5): 51–59.

Kenton, Jacob Devlin Ming-Wei Chang, and Lee Kristina Toutanova. 2019. Bert: Pre-training of deep bidirectional transformers for language understanding. In *Proceedings of NAACL-HLT*, 4171–4186.

Kerner, Hannah R., Danika F. Wellington, Kiri L. Wagstaff, James F. Bell, Chiman Kwan, and Heni Ben Amor. 2019. Novelty detection for multispectral images with application to planetary exploration. In *Proceedings of the AAAI Conference on Artificial Intelligence*, vol. 33, 9484–9491.

Khattar, Dhruv, Jaipal Singh Goud, Manish Gupta, and Vasudeva Varma. 2019. MVAE: Multimodal variational autoencoder for fake news detection. In *The World Wide Web Conference*, 2915–2921. ACM.

Khosla, Prannay, Piotr Teterwak, Chen Wang, Aaron Sarna, Yonglong Tian, Phillip Isola, Aaron Maschinot, Ce Liu, and Dilip Krishnan. 2020. Supervised contrastive learning. *Advances in Neural Information Processing Systems* 33: 18661–18673.

Kim, Dong-Hyun, and Hae-Yeoun Lee. 2017. Image manipulation detection using convolutional neural network. *International Journal of Applied Engineering Research* 12 (21): 11640–11646.

Kim, Jin-Hwa, Kyoung Woon On, Woosang Lim, Jeonghee Kim, JungWoo Ha, and Byoung-Tak Zhang. 2016. Hadamard product for low-rank bilinear pooling. *CoRR* abs/1610.04325. http://arxiv.org/abs/1610.04325

Kingma, Diederik P., and Jimmy Ba. 2015. Adam: A method for stochastic optimization. In ed. Yoshua Bengio and Yann LeCun, *3rd International Conference on Learning Representations, ICLR 2015, San Diego, CA, USA, May 7–9, 2015, Conference Track Proceedings.* http://arxiv. org/abs/1412.6980

Klinger, Roman, et al. 2018. An analysis of annotated corpora for emotion classification in text. In *Proceedings of the 27th International Conference on Computational Linguistics,* 2104–2119.

Kouzy, Ramez, Joseph Abi Jaoude, Afif Kraitem, Molly B. El Alam, Basil Karam, Elio Adib, Jabra Zarka, Cindy Traboulsi, Elie W. Akl, and Khalil Baddour. 2020. Coronavirus goes viral: Quantifying the COVID-19 misinformation epidemic on twitter. *Cureus* 12 (3): e7255.

Kula, Sebastian, Michał Choraś, Rafał Kozik, Paweł Ksieniewicz, and Michał Woźniak. 2020. Sentiment analysis for fake news detection by means of neural networks. In *International Conference on Computational Science,* 653–666. Springer.

Kumar, Sushil, and Komal Kumar Bhatia. 2020. Semantic similarity and text summarization based novelty detection. *SN Applied Sciences* 2 (3): 332.

Kumari, Rina, Nischal Ashok, Tirthankar Ghosal, and Asif Ekbal. 2021. Misinformation detection using multitask learning with mutual learning for novelty detection and emotion recognition. *Information Processing & Management* 58 (5): 102631.

Kumari, Rina, Nischal Ashok, Pawan Kumar Agrawal, Tirthankar Ghosal, and Asif Ekbal. 2023. Identifying multimodal misinformation leveraging novelty detection and emotion recognition. *Journal of Intelligent Information Systems* 61: 1–22.

Kwon, Sejeong, Meeyoung Cha, Kyomin Jung, Wei Chen, and Yajun Wang. 2013. Prominent features of rumor propagation in online social media. In *2013 IEEE 13th International Conference on Data Mining,* 1103–1108. IEEE.

Lakmal, Dimuthu, Surangika Ranathunga, Saman Peramuna, and Indu Herath. 2020. Word embedding evaluation for Sinhala. In *Proceedings of the 12th Language Resources and Evaluation Conference,* 1874–1881.

Lee, Sungjin. 2015. Online sentence novelty scoring for topical document streams. In *Proceedings of the 2015 Conference on Empirical Methods in Natural Language Processing,* 567–572.

Lei, Jingsheng, Yanghui Rao, Qing Li, Xiaojun Quan, and Liu Wenyin. 2014. Towards building a social emotion detection system for online news. *Future Generation Computer Systems* 37: 438–448.

Li, Yanran, Hui Su, Xiaoyu Shen, Wenjie Li, Ziqiang Cao, and Shuzi Niu. 2017. DailyDialog: A manually labelled multi-turn dialogue dataset. In *Proceedings of the Eighth International Joint Conference on Natural Language Processing (Volume 1: Long Papers),* 986–995.

Li, Guanyu, Pengfei Zhang, and Caiyan Jia. 2018. Attention boosted sequential inference model. *CoRR* abs/1812.01840. http://arxiv.org/abs/1812.01840

Li, Liunian Harold, Mark Yatskar, Da Yin, Cho-Jui Hsieh, and Kai-Wei Chang. 2019. Visualbert: A simple and performant baseline for vision and language. *CoRR* abs/1908.03557. http://arxiv. org/abs/1908.03557

Li, Yichuan, Bohan Jiang, Kai Shu, and Huan Liu. 2020a MM-COVID: A multilingual and multimodal data repository for combating COVID-19 disinformation. *CoRR* abs/2011.04088. https://arxiv.org/abs/2011.04088

Li, Yichuan, Bohan Jiang, Kai Shu, and Huan Liu. 2020b. MM-COVID: A multilingual and multimodal data repository for combating COVID-19 disinformation. *arXiv preprint arXiv:2011.04088.*

Li, Haifeng, Yi Li, Guo Zhang, Ruoyun Liu, Haozhe Huang, Qing Zhu, and Chao Tao. 2022. Global and local contrastive self-supervised learning for semantic segmentation of hr remote sensing images. *IEEE Transactions on Geoscience and Remote Sensing* 60: 1–14.

Liew, Jasy Suet Yan, and Howard R. Turtle. 2016. Exploring fine-grained emotion detection in tweets. In *Proceedings of the NAACL Student Research Workshop,* 73–80.

Liu, Shuaipeng, Shuo Liu, and Lei Ren. 2019a Trust or suspect? An empirical ensemble framework for fake news classification. In *Proceedings of the 12th ACM International Conference on Web Search and Data Mining, Melbourne, Australia,* 11–15.

Liu, Yahui, Xiaolong Jin, and Huawei Shen. 2019b. Towards early identification of online rumors based on long short-term memory networks. *Information Processing & Management* 56 (4): 1457–1467.

Lu, Yi-Ju, and Cheng-Te Li. 2020. GCAN: Graph-aware co-attention networks for explainable fake news detection on social media. In ed. Dan Jurafsky, Joyce Chai, Natalie Schluter, and Joel R. Tetreault, *Proceedings of the 58th Annual Meeting of the Association for Computational Linguistics, ACL 2020, Online, July 5–10, 2020*, 505–514. Association for Computational Linguistics. https://doi.org/10.18653/v1/2020.acl-main.48

Lugosch, Loren, Tatiana Likhomanenko, Gabriel Synnaeve, and Ronan Collobert. 2022. Pseudo-labeling for massively multilingual speech recognition. In *ICASSP 2022-2022 IEEE International Conference on Acoustics, Speech and Signal Processing (ICASSP)*, 7687–7691. IEEE.

Ma, Jing, Wei Gao, Prasenjit Mitra, Sejeong Kwon, Bernard J. Jansen, Kam-Fai Wong, and Meeyoung Cha. 2016. Detecting rumors from microblogs with recurrent neural networks. In *IJCAI*, 3818–3824.

Ma, Jing, Wei Gao, and Kam-Fai Wong. 2018. Rumor detection on twitter with tree-structured recursive neural networks. In *ACL (1)*.

Ma, Hui, Jian Wang, Hongfei Lin, Bo Zhang, Yijia Zhang, and Bo Xu. 2023. A transformer-based model with self-distillation for multimodal emotion recognition in conversations. *IEEE Transactions on Multimedia* abs/2310.20494: 1–13.

MacCartney, Bill. 2009. *Natural language inference*. Stanford: Stanford University.

Machajdik, Jana, and Allan Hanbury. 2010. Affective image classification using features inspired by psychology and art theory. In *Proceedings of the 18th ACM international conference on Multimedia*, 83–92.

Maclin, Richard, and David Opitz. 1997. An empirical evaluation of bagging and boosting. *AAAI/IAAI* 1997: 546–551.

Magdy, Amr, and Nayer Wanas. 2010. Web-based statistical fact checking of textual documents. In *Proceedings of the 2nd International Workshop on Search and Mining User-Generated Contents*, 103–110.

Mai, Sijie, Haifeng Hu, and Songlong Xing. 2019. Divide, conquer and combine: Hierarchical feature fusion network with local and global perspectives for multimodal affective computing. In *Proceedings of the 57th Annual Meeting of the Association for Computational Linguistics*, 481–492.

Maigrot, Cédric, Vincent Claveau, Ewa Kijak, and Ronan Sicre. 2016. Mediaeval 2016: A multimodal system for the verifying multimedia use task. In *MediaEval 2016: "Verifying Multimedia Use" task*.

Mamta, Asif Ekbal, and Pushpak Bhattacharyya. 2022. Exploring multi-lingual, multi-task, and adversarial learning for low-resource sentiment analysis. *Transactions on Asian and Low-Resource Language Information Processing* 21 (5): 1–19.

Manocha, Pranay, Zeyu Jin, Richard Zhang, and Adam Finkelstein. 2021. CDPAM: Contrastive learning for perceptual audio similarity. In *ICASSP 2021-2021 IEEE International Conference on Acoustics, Speech and Signal Processing (ICASSP)*, 196–200. IEEE.

Mitra, Tanushree, and Eric Gilbert. 2015. CREDBANK: A large-scale social media corpus with associated credibility annotations. In *Proceedings of the International AAAI Conference on Web and Social Media*, vol. 9, 258–267.

Mocanu, Bogdan, Ruxandra Tapu, and Titus Zaharia. 2023. Multimodal emotion recognition using cross modal audio-video fusion with attention and deep metric learning. *Image and Vision Computing* 133: 104676.

Mohammad, Saif. 2021. # emotional tweets. In ** SEM 2012: The First Joint Conference on Lexical and Computational Semantics–Volume 1: Proceedings of the Main Conference and the Shared Task, and Volume 2: Proceedings of the Sixth International Workshop on Semantic Evaluation (SemEval 2012)*, 246–255.

Mohammad, Saif M., and Felipe Bravo-Márquez. 2017. Wassa-2017 shared task on emotion intensity. In *8th Workshop on Computational Approaches to Subjectivity, Sentiment and Social Media Analysis WASSA 2017: Proceedings of the Workshop*, 34–49. The Association for Computational Linguistics.

Mohammad, Saif M., Xiaodan Zhu, Svetlana Kiritchenko, and Joel Martin. 2015. Sentiment, emotion, purpose, and style in electoral tweets. *Information Processing & Management* 51 (4): 480–499.

Mohawesh, Rami, Xiao Liu, Hilya Mudrika Arini, Yutao Wu, and Hui Yin. 2023a. Semantic graph based topic modelling framework for multilingual fake news detection. *AI Open* 4: 33–41.

Mohawesh, Rami, Sumbal Maqsood, and Qutaibah Althebyan. 2023b. Multilingual deep learning framework for fake news detection using capsule neural network. *Journal of Intelligent Information Systems* 60: 1–17.

Mosallanezhad, Ahmadreza, Mansooreh Karami, Kai Shu, Michelle V. Mancenido, and Huan Liu. 2022. Domain adaptive fake news detection via reinforcement learning. *CoRR* abs/2202.08159. https://arxiv.org/abs/2202.08159

Mutlu, Ece C., Toktam Oghaz, Jasser Jasser, Ege Tutunculer, Amirarsalan Rajabi, Aida Tayebi, Ozlem Ozmen, and Ivan Garibay. 2020. A stance data set on polarized conversations on twitter about the efficacy of hydroxychloroquine as a treatment for COVID-19. *Data in Brief* 33: 106401.

Nakamura, Kai, Sharon Levy, and William Yang Wang. 2020. Fakeddit: A new multimodal benchmark dataset for fine-grained fake news detection. In *Proceedings of the Twelfth Language Resources and Evaluation Conference*, 6149–6157.

Nasharuddin, Nurul Amelina, and Muhamad Taufik Abdullah. 2010. Cross-lingual information retrieval. *Electronic Journal of Computer Science and Information Technology* 3 (1).

Nielsen, Dan S. and Ryan McConville. 2022. Mumin: A large-scale multilingual multimodal fact-checked misinformation social network dataset. In *Proceedings of the 45th International ACM SIGIR Conference on Research and Development in Information Retrieval*, 3141–3153.

Nørregaard, Jeppe, Benjamin D Horne, and Sibel Adalı. 2019. NELA-GT-2018: A large multi-labelled news dataset for the study of misinformation in news articles. In *Proceedings of the International AAAI Conference on Web and Social Media*, vol. 13, 630–638.

Ogundepo, Odunayo, Xinyu Zhang, Shuo Sun, Kevin Duh, and Jimmy Lin. 2022. AfriCLIRMa-trix: Enabling cross-lingual information retrieval for african languages. In *Proceedings of the 2022 Conference on Empirical Methods in Natural Language Processing*, 8721–8728.

Palani, Balasubramanian, Sivasankar Elango, Vignesh Viswanathan K, et al. 2021. CB-Fake: A multimodal deep learning framework for automatic fake news detection using capsule neural network and bert. *Multimedia Tools and Applications* 81: 1–34.

Pan, Tian, Yibing Song, Tianyu Yang, Wenhao Jiang, and Wei Liu. 2021. VideoMoCo: Contrastive video representation learning with temporally adversarial examples. In *Proceedings of the IEEE/CVF Conference on Computer Vision and Pattern Recognition*, 11205–11214.

Panda, Rameswar, Jianming Zhang, Haoxiang Li, Joon-Young Lee, Xin Lu, and Amit K. Roy-Chowdhury. 2018. Contemplating visual emotions: Understanding and overcoming dataset bias. In *European Conference on Computer Vision*.

Pant, Manish, and Ankush Chopra. 2022. Multilingual financial documentation summarization by team_tredence for FNS2022. In *Proceedings of the 4th Financial Narrative Processing Workshop@ LREC2022*, 112–115.

Patwa, Parth, Shivam Sharma, Srinivas Pykl, Vineeth Guptha, Gitanjali Kumari, Md. Shad Akhtar, Asif Ekbal, Amitava Das, and Tanmoy Chakraborty. 2021. Fighting an infodemic: COVID-19 fake news dataset. In *Combating Online Hostile Posts in Regional Languages during Emergency Situation: First International Workshop, CONSTRAINT 2021, Collocated with AAAI 2021, Virtual Event, February 8, 2021, Revised Selected Papers 1*, 21–29. Springer.

Patwa, Parth, Sathyanarayanan Ramamoorthy, Nethra Gunti, Shreyash Mishra, S. Suryavardan, Aishwarya Reganti, Amitava Das, Tanmoy Chakraborty, Amit Sheth, Asif Ekbal, et al. 2022. Findings of Memotion 2: Sentiment and emotion analysis of memes. In *Proceedings of De-Factify: Workshop on Multimodal Fact Checking and Hate Speech Detection, CEUR*.

Pennycook, Gordon, and David G. Rand. 2019. Lazy, not biased: Susceptibility to partisan fake news is better explained by lack of reasoning than by motivated reasoning. *Cognition* 188: 39–50.

Pennycook, Gordon, Jonathon McPhetres, Yunhao Zhang, Jackson G. Lu, and David G. Rand. 2020. Fighting COVID-19 misinformation on social media: Experimental evidence for a scalable accuracy-nudge intervention. *Psychological Science* 31: 0956797620939054.

Pérez-Rosas, Verónica, Bennett Kleinberg, Alexandra Lefevre, and Rada Mihalcea. 2018. Automatic detection of fake news. In *Proceedings of the 27th International Conference on Computational Linguistics*, 3391–3401.

Pham, Lam. 2019. Transferring, transforming, ensembling: the novel formula of identifying fake news. In *Proceedings of the 12th ACM International Conference on Web Search and Data Mining, Melbourne, Australia*, 11–15.

Pham, Ngoc-Quan, Alex Waibel, and Jan Niehues. 2022. Adaptive multilingual speech recognition with pretrained models. *arXiv preprint arXiv:2205.12304*.

Potthast, Martin, Johannes Kiesel, Kevin Reinartz, Janek Bevendorff, and Benno Stein. 2018. A stylometric inquiry into hyperpartisan and fake news. In *Proceedings of the 56th Annual Meeting of the Association for Computational Linguistics (Volume 1: Long Papers)*, 231–240.

Preoţiuc-Pietro, Daniel, H. Andrew Schwartz, Gregory Park, Johannes Eichstaedt, Margaret Kern, Lyle Ungar, and Elisabeth Shulman. 2016. Modelling valence and arousal in Facebook posts. In *Proceedings of the 7th Workshop on Computational Approaches to Subjectivity, Sentiment and Social Media Analysis*, 9–15.

Preston, Stephanie, Anthony Anderson, David J. Robertson, Mark P. Shephard, and Narisong Huhe. 2021. Detecting fake news on Facebook: The role of emotional intelligence. *Plos one* 16 (3): e0246757.

Qi, Peng, Juan Cao, Tianyun Yang, Junbo Guo, and Jintao Li. 2019. Exploiting multi-domain visual information for fake news detection. In *2019 IEEE International Conference on Data Mining (ICDM)*, 518–527. IEEE.

Qin, Yumeng, Dominik Wurzer, Victor Lavrenko, and Cunchen Tang. 2016. Spotting rumors via novelty detection. *CoRR* abs/1611.06322. http://arxiv.org/abs/1611.06322

Radford, Alec, Jong Wook Kim, Chris Hallacy, Aditya Ramesh, Gabriel Goh, Sandhini Agarwal, Girish Sastry, Amanda Askell, Pamela Mishkin, Jack Clark, et al. 2021. Learning transferable visual models from natural language supervision. In *International Conference on Machine Learning*, 8748–8763. PMLR.

Rashkin, Hannah, Eunsol Choi, Jin Yea Jang, Svitlana Volkova, and Yejin Choi. 2017. Truth of varying shades: Analyzing language in fake news and political fact-checking. In *Proceedings of the 2017 Conference on Empirical Methods in Natural Language Processing*, 2931–2937.

Reimers, Nils, and Iryna Gurevych. 2020. Making monolingual sentence embeddings multilingual using knowledge distillation. In *Proceedings of the 2020 Conference on Empirical Methods in Natural Language Processing (EMNLP)*, 4512–4525.

Reiter, Ehud, and Robert Dale. 1997. Building applied natural language generation systems. *Natural Language Engineering* 3 (1): 57–87.

Ren, Gang, and Taeho Hong. 2019. Examining the relationship between specific negative emotions and the perceived helpfulness of online reviews. *Information Processing & Management* 56 (4): 1425–1438.

Rish, Irina et al. 2001. An empirical study of the naive bayes classifier. In *IJCAI 2001 Workshop on Empirical Methods in Artificial Intelligence*, vol. 3, 41–46.

Rohit, Wankhede, Sachin Deshmukh, and Rajkumar Jagdale. 2018. Novelty detection in BBC sports news streams. *International Journal of Scientific Research in Computer Science Applications and Management Studies* 7 (2).

Rubin, Victoria L., Yimin Chen, and Nadia K. Conroy. 2015. Deception detection for news: three types of fakes. *Proceedings of the Association for Information Science and Technology* 52 (1): 1–4.

Ruchansky, Natali, Sungyong Seo, and Yan Liu. 2017. CSI: A hybrid deep model for fake news detection. In *Proceedings of the 2017 ACM on Conference on Information and Knowledge Management*, 797–806.

Ruder, Sebastian, Ivan Vulić, and Anders Søgaard. 2022. Square one bias in NLP: Towards a multi-dimensional exploration of the research manifold. *arXiv preprint arXiv:2206.09755*.

Ruiz, Nataniel, Yuanzhen Li, Varun Jampani, Yael Pritch, Michael Rubinstein, and Kfir Aberman. 2023. DreamBooth: Fine tuning text-to-image diffusion models for subject-driven generation. In *Proceedings of the IEEE/CVF Conference on Computer Vision and Pattern Recognition*, 22500–22510.

Sachan, Tanmay, Nikhil Pinnaparaju, Manish Gupta, and Vasudeva Varma. 2021. Scate: Shared cross attention transformer encoders for multimodal fake news detection. In *Proceedings of the 2021 IEEE/ACM International Conference on Advances in Social Networks Analysis and Mining*, 399–406.

Sadeghi, Fariba, Amir Jalaly Bidgoly, and Hossein Amirkhani. 2022. Fake news detection on social media using a natural language inference approach. *Multimedia Tools and Applications* 81 (23): 33801–33821.

Saikh, Tanik, Tirthankar Ghosal, Asif Ekbal, and Pushpak Bhattacharyya. 2017. Document level novelty detection: Textual entailment lends a helping hand. In *Proceedings of the 14th International Conference on Natural Language Processing (ICON-2017)*, 131–140.

Saikh, Tanik, Arkadipta De, Asif Ekbal, and Pushpak Bhattacharyya. 2020. A deep learning approach for automatic detection of fake news. *CoRR* abs/2005.04938. https://arxiv.org/abs/2005.04938

Salem, Fatima K. Abu, Roaa Al Feel, Shady Elbassuoni, Mohamad Jaber, and May Farah. 2019. FA-KES: A fake news dataset around the Syrian war. In *Proceedings of the International AAAI Conference on Web and Social Media*, vol. 13, 573–582.

Santia, Giovanni, and Jake Williams. 2018. BuzzFace: A news veracity dataset with Facebook user commentary and egos. In *Proceedings of the International AAAI Conference on Web and Social Media*, vol. 12, 531–540.

Scherer, Klaus R., and Harald G. Wallbott. Evidence for universality and cultural variation of differential emotion response patterning. *Journal of Personality and Social Psychology* 66 (2): 310.

Schuff, Hendrik, Jeremy Barnes, Julian Mohme, Sebastian Padó, and Roman Klinger. 2017. Annotation, modelling and analysis of fine-grained emotions on a stance and sentiment detection corpus. In *Proceedings of the 8th Workshop on Computational Approaches to Subjectivity, Sentiment and Social Media Analysis*, 13–23.

Seyeditabari, Armin, Narges Tabari, Shafie Gholizadeh, and Wlodek Zadrozny. 2019. Emotion detection in text: Focusing on latent representation. *CoRR* abs/1907.09369.

Shaha, Manali, and Meenakshi Pawar. 2018. Transfer learning for image classification. In *2018 Second International Conference on Electronics, Communication and Aerospace Technology (ICECA)*, 656–660. IEEE.

Shahi, Gautam Kishore, and Durgesh Nandini. 2020. FakeCovid–a multilingual cross-domain fact check news dataset for COVID-19. *arXiv preprint arXiv:2006.11343*.

Sharma, Dilip Kumar, and Sunidhi Sharma. 2021. Comment filtering based explainable fake news detection. In *Proceedings of Second International Conference on Computing, Communications, and Cyber-Security*, 447–458. Springer.

Shrestha, Maniz. 2018. Detecting fake news with sentiment analysis and network metadata. *Earlham College, Richmond*.

Shu, Kai, Limeng Cui, Suhang Wang, Dongwon Lee, and Huan Liu. 2019a defend: Explainable fake news detection. In ed. Ankur Teredesai, Vipin Kumar, Ying Li, Rómer Rosales, Evimaria Terzi, and George Karypis, *Proceedings of the 25th ACM SIGKDD International Conference on Knowledge Discovery & Data Mining, KDD 2019, Anchorage, AK, USA, August 4–8, 2019*, 395–405. ACM. https://doi.org/10.1145/3292500.3330935

Shu, Kai, Suhang Wang, and Huan Liu. 2019b. Beyond news contents: The role of social context for fake news detection. In *12th ACM International Conference on Web Search and Data Mining, WSDM 2019*, 312–320. Association for Computing Machinery.

Shu, Kai, Deepak Mahudeswaran, Suhang Wang, Dongwon Lee, and Huan Liu. 2020. FakeNews-Net: A data repository with news content, social context, and spatiotemporal information for studying fake news on social media. *Big Data* 8 (3): 171–188.

Simonyan, Karen, and Andrew Zisserman. 2014. Very deep convolutional networks for large-scale image recognition. *arXiv preprint arXiv:1409.1556*.

Singhal, Shivangi, Rajiv Ratn Shah, Tanmoy Chakraborty, Ponnurangam Kumaraguru, and Shin'ichi Satoh. 2019. SpotFake: A multi-modal framework for fake news detection. In *2019 IEEE Fifth International Conference on Multimedia Big Data (BigMM)*, 39–47. IEEE.

Singhal, Shivangi, Rajiv Ratn Shah, and Ponnurangam Kumaraguru. 2021. Factorization of fact-checks for low resource indian languages. *arXiv preprint arXiv:2102.11276*.

Sivasangari, V., Ashok Kumar Mohan, M. Sethumadhavan, and K. Suthendran. 2018. Isolating rumors using sentiment analysis. *Journal of Cyber Security and Mobility* 7: 181–200.

Slovikovskaya, Valeriya, and Giuseppe Attardi. 2020. Transfer learning from transformers to fake news challenge stance detection (FNC-1) task. In *Proceedings of the Twelfth Language Resources and Evaluation Conference*, 1211–1218.

Soleymani, Mohammad, Maja Pantic, and Thierry Pun. 2011. Multimodal emotion recognition in response to videos. *IEEE Transactions on Affective Computing* 3 (2): 211–223.

Song, Yan-Yan, and LU Ying. 2015. Decision tree methods: Applications for classification and prediction. *Shanghai Archives of Psychiatry* 27 (2): 130.

Song, Chenguang, Nianwen Ning, Yunlei Zhang, and Bin Wu. 2021a. Knowledge augmented transformer for adversarial multidomain multiclassification multimodal fake news detection. *Neurocomputing* 462 :88–100.

Song, Chenguang, Nianwen Ning, Yunlei Zhang, and Bin Wu. 2021b. A multimodal fake news detection model based on crossmodal attention residual and multichannel convolutional neural networks. *Information Processing & Management* 58 (1): 102437.

Sotthisopha, Natthapat, and Peerapon Vateekul. 2018. Improving short text classification using fast semantic expansion on multichannel convolutional neural network. In *2018 19th IEEE/ACIS International Conference on Software Engineering, Artificial Intelligence, Networking and Parallel/Distributed Computing (SNPD)*, 182–187. IEEE.

Strapparava, Carlo, and Rada Mihalcea. 2007. Semeval-2007 task 14: Affective text. In *Proceedings of the Fourth International Workshop on Semantic Evaluations (SemEval-2007)*, 70–74.

Suryavardan, S., Shreyash Mishra, Parth Patwa, Megha Chakraborty, Anku Rani, Aishwarya Reganti, Aman Chadha, Amitava Das, Amit Sheth, Manoj Chinnakotla, et al. 2022. Factify 2: A multimodal fake news and satire news dataset. *Proceedings ISSN* 1613: 0073. http://ceur-ws.org

Tacchini, Eugenio, Gabriele Ballarin, Marco L. Della Vedova, Stefano Moret, and Luca de Alfaro. 2017. Some like it hoax: Automated fake news detection in social networks. *CoRR* abs/1704.07506. http://arxiv.org/abs/1704.07506

Tammina, Srikanth. 2019. Transfer learning using VGG-16 with deep convolutional neural network for classifying images. *International Journal of Scientific and Research Publications (IJSRP)* 9 (10): 143–150.

Taunk, Dhaval, and Vasudeva Varma. 2023. Summarizing Indian languages using multilingual transformers based models. *arXiv preprint arXiv:2303.16657*.

The now: What is clickbait? https://edu.gcfglobal.org/en/thenow/what-is-clickbait/1/. (Accessed on 12/06/2023).

Thorne, James, Andreas Vlachos, Christos Christodoulopoulos, and Arpit Mittal. 2018. Fever: A large-scale dataset for fact extraction and verification. *arXiv preprint arXiv:1803.05355*.

van Esch, Daan, Tamar Lucassen, Sebastian Ruder, Isaac Caswell, and Clara Rivera. 2022. Writing system and speaker metadata for 2,800+ language varieties. In *Proceedings of the Thirteenth Language Resources and Evaluation Conference*, 5035–5046.

Vaswani, Ashish, Noam Shazeer, Niki Parmar, Jakob Uszkoreit, Llion Jones, Aidan N. Gomez, Łukasz Kaiser, and Illia Polosukhin. 2017. Attention is all you need. In *Advances in Neural Information Processing Systems*, 5998–6008.

Velankar, Abhishek, Hrushikesh Patil, and Raviraj Joshi. 2022. Mono vs multilingual BERT for hate speech detection and text classification: A case study in Marathi. In *IAPR Workshop on Artificial Neural Networks in Pattern Recognition*, 121–128. Springer.

Vlachos, Andreas, and Sebastian Riedel. 2014. Fact checking: Task definition and dataset construction. In *Proceedings of the ACL 2014 Workshop on Language Technologies and Computational Social Science*, 18–22.

Vosoughi, Soroush, Deb Roy, and Sinan Aral. 2018. The spread of true and false news online. *Science* 359 (6380): 1146–1151.

Wang, William Yang. 2017. "liar, liar pants on fire": A new benchmark dataset for fake news detection. *arXiv preprint arXiv:1705.00648.*

Wang, Yichen, and Aditya Pal. 2015. Detecting emotions in social media: A constrained optimization approach. In *Twenty-Fourth International Joint Conference on Artificial Intelligence.*

Wang, Yaqing, Fenglong Ma, Zhiwei Jin, Ye Yuan, Guangxu Xun, Kishlay Jha, Lu Su, and Jing Gao. 2018. Eann: Event adversarial neural networks for multi-modal fake news detection. In *Proceedings of the 24th ACM SIGKDD International Conference on Knowledge Discovery & Data Mining*, 849–857. ACM.

Wang, Jingzi, Hongyan Mao, and Hongwei Li. 2022. FMFN: Fine-grained multimodal fusion networks for fake news detection. *Applied Sciences* 12 (3): 1093.

Wu, Lianwei, Yuan Rao, Ambreen Nazir, and Haolin Jin. 2020. Discovering differential features: Adversarial learning for information credibility evaluation. *Information Sciences* 516: 453–473.

Wu, Kun, Xu Yuan, and Yue Ning. 2021. Incorporating relational knowledge in explainable fake news detection. In *Pacific-Asia Conference on Knowledge Discovery and Data Mining*, 403–415. Springer.

Xiaoye, SHI. 2019. *Analysis of ByteDance*. PhD thesis, Ph. D. Dissertation. Swiss Federal Institute of Technology Zurich.

Xie, Enze, Jian Ding, Wenhai Wang, Xiaohang Zhan, Hang Xu, Peize Sun, Zhenguo Li, and Ping Luo. 2021. DetCo: Unsupervised contrastive learning for object detection. In *Proceedings of the IEEE/CVF International Conference on Computer Vision*, 8392–8401.

Xiong, Xi, Yuanyuan Li, Rui Zhang, Zhan Bu, Guiqing Li, and Shenggen Ju. 2020. DGI: Recognition of textual entailment via dynamic gate matching. *Knowledge-Based Systems* 194: 105544.

Xu, Zheng, M.M. Kamruzzaman, and Jinyao Shi. 2022. Method of generating face image based on text description of generating adversarial network. *Journal of Electronic Imaging* 31 (5): 051411.

Yang, Zichao, Diyi Yang, Chris Dyer, Xiaodong He, Alex Smola, and Eduard Hovy. 2016. Hierarchical attention networks for document classification. In *Proceedings of the 2016 Conference of the North American Chapter of the Association for Computational Linguistics: Human Language Technologies*, 1480–1489.

Yang, Jufeng, Yan Sun, Jie Liang, Yong-Liang Yang, and Ming-Ming Cheng. 2018a. Understanding image impressiveness inspired by instantaneous human perceptual cues. In *Proceedings of the AAAI Conference on Artificial Intelligence*, vol. 32.

Yang, Yang, Lei Zheng, Jiawei Zhang, Qingcai Cui, Zhoujun Li, and Philip S. Yu. 2018b TI-CNN: Convolutional neural networks for fake news detection. *CoRR* abs/1806.00749. http://arxiv.org/abs/1806.00749

Yang, Yang, Lei Zheng, Jiawei Zhang, Qingcai Cui, Zhoujun Li, and Philip S. Yu. 2018c. Ti-CNN: Convolutional neural networks for fake news detection. *arXiv preprint arXiv:1806.00749.*

Yang, K.-C., T. Niven, and Hung-Yu Kao. 2019a Fake news detection as natural language inference. In *12th ACM International Conference on Web Search and Data Mining (WSDM-2019)(in Fake News Classification Challenge, WSDM Cup 2019).*

Yang, Runqi, Jianhai Zhang, Xing Gao, Feng Ji, and Haiqing Chen. 2019b. Simple and effective text matching with richer alignment features. In *Proceedings of the 57th Annual Meeting of the Association for Computational Linguistics*, 4699–4709.

Yang, Chen, Xinyi Zhou, and Reza Zafarani. 2021. Checked: Chinese COVID-19 fake news dataset. *Social Network Analysis and Mining* 11 (1): 1–8.

Ye, Junjie, Jie Zhou, Junfeng Tian, Rui Wang, Jingyi Zhou, Tao Gui, Qi Zhang, and Xuanjing Huang. 2022. Sentiment-aware multimodal pre-training for multimodal sentiment analysis. *Knowledge-Based Systems* 258: 110021.

You, Yang, Igor Gitman, and Boris Ginsburg. 2017. Large batch training of convolutional networks. *arXiv preprint arXiv:1708.03888*.

Yu, Feng, Qiang Liu, Shu Wu, Liang Wang, Tieniu Tan, et al. 2017a. A convolutional approach for misinformation identification. In *IJCAI*, 3901–3907.

Yu, Zhou, Jun Yu, Jianping Fan, and Dacheng Tao. 2017b. Multi-modal factorized bilinear pooling with co-attention learning for visual question answering. In *Proceedings of the IEEE International Conference on Computer Vision*, 1821–1830.

Yu, Zhou, Jun Yu, Yuhao Cui, Dacheng Tao, and Qi Tian. 2019. Deep modular co-attention networks for visual question answering. In *Proceedings of the IEEE/CVF Conference on Computer Vision and Pattern Recognition*, 6281–6290.

Yu, Jiahui, Yuanzhong Xu, Jing Yu Koh, Thang Luong, Gunjan Baid, Zirui Wang, Vijay Vasudevan, Alexander Ku, Yinfei Yang, Burcu Karagol Ayan, et al. 2022. Scaling autoregressive models for content-rich text-to-image generation. *arXiv preprint arXiv:2206.10789* 2 (3): 5.

Zarrabian, Shahram, and Peyman Hassani-Abharian. 2020. COVID-19 pandemic and the importance of cognitive rehabilitation. *Basic and Clinical Neuroscience* 11: 189–190.

Zhang, Zhongheng. 2016. Introduction to machine learning: k-nearest neighbors. *Annals of Translational Medicine* 4 (11): 218.

Zhang, Wen, Taketoshi Yoshida, and Xijin Tang. 2011. A comparative study of TF*IDF, LSI and multi-words for text classification. *Expert Systems with Applications* 38 (3): 2758–2765.

Zhang, Pingping, Dong Wang, Huchuan Lu, Hongyu Wang, and Xiang Ruan. 2017. Amulet: Aggregating multi-level convolutional features for salient object detection. In *Proceedings of the IEEE International Conference on Computer Vision*, 202–211.

Zhang, Jiawei, Limeng Cui, Yanjie Fu, and Fisher B. Gouza. 2018. Fake news detection with deep diffusive network model. *arXiv preprint arXiv:1805.08751*.

Zhang, Jiawei, Bowen Dong, and S. Yu Philip. 2020. FAKEDETECTOR: Effective fake news detection with deep diffusive neural network. In *2020 IEEE 36th International Conference on Data Engineering (ICDE)*, 1826–1829. IEEE.

Zhang, Biao, Ankur Bapna, Rico Sennrich, and Orhan Firat. 2021a. Share or not? Learning to schedule language-specific capacity for multilingual translation. In *Ninth International Conference on Learning Representations 2021*.

Zhang, Xueyao, Juan Cao, Xirong Li, Qiang Sheng, Lei Zhong, and Kai Shu. 2021b Mining dual emotion for fake news detection. In *Proceedings of the Web Conference 2021*, 3465–3476.

Zhang, Chao, Bo Li, Tara Sainath, Trevor Strohman, Sepand Mavandadi, Shuo-yiin Chang, and Parisa Haghani. 2022. Streaming end-to-end multilingual speech recognition with joint language identification. *arXiv preprint arXiv:2209.06058*.

Zhao, Xiangyun, Raviteja Vemulapalli, Philip Andrew Mansfield, Boqing Gong, Bradley Green, Lior Shapira, and Ying Wu. 2021. Contrastive learning for label efficient semantic segmentation. In *Proceedings of the IEEE/CVF International Conference on Computer Vision*, 10623–10633.

Zheng, Wenfeng, Lirong Yin, Xiaobing Chen, Zhiyang Ma, Shan Liu, and Bo Yang. 2021. Knowledge base graph embedding module design for visual question answering model. *Pattern Recognition* 120: 108153.

Zhou, Deyu, Xuan Zhang, Yin Zhou, Quan Zhao, and Xin Geng. 2016. Emotion distribution learning from texts. In *Proceedings of the 2016 Conference on Empirical Methods in Natural Language Processing*, 638–647.

Zhong, Zilong, Jonathan Li, Lingfei Ma, Han Jiang, and He Zhao. 2017. Deep residual networks for hyperspectral image classification. In *2017 IEEE International Geoscience and Remote Sensing Symposium (IGARSS)*, 1824–1827. IEEE.

Zhou, Xinyi, Apurva Mulay, Emilio Ferrara, and Reza Zafarani. 2020a. Recovery: A multimodal repository for COVID-19 news credibility research. In *Proceedings of the 29th ACM International Conference on Information & Knowledge Management*, 3205–3212.

Zhou, Xinyi, Jindi Wu, and Reza Zafarani. 2020b [. . . formula. . .]: Similarity-aware multi-modal fake news detection. *Advances in Knowledge Discovery and Data Mining* 12085: 354.

Zhou, Yufan, Zhang, Ruiyi, Chen, Changyou, Li, Chunyuan, Tensmeyer, Chris, Yu, Tong, Gu, Jiuxiang, Xu, Jinhui, and Sun, Tong. 2022. Towards language-free training for text-to-image generation. In *Proceedings of the IEEE/CVF Conference on Computer Vision and Pattern Recognition*, 17907–17917.

Zhu, Tong, Leida Li, Jufeng Yang, Sicheng Zhao, Hantao Liu, and Jiansheng Qian. 2022. Multimodal sentiment analysis with image-text interaction network. *IEEE Transactions on Multimedia* 25: 3375–3385.

Zlatkova, Dimitrina, Preslav Nakov, and Ivan Koychev. 2019. Fact-checking meets fauxtography: Verifying claims about images. In *Proceedings of the 2019 Conference on Empirical Methods in Natural Language Processing and the 9th International Joint Conference on Natural Language Processing (EMNLP-IJCNLP)*, 2099–2108.

Zubiaga, Arkaitz, Maria Liakata, Rob Procter, Geraldine Wong Sak Hoi, and Peter Tolmie. 2016. Analysing how people orient to and spread rumours in social media by looking at conversational threads. *PloS one* 11 (3): e0150989.

Zubiaga, Arkaitz, Elena Kochkina, Maria Liakata, Rob Procter, Michal Lukasik, Kalina Bontcheva, Trevor Cohn, and Isabelle Augenstein. 2018. Discourse-aware rumour stance classification in social media using sequential classifiers. *Information Processing & Management* 54 (2): 273–290.

Printed in the United States
by Baker & Taylor Publisher Services